SHITO RYU MASTERS

Jose M. Fraguas

EMPIRE Books
P.O. Box 491788, Los Angeles, CA 90049

Disclaimer
Please note that the author and publisher of this book are NOT RESPONSIBLE in any manner whatsoever for any injury that may result from practicing the techniques and/or following the instructions given within. Since the physical activities described herein may be too strenuous in nature for some readers to engage in safely, it is essential that a physician be consulted prior to training.

First publish in 2017 by AWP LLC/Empire Books. Copyright (c) 2017 by Jose M. Fraguas.

All rights reserved. No part of this publication may be reproduced or utilized in any form or by any means, electronic or mechanical, including photocopying, recording, or by any information storage and retrieval system, without prior written permission from AWP LLC/Empire Books.

EMPIRE BOOKS

P.O. Box 491788
Los Angeles, CA 90049

First edition
Library of Congress Catalog Number: ISBN-13: 978-1-933901-61-9

17 16 15 14 13 12 11 10 09 08 07 06 05 04

Library of Congress Cataloging-in-Publication Data

Names: Fraguas, Jose M., author.
Title: Shito ryu masters / by Jose M. Fraguas.
Description: Los Angeles, California : Empire Books, 2017.
Identifiers: LCCN 2017048818 (print) | LCCN 2017050689 (ebook) | ISBN 9781933901619 (ebook) | ISBN 9781933901619 (pbk.)
Subjects: LCSH: Martial artists–Interviews. | Martial artists–Biography.
Classification: LCC GV1114.3 (ebook) | LCC GV1114.3 .F7155 2017 (print) | DDC 796.8–dc23
LC record available at https://lccn.loc.gov/2017048818

Printed in the United States of America.

*"Clearing my mind of everything
with devotion and joyful anticipation
I row my boat toward the island of Budo."*

- Kenwa Mabuni (1889 – 1952)

Dedication

I dedicate this book to the memory of Yoshiaki Tsujikawa Sensei.

Acknowledgments

Many people were responsible for making this book possible, some more directly than others. I want to extend my gratitude to all those whom so generously contributed their time and experience to the preparation of this work. A very special thanks to my teacher, Masahiro Okada Sensei, whose flights of guidance throughout my Budo life and karate-do journey, have been always on the wings of excitement and self-discovery. I also want to thank France's Thierry Plee, long-time friend and president of Sedirep and Budo Editions; Mr. Schlatt, kind friend and founder of Schlatt-Books in Germany; Germany's Norbert Schiffer (director of Satori-Verlag and Budo magazine); Don Warrener (director of Rising Sun Productions); Isaac Florentine (film director and passionate Shito Ryu karateka); and finally to Oleg Larinov, a great karateka, impeccable filmmaker and better human being; I truly admire your passion for the art of karate-do.

A word of appreciation is also due to my good friend Masahiro Ide, president of JK Fan and Champ videos, for his generosity and cooperation in this project; I also want to thank the publishers of Gekkan Karate-do magazine (Fukushodo, Ltd., Japan), for their assistance, kindness and supply of great photographic material for some of the chapters. Without their support, kindness and commitment to preserve the art of karate-do, this book would not exist.

And last but not least, to all the instructors who shared their knowledge and experience with me, past and present, for giving me the understanding and knowledge to undertake all the karate-do projects I've done during my life. My understanding of the art has grown over the years thanks to the questions they made me ask myself. These questions — both perceptive and practical — have sent me further and deeper in search for answers. This book would not exist without you.

You all have my enduring thanks.

— Jose M. Fraguas

About the Author

Born and raised in Madrid, Spain, Jose M. Fraguas began his martial arts studies with judo, in grade school, at age 9. From there he moved to study Shito Ryu karate-do under his teacher, Masahiro Okada Sensei, eventually receiving a seventh-degree black belt and the Shihan certificate from Soke K. Mabuni. He began his career as a writer at age 16 as a regular contributor to martial arts magazines in Great Britain, France, Spain, Italy, Germany, Portugal, Holland and Australia. In 1980, he moved to Los Angeles, California, where his open-minded mentality helped him to develop a more elaborated approach to the martial arts.

Fraguas founded his first publishing company in Europe, authoring dozens of books and distributing his magazines to 35 countries in three different languages. His reputation and credibility as a martial artist and publisher became well known to the top masters around the world. Considering himself a martial artist first and a writer and publisher second, Fraguas feels fortunate to have had the opportunity to interview many legendary martial artists. He recognizes that much of the information given in the interviews helped him to discover new dimensions in the martial arts. "I was constantly absorbing knowledge from the great masters," he recalls. "I only trained with a few of them, but intellectually, academically and spiritually all of them have made very important contributions to my growth as a complete martial artist."

Steeped in tradition yet looking to the future, Fraguas understands and appreciates martial arts history and philosophy and feels this rich heritage is a necessary steppingstone to personal growth and spiritual evolution. His desire to promote both ancient philosophy and modern thinking provided the motivation for writing this book. "If the motivation is just money, a book cannot be of good quality," Fraguas says. "If the book is written to just make people happy, it cannot be deep. I want to write books so I can learn as well as teach. Karate-do, like human life itself, is filled with experiences that seem quite ordinary at the time and assume a fabled stature only with the passage of the years. I hope this work will be appreciated by future practitioners not only of the art of Shito Ryu style but karate in general, regardless of the style."

It is clear that every one of us will some kind of leave a legacy behind when we die. The challenge is the same for all of us. For Fraguas, who has authored more than 30 books, the important question is what kind of legacy will I leave? "I believe our main legacy as writers is to educate or even just re-echo those things that we believe are worthwhile - a subjective matter. Even if the idea is obvious or simple, we believe it deserves to be kept alive, and we do that using different ways current with the times; we broadcast our worldview with our family, friends, co-workers, and so on," he says. "Ideally we live by our beliefs so as to lend them credence; the "unfollowing adherent" is just a meaningless mouthpiece - a preacher not following his own sermon. A legacy of values proven out by the bearer's own life would be a very good legacy for anyone. Life is motion, and the real goal of a writer should be to arrest that motion [which is life] and preserve knowledge [the words of these masters in this book] by artificial means, and hold it fixed so that a hundred years later, when a stranger opens a book and reads it, it moves again since it is life. Since man is mortal, the only immortality possible for a writer is to leave something behind him that is immortal since it will always move. This is the writer's way of scribbling "I was here" on the wall of the final and irrevocable oblivion through which we all must someday pass."

Jose M. Fraguas lives in Los Angeles, California.

Introduction

Some of my best days were spent interviewing and meeting the Shito Ryu masters in this book. There is little I enjoy more than reading a great interview while time slows and sometimes even seems to stop. Having the opportunity to meet and interview the most prestigious Shito Ryu icons of the past five decades is something that every karateka doesn't have the chance to do. Hopefully, in some small way, this will help make up for that. Meeting the masters and having long conversations with them allowed me to do more than simply scratch the surface of the technical aspects of the art; it also allowed me to understand the human beings behind the teachers. Some of the dialogues and interviews began by simply commenting about the superficial techniques of fighting, and ended up turning into a spiritual conversation about the philosophical aspects of karate-do. Although these masters are all very different, they share a common thread of traditional values such as discipline, respect, positive attitude, dedication and etiquette.

For more than 40 years I've interviewed great karate-do masters, one-on-one, face-to-face, with no place to run if I asked a stupid question. Many times it was a real challenge to not just talk to them, but to make the questions interesting enough to bring out their deepest knowledge. I tried to absorb as much knowledge as I could, ranging from their training methods, to their system, to their philosophies about life itself. Their personal cultural backgrounds never prevented them from analyzing, researching or modifying anything they considered important. They always kept their minds open to improving the art and themselves. From a formal philosophical point of view, many of them followed classical philosophies and religions—but they all tempered that with vast amounts of common sense.

They devoted themselves to the art of karate-do, often in solitude, to the exclusion of other "normal" pursuits. They worked themselves into extraordinary physical condition. They ignored distractions and diversions and concentrated on their mental and physical training. They got as good as they could possibly get at performing and teaching the art while the rest of us watched them, leading our "balanced lives," and wondering how good we might have gotten at something had we devoted ourselves to it as ferociously as these masters embraced their journey. In that respect, they bear our dreams.

If you read carefully between the lines, you'll see that none of these men were trying to become a fighting machine, or create the most devastating martial arts system known to man. They focused, rather, on how to use karate-do to become a better person. There are many principles that once discovered open a wide spectrum of possibilities, not only to karate, but to a better existence as individuals.

The interviews often lasted as long as three or four hours. I would begin at their school and finish the conversation at a restaurant or coffee shop. Much of this information had never been published before and some had to be trimmed either at the master's request or edited to avoid misunderstandings. It is not the questions that make an interview. An interview is either good or bad depending on the answers. Considering the masters in this book, I had an easy job. My goal was to make them comfortable talking about life and karate training.

"The great old masters are gone," many like to say. But as long as we keep their teachings in our heart, they will live forever. To understand karate-do properly, it is necessary to take into account its philosophical methods as well as its physical techniques. There is a deep distinction between a fighting system and a martial art. Unfortunately, the roots of karate-do have been de-emphasized, neglected or totally abandoned today.

Karate-do is not a sport, although it can be useful as such in our modern society. Someone who chooses to devote himself to a sport such as basketball, tennis, soccer or football—which is based on youth, strength, and speed—chooses to die twice. When you can no longer do that sport, due to the lack of their required attributes, waking up in the morning without the activity that has been the center of your life for 35 years is troubling and unsettling. In contrast, karate-do can and should be practiced for life—it never leaves you.

All the masters have expressed similar ideas in very different ways. Regardless of the words they used, there must be truth in the philosophies and principles that so many different people have believed in and lived by — and in some cases — died for. The more I interviewed them, the more I realized that those great masters are more like you and me than they are different. They had difficult days and seemingly impossible hurdles, yet they endured and prevailed. Most of what passed as human wisdom is merely the post-examination gabble of excited individuals trying to guess how the new lessons will explain the old questions of life and karate-do training. Anything is fresh on the first hearing ... even though others may have heard it a thousand times through a score of generations.

A true karate-do practitioner is like a musician, painter, writer or actor—their art is an expression of themselves. The need to discover who they are becomes the reason for an endless search for the perfect

technique, great melody, inspiring poetry, amazing painting or Academy Award performance. It is this motivation to reach that impossible dream that allows a simple individual to become an exceptional artist and master of his craft.

Many of the greatest teachers share a commonly misunderstood teaching methodology. They know the words they could use to teach their students have little or no meaning. They know that to try "self-discovery" in quantitative or empirical terms is a useless task. A great deal of knowledge and wisdom comes from oral traditions, which karate-do, like every other cultural expression, has. These oral traditions have always been reserved for a certain kind of student and considered "secrets," given only to a special few who have the minds and attitudes to fully grasp them. Alexandra David-Neel wrote: "It is not on the master that the secret depends but on the hearer. Truth learned from others is of no value, the only truth which is effective and of value is self-discovered … the teacher can only guide to the point of discovery." In the end, "the only secret is that there is no secret." As Kato Tokuro, arguably the finest potter of the last century, a great art scholar, and the teacher of Pablo Picasso said: "The sole cause of secrets in craftsmanship is the student's inability to learn." To find out what karate-do means to you, what it does for you, and what it holds for you, is a deeply personal process. Each path is different and we all have to find a personal rhythm that fit us individually, according to what surround us.

As human beings, we are always tempted to follow linear logic towards ultimate self-improvement—but the truth is that there are no absolute truths. You have to find your own way in life whether it be in martial arts, business or cherry picking. Whatever path you pursue, you have to distill the personal truths that are right for you, according to your own nature. The quest for perfection is very imperfect, and not in tune with human nature or experience. To have any hope of attaining even a single perfection, you have to concentrate on a single pursuit and direct all your energy towards it. In this sense, perfection comes from appreciating endeavors for their own sake—not to impress anyone—but for your own inner satisfaction and sense of accomplishment. It is important to have a feeling of responsibility; and putting yourself into an art as genuinely as you can, without any sense that you are going to get something back in return, reverberates throughout time and space. We need to honor those who came before us, as well as nurture those who will come after, so the art can grow and expand—you've got to send the elevator back down.

Karate is a large part of my life and I draw inspiration from it. I really don't know the "how" or the "why" of its effect on me, but I feel its influence in even my most mundane activities. All human beings have sources or principles that keep them grounded, and karate is mine. That is when the term "way of life" becomes real. In bushido, the self-discipline required to pursue mastery is more important than mastery itself—the struggle is more important than the reward. A common thread throughout the lives of all the masters appearing in this book is their constant struggle towards self-mastery. They realized that life is an ongoing process, and once you achieve all your goals you are as good as dead. But this process is not all driven by action. Often the greatest action is inaction, and the hardest voice to hear is the sound of your own thoughts. You need to sit alone and collect yourself, free from technology and distraction, and just think. This is perhaps the only way to achieve mental and spiritual clarity.

I don't believe that books are meant to be read fast. I've always thought that writing is timeless and that reading is not a detraction. So take your time. Books are an essential part of our existence and they open new and exciting avenues of life. My goal is to share these interviews with as many people as possible. I hope this collection provides comfort and inspiration for the karate practitioner, the martial artist — regardless of style — and for the casual reader. If you, the reader, find this work useful as both a guide and a reference work and discover some unexpected thoughts and philosophies, the book will have served its purpose.

Approach this book with the Zen "beginner's mind" and "empty cup" mentality and soak up the words of these great Shito Ryu karate teachers. They will help you to not only grow as a karateka but as a human being as well.

The Founding of Shito Ryu

"When the spirit of karate-do is deeply embraced, it becomes the vehicle in which one is ferried across the great void in order to discover the purpose or meaning of life."
– Kenwa Mabuni–

The late 19th century was the heyday of Okinawan Karate. As previously isolated and hidden teachings became increasingly more available to the public, practitioners and instructors were able to train in multiple styles and blend and refine them into new systems.

One of the most prominent and effective systems to emerge during this period was shito-ryu, founded by Kenwa Mabuni. Mabuni was born in 1889 in Shuri, Okinawa, and was of the samurai class. A frail and somewhat weak youth, he began training in martial arts as both a means of self-defense and to improve his physical condition. He first began training in the system of shuri-te under Yasutsune Itosu when he was 13.

From the beginning, he plunged into his study of the art with a tremendous dedication. As his physical condition improved, he displayed a tremendous aptitude for martial arts and spent the next ten years training with Itosu. According to those close to Mabuni, when Itosu passed away, Mabuni spent an entire year visiting Itosu's grave and practicing his kata almost daily.

Mabuni's next instruction was not in Okinawa-te at all, but rather kung-fu. Wu Xian Gu, a Chinese tea merchant settled in Okinawa, took the name of Gokenki, and began actively teaching Fukien-style White Crane. It is believed that this is how the famous

"crane stance" associated with Okinawa martial arts was incorporated into several systems.

A close friend of many masters, Mabuni was referred to famed naha-te master Higashionna by none other than the legendary founder of goju-ryu, Chojun Miyagi. He perfected his sanchin kata under Higashionna, and proceeded to study from Seisho Arakaki, who was also the instructor of Gichin Funakoshi, Tsuyoshi Chitose and Kanken Toyama. Under Arakaki, Mabuni perfected the niseshi, unshu, sochin, aragaki-sai and aragaki-bo kata.

To learn the applications of Okinawan weaponry, Mabuni trained under the great Seisho of Naha, in ryukyu kobujutsu, which is the reason why the shito-ryu styles stress the study and training of weapons. Mabuni was one of the world's first martial arts instructors to design and incorporate protective equipment into his weapons training.

When he formed his own system, Mabuni originally called it hanko ryu (half-hard style) but later he changed the name to shito ryu to honor his instructors. Shito is a combination of shi from Itosu's name and ito from Higashionna's name.

By combining the systems under which he had become proficient, Mabuni had a tremendous number of kata in his curriculum. However, he did not blend the two systems together, he linked them together into one style, with shuri-te being taught to the beginning students and naha-te to the advanced. Mabuni was so highly respected that Shotokan founder Gichin Funakoshi studied from him and sent one of his top students, Masatoshi Nakayama to train under him as well.

Mabuni was instrumental in founding the Kenyokukai, hosting at his home such promiment masters as Tokuda Anbun, Gichin Funakoshi, Chibana Chosin, Shiroma Shinpan, Ishikawa Hoko, Oshiro Choju, and Tokumura Seicho. They would periodically gather to research and perpetuate Okinawan martial arts.

Eventually, on advice from judo founder Jigoro Kano, Mabuni decided to go to Japan to teach his art. Relocating in the city of Osaka, he taught naha-te at the University, and, over the next few years, dedicated himself to promoting shito-ryu in the Osaka area. This led to the formation of the "Dai Nihon Karatedo Kai", which later became the "World Shito-Ryu Karatedo Federation."

Unfortunately, like many of the great masters, Mabuni's life was disrupted by the Second World War. Impoverished after the war, Mabuni occupied himself with trying to expand the shito-ryu system. Eventually, as the post-war universities began to reopen, shito-ryu's popularity began to grow.

The year that the American occupation of Japan ended, 1952, also saw the passing of Kenwa Mabuni. Although he left behind an impressive number of followers, such as Sakagami Ryusho, Tani Chojiro, Konishi Yasuhiro, Kanei Uechi (not to be confused with Kanei Uechi of Uechi-ryu) Iwata Manzo, Yoshiaki Tsujikawa, Kuniba Kosei, Hisatomi Tokio and his sons Kenzo Mabuni and Kenei Mabuni. Kenei the eldest son, was the Soke of the "World Shito Kai Karatedo Federation" with headquarters in the Honbu dojo in Tokyo, and passed away on December, 2015. Kenzo Mabuni, the youngest son, was asked by his mother Kamae

Mabuni to take over the style. Uncertain about accepting, Kenzo went into seclusion in the city of Nagoya and after training in a number of arts, he accepted the responsibility. He lived in the original family home in Osaka, where the headquarters of his shito ryu organization, the "Nippon Karate Do Kai" were and passed away on June 26, 2005.

Today, shito-ryu is considered one of the four most practiced systems in the world.

KENWA MABUNI

THE FOUNDER OF SHITO-RYU

KENWA MABUNI WAS BORN ON NOVEMBER 14, 1889, IN THE TOWN OF SHURI, ON THE ISLAND OF OKINAWA. A DESCENDANT OF ONIGUSIKUNI, A FAMOUS SAMURAI, MABUNI STARTED HIS STUDIES UNDER THE GREAT SHURI-TE MASTER YASUTSUNE ITOSU (1830-1915) AT AGE 13. ALTHOUGH VERY WEAK PHYSICALLY, MABUNI TOOK HIS TRAINING UNDER THE 70-YEAR-OLD MASTER VERY SERIOUSLY AND PROGRESSED QUICKLY, LEARNING MORE THAN 20 DIFFERENT KATA. THIS TRAINING STRENGTHENED HIS BODY AND ALLOWED HIM TO DEAL WITH THE HARD PHYSICAL DEMANDS IMPOSED BY HIS ITOSU'S RIGOROUS METHODS. MABUNI PRACTICED UNDER ITOSU'S GUIDANCE FOR MORE THAN 10 YEARS UNTIL ITOSU'S DEATH. ITOSU TOOK A STRONG LIKING TO HIS YOUNG STUDENT AND TAUGHT HIM 23 KATA. LEGEND HAS IT THAT WHEN ITOSU PASSED AWAY, MABUNI WAS SO SAD THAT HE SPENT A WHOLE YEAR BY ITOSU'S GRAVE, PRACTICING ALL THE KATA THAT ITOSU HAD TAUGHT HIM AS A SIGN OF LOVE AND DEVOTION TOWARD HIS TEACHER.

Before training under naha-te master Kanryo Higashionna (1851-1915), Mabuni went to study under master Gokenki (Wu Xian Gui), who was a tea merchant from Fukien Province and teacher of Chinese kempo. Gokenki arrived in Okinawa around 1915, married an Okinawan girl and taught Fukien-style white crane fist (hakutsuruken) to Mabuni. This Shaolin method featured standing on one leg and yelling "kiai," which was intended to resemble the cry of a crane. This method includes a form named hakkucho that is still practiced in the shito-ryu style all over the world. Later in his life, Gokenki changed his name to Yoshikawa.

Later on, and after the recommendation of his good friend Chojun Miyagi, Mabuni went to study under Higashionna, who taught him the method of naha-te. He was pleased with this style of karate because it gave him a different perspective on how to approach training and fighting. Under Higashionna, he perfected the sanchin kata, but it was from his studies under Seisho (Kamadeunchu) Arakaki (1840-1918) — who also taught Tsuyoshi Chitose, the founder of Chito Ryu, Gichin Funakoshi of Shoto Kan and Kanken Toyama of the Shudokan school — that Mabuni Kenwa perfected the kata known today as niseshi, unshu, sochin, aragaki-sai and aragaki-bo.

Years later and with the opposition of masters like Kanken Toyama, who considered it useless to name the styles with "funny-sounding names," the Dai Nippon Butoku-Kai demanded a more specific description of several group's karate systems. Mabuni decided to call his own method hanko ryu (half-hard style) but later he changed the name to shito-ryu as a sign of gratitude and respect for his former teachers. The word shito is a combination of "shi" from Higashionna's name and "ito" from Itosu's name. Mabuni started teaching students in a local high school, as well as to the police in Okinawa where he was working as an officer.

Mabuni combined the two major streams of Okinawa karate and incorporated them into his new style. This gave him a vast store of kata from which to draw. However, he did not just throw a grab-bag style of techniques into a melting pot. He taught pure shuri-te, with it's basic, linear approach to his lower level students, and naha-te to his advanced students. This is the reason why he was highly respected in karate circles as an expert in kata. Master Gichin Funakoshi, a contemporary of Mabuni, not only learned various kata from him but also sent his top student, Masatoshi Nakayama, and his own son, Yoshitaka (Giko) Funakoshi, to Mabuni to learn useshi, niseshi and unshu kata. These were later incorporated and modified to fit into his shotokan method as gojushiho, nijushiho and unsu. Funakoshi described Mabuni as "a leading expert who has collected a myriad of research material and is unsurpassed among others because of his mastery of kata." This is a good proof of the lack of ego shown by the true karate masters. An expert in kata, Mabuni influenced the development of modern shotokan and wado-ryu styles in Japan. Both Funakoshi and Othsuka Hinori looked to him as a source of great knowledge. Unfortunately, many other karate-do teachers envied Mabuni because of how much he knew and his deep level of understanding of the art.

Under master Seisho Arakaki (1840-1918) of Naha, Mabuni also learnt ryukyu kobujutsu, which is the reason why the shito-ryu styles stress the study and training of weapons. He was very interested in a variety of martial arts as well as sports. From these he applied certain athletic training principles to his karate teachings. As a pioneer and innovator, Mabuni developed protector equipment to spar more realistically. He took ideas from kendo, boxing and baseball and designed protective equipment for kumite training.

Later on he formed the Kenyokukai, a group that would gather at Mabuni's home to research karate history and further technical development. This group was formed by members such as Tokuda Anbun, Gichin Funakoshi, Chibana Chosin, Shiroma Shinpan, Ishikawa Hoko, Oshiro Choju and Tokumura Seicho. In 1918, Mabuni was granted the honor of demonstrating in the presence of Prince Kuni and Prince Kacho at the Okinawa Normal School. When Funakoshi was sent to Japan to officially introduce Okinawan tode, Mabuni and the research group continued training together.

During his days in Okinawa, Mabuni traveled extensively with his good friend Yasuhiro Konishi, a friend and student who later developed his own karate system called shindo jinen ryu. In 1925, both Mabuni and Konishi visited Wakayama Prefecture, where Kanbun Uechi (founder of Uechi-ryu) was teaching. After spending a great deal of time with him, Mabuni created a kata named shinpa.

Kenwa Mabuni, like other Okinawa teachers, eventually decided to go to Japan to propagate the art of karate. This happened after Jigoro Kano observed a demonstration given by Mabuni Kenwa. The founder of judo told Mabuni he should go to Japan to spread the art. When Mabuni arrived to Japan, Funakoshi had been in Tokyo for more than six years. Out of respect to Funakoshi's seniority in age, Mabuni decided to relocate to Osaka where one of his close friends, Master Motobu, was living. This was very helpful to Funakoshi Gichin, whose life was already difficult at that time in Tokyo. The estab-

lishment of another karate instructor in the area would have made it much harder.

At Donisha University in Osaka, Mabuni taught strictly naha-te on behalf of his close friend Sensei Miyagi, who had taught there before returning to Okinawa. Mabuni strictly adhered to the naha-te method and system. It is interesting to observe that in an advertisement for his book, "Seipai No Kenkyu Goshijitsu" (Hiden Karate-Do Kenpo and originally published in 1934), Mabuni described himself as a shihan of goju-ryu. Also, the Otaru newspaper described him as "a great goju-ryu karate-do master." Mabuni also had the intention of finishing a book titled, "Goju-Ryu Karate-Do Kempo" (Sochin and Kururunfa). From this, it seems more than evident that Mabuni always kept a close link with the art taught by Kanryo Higashionna.

At the beginning of his days in Osaka, he taught at various dojo, including the Seishinkai School of Kosei Kuniba, who later formed the Motobu-ha faction of the shito-ryu style.

For the next few years, Mabuni dedicated himself to the promotion of his karate style in the Osaka area at his Yoshukan dojo. In order to attract people to his school, he gave demonstrations in which he would break bricks and boards to show the power and effectiveness of karate. With the establishment of the Dai Nihon Karate-do Kai, his enormous efforts began to pay off. As Mabuni's style began to be universally accepted, he started to teach more frequently at both his home and different universities that requested his services.

During the war, many karate masters went through a phase of privations trying to make a decent living. Much more concerned about supporting their families and paying the rent, these masters were much less preoccupied about creating an organization for karate expansion. Mabuni barely survived the post-war turmoil and afterwards devoted himself to the further expansion of shito-ryu. It was only after few years after the war, when some universities and colleges began to reopen, that the future of the art was assured. Mabuni always stressed that karate involves three important aspects: shin (heart-spirit), gi (technique) and tai (body). Thus, a good karate-ka should strive to balance the heart, the body and the physical technique.

Kenwa Mabuni passed away May 23, 1952, at 63 years of age. This was the same year the American occupation of Japan ended. He never had a chance to witness the economic revival that eventually fueled karate's explosive growth in later years. When he died, Mabuni left behind an impressive group of

followers to carry on his legacy: Sakagami Ryusho, Tani Chojiro, Konishi Yasuhiro, Kanei Uechi (not to be confused with Kanei Uechi of Uechi-ryu) Iwata Manzo, Yoshiaki Tsujikawa, Kuniba Kosei, Hisatomi Tokio, and his sons Kenzo Mabuni and Kenei Mabuni. Kenei, Kenwa's oldest son, joined forces with Tokyo University graduates Manzo Iwata and Ken Saiko and created the "World Shito Kai Karate-do Federation". The headquarters were in the Honbu Dojo in Tokyo. Kenzo Mabuni, the youngest son, was asked by his mother, Kamae Mabuni, and numerous karate seniors to take over the style. Unsure about his final decision, Kenzo Mabuni went into seclusion in the city of Nagoya. He trained diligently for more than two years and then retreated and spent some time training with Ryusho Sakagami and Watanabe Kenichi. After this, he decided to accept and fully commit himself to the task of being the inheritor of his father's lineage. Kenzo Mabuni lived in the original family home in Osaka, where he had the headquarters of the Nippon Karate Do Kai. He kept the founder's syllabus, personnel technical notes, textbooks and records. He felt that his mission was to teach what his father left for the world. He passed away on June 26, 2005, and was recognized as the true heir of his father's art.

Although Kenwa Mabuni authored several books and manuscripts, all of his books were already out of print before the war and were never translated into English. In like manner, some of his manuscripts are untraceable. After the acknowledgement of his tremendous influence and contribution to the modern world of karate-do, some of his works have been reprinted in Japanese.

After the death of Kenwa Mabuni, the shito-ryu style became one of the four most practiced karate systems in the world and is considered as the true repository of traditional kata. Different branches of the art such as tani-ha shito-ryu (shukokai), hayashi-ha shito-ryu, seishin-kai, motobu-ha shito-ryu, itosu-kai and shito-kai spread his original message in slightly different forms, but all of them retain the essence of a great karate master named Kenwa Mabuni.

Contents

1
RUDY CROSSWELL
SEARCHING FOR MEANING

19
DEL SAITO
A JOURNEY OF WISDOM

37
FUMIO DEMURA
LEADING BY EXAMPLE

45
TERUO HAYASHI
IN PURSUIT OF EXCELLENCE

53
JAMES HERDON
FORWARD THINKING

61
YOSHIMI INOUE
RETURNING TO THE SOURCE

69
YASHUNARI ISHIMI
THE INTERNAL SERENITY

77
GENZO IWATA
THE SHITO KAI LEGACY

83
SANAUOV JASTALAP
UNCOMMON WISDOM

91
CHUZO KOTAKA
A LONG JOURNEY

97
KENEI MABUNI
THE POWER OF INNER STRENGTH

105
KENZO MABUNI
STAYING THE COURSE

113
MINOBU MIKI
A MODERN TRADITIONALIST

123
AKIO MINAKAMI
A WARRIOR'S JOURNEY

133
SEINOSUKE MITSUYA
THE DISTANT DREAM

143
KUNIO MIYAKE
THE POWER OF WILL

153
SAM MOLEDZKI
NOT AN ORDINARY MAN

159
KUNIO MURAYAMA
A SOULFUL JOURNEY

167
HIDETOSHI NAKAHASHI
BUDO SIMPLICITY

173
YOSHINAO NANBU
WALKING HIS OWN PATH

181
YUISHI NEGISHI
A MODERN SAMURAI

189
TED RABINO
IN THE SPIRIT OF SHITO KAI

201
RYUSHO SAKAGAMI
THE GENTLE MASTER

209
SADAAKI SAKAGAMI
IN THE NAME OF ITOSU

217
SHOKO SATO
MOVING FORWARD

223
SHIGERU SAWABE
A LEGACY OF EXCELLENCE

233
GEORGE TAN
KARATE PILLARS

241
KATSUTAKA TANAKA
THE TRUE WAY OF BUDO

249
ALLEN TANZADEH
A WEALTH OF KNOWLEDGE

265
KEIJI TOMIYAMA
THE CHALLENGES OF BUDO

277
ERIC TOMLINSON
THE WAY FOR PERFECTION

285
TAMAS WEBER
BUDO ON THE BATTLEFIELD

295
JOSE M. FRAGUAS
ONE ON ONE

RUDY CROSSWELL

SEARCHING FOR MEANING

Shihan Rudy Crosswell began his martial arts training just outside of New York City at the age of thirteen. The year was 1960, and his first dojo offered the arts of Isshin-ryu karate and Judo. He went on to study Shotokan and Chito-ryu karate during this period before joining the US Air Force in 1965. During his first three years with the US military, he studied Shorin-ryu, Tang Soo Do and Goju-ryu karate. Shihan Crosswell was awarded his first black belt in the art of Goju-ryu karate in 1967, having already embarked on what was to become a lifetime of dedication to traditional martial arts.

In 1968, destiny favored Shihan Crosswell with a rare wartime assignment to the US Air Force base in Fuchu, Japan. While living just outside Tokyo, he met and became a student of the legendary Soke Shogo Kuniba (Kokuba) and Soke Teruo Hayashi and his life changed forever. Later on, Shihan Crosswell began to host and train with Soke K. Mabuni on regular basis and this effort led to a Shihan certificate in the exclusive "Seito Shito-ryu Shihan-kai". Shihan Crosswell continued to train with Kenzo Mabuni and continued to actively expand his now formidable kobudo syllabus.

As he entered his fifth consecutive decade of unbroken martial arts training "The International Seibukan Martial Arts Association", headquartered in Kyoto, Japan, recognized his contributions to both the art of Shito-ryu karate and Okinawan kobudo by awarding him the ultimate rank of 10th dan, Hanshi, in Shito-ryu Karate and 9th dan, Kyoshi, in Okinawan kobudo.

By now highly sought-after as one of the world's premier traditional martial arts experts, Shihan Crosswell continues actively seeking out new karate, kobudo, and sword knowledge—all the while devoting his heart and soul to nurturing individual students at the Arizona Budokan Dojo. His searching for 'Budo meaning' still continues..

SHITO RYU MASTERS

How long have you been practicing karate?

I started training in 1960, so I'm entering my fifty-second year.

How many styles karate or other Martial Arts methods have you trained in and who were your teachers? Do you practice any other art in conjunction with karate?

In the early years I trained in several styles. Schools were unstable and would close because they couldn't keep enough students to pay the rent. I did some Shotokan, Isshin-ryu, Chito-ryu, Tong Soo Do, Goju-ryu, and even some judo. My early sensei included Orito, Don Nagle, James Cheatam, Col. Asa Herring, and Robert Coryer.

In 1968 the U.S. Air Force stationed me in Fuchu, Japan for three years. I was in communications at the Headquarters 5th Air Force in support of the Vietnam War. That is when I started my

studies of Shito-ryu karate, Okinawan kobudo, aiki-jutsu, and Japanese sword. I was fortunate because my sensei were multifaceted. They were graded in several arts and so I was able learn a variety of things. My primary teachers in Japan were Shogo Kuniba and Teruo Hayashi. Their karate included a lot of grappling-based gyaku-waza, aiki-jutsu, and ju-jitsu-type techniques and we always utilized these in breaking down the movements within kata to see how they actually applied. They were both weapons masters as well, so my study of Okinawan kobudo began with them.

Would you tell us some interesting stories of your early days in karate?

I remember that the training was quite severe—in fact, if we taught that way today we would have very few students and a lot of lawsuits. James Cheatam was the sensei at the Chito-ryu dojo that I joined in Newark, New Jersey in 1963. He was a talented martial artist who studied under Tsuroka Sensei in Canada. Anyway he was black, all his black belts were black, and these were the days of some pretty heated civil rights battles and racial tension in the US. I didn't feel any animosity from the dojo as a whole, but when it came to sparring it was every man for himself—and here I was a skinny little white kid from the Jersey streets. During sparring matches they would line towels along the sides of the room every few feet—not to wipe up the sweat necessarily, but to mop up the blood. I had my ribs broken when a guy called "Little Richard" hit me with a flying side kick. Sensei Cheatam told me, "I keep telling you to keep yourself covered. I guess that'll teach you." He was right, but I couldn't tell my mom about it, because I knew she would probably make me quit. So I taped them up myself, laid low for a few weeks, and then went back for more. My high school buddy told me I was crazy. He said, "Rudy, you're paying these guys to beat you up when you could go out in the street and get beat up for free!

In 1967, I was studying Tang Soo Do in Arizona. My sensei told us to meet him at the dojo early Saturday morning. When we got there, he said, "Today we're going learn how to break rocks." Seriously. We drove his Mercedes down to the dry riverbed and loaded up his trunk with river rocks. Then he took us back to the dojo and showed us how to hold a rock in one hand and chop it in half with the other.

In 1969 while I was living Japan, I had established a dojo on the Fuchu Air Station in Higashi Fuchu, just outside of Tokyo. This was the Vietnam era, and Fuchu was a communications center as well as the headquarters for the 5th Air Force. Soke Shogo Kuniba would come and teach at my dojo for a few days and then visit a few other dojos in the Kanto area as well. As usual, I scheduled time off my duties so that I could travel with him, not wanting to miss an opportunity to gain more knowledge and experience. Just days before his arrival, a white belt student decided to kick me in the left leg during a kumite match, exploding my knee and causing the doctors to put me in a cast that extended from my ankle to my thigh. I refused to cancel Soke's visit—and in fact didn't even tell him about the severe injury. With pants covering the cast, all he knew was that I was limping a bit. We took a train up to Johnson Air Base where he had another branch dojo and proceeded to enter the gym. I dressed in a stall and joined the group on the floor. We did basics up and down the floor and kata, and with my awkward footing they probably thought that I was just another American with lousy stances. Later we were instructed to do a circle sparring exercises where ten guys or so form a circle with one guy in the middle. Everyone in the outer circle gets to attack. When I got in the middle of the circle, I realized that I couldn't kick with the bad leg—nor could I stand on the bad leg and kick with the good leg. What I did was keep shifting my body, blocking and punching and hoping for the best. I'm happy to report that I was still standing when it was over, but feeling a little embarrassed about my clumsy technique. Soke ended class and we all went to the dressing room. When I took my gi off the Japanese students went wild. They all stared and came over to feel my cast. When they realized it was completely solid, they said, "you trained with that on your leg?! A Japanese would never do that!" I was a little surprised at what all the fuss was about. I had just wanted to train and take advantage of another opportunity to learn. It didn't occur to me that I shouldn't just because I had a cast on my leg. I honestly didn't think about it. I was not out to impress anyone—I had a chance to learn and I was not going to sit on the bench. Thinking about the incident in hindsight, I think Soke Kuniba was pretty proud of his American student that day as all the Japanese students stood around shaking their heads in disbelief.

One of my favorite stories of Hayashi-sensei (though it was not at all pleasant at the time) was when I tested for my godan in karate. Hayashi-sensei had taught me a kata a year earlier, which I had practiced diligently that entire year to prepare for my test, only to find out days before that Sensei wanted me to perform a completely different version of it. It wasn't a matter of fixing some details—the kata has essentially completely changed, and I needed it to be as close to perfect as possible in just a few days for my test. I never found out whether this was an intentional last-minute switch or not, but looking back I can't help but be reminded of Hayashi-sensei's experience with Nakaima-sensei and a particular bo kata that he was asked to perform a year after the old master begrudgingly taught him the form. The story goes that after Hayashi performed the kata, Nakaima-sensei told him that he would now teach him the "real" version--one completely different from the sequence Nakaima had originally taught. Sometimes the lessons of our teachers are mysterious—even decades later—but knowing Hayashi-sensei, I would not be surprised if this was his way of passing on some of his own important experiences and lessons to me. Lots of crazy times, but good memories.

SHITO RYU MASTERS

Were you a 'natural' at karate – did the movements come easily to you?

Yes. I had a huge desire to learn and I picked up movements quickly. For some reason, I always seemed to learn kata sequences and kumite combinations easily. I have wondered if this might be a result of good genes from my mother, who was an accomplished ballerina and taught at the famous Takarazuka Theater in Kobe during the pre-WWII era.

Please, explain for us the main points of Shito Ryu and its differences with other styles like Shotokan or Goju Ryu?

Well, first you have to understand that Shito-ryu includes the entire kata syllabus of both Shorin-ryu (which is the basis of Shotokan) and Goju-ryu. Kenwa Mabuni studied both schools and then added some Southern White Crane forms that he got from Gokenki and Aragaki, as well as some kata that he created himself. Mabuni was a walking kata dictionary, and the masters of his day—including Gichin Funakoshi—went to him to study kata. As a result, most Shito-ryu schools include fifty or more kata on their required list. Within all these kata, we find a wealth of information in terms of application or self-defense concepts, including a lot of grappling techniques and takedowns. Because we think of kata as encyclopedias or reference books full of technique and potential applications, our roots give us a wider range of material to work with. In terms of body language and the general "feel" of the style, Shito-ryu incorporates both the quick, snappy, straight-line movements that characterize the Shorin-ryu side and its offshoots as well as the circular, close-fighting, grappling, and breath control concepts from the Goju-ryu side.

When Shotokan evolved in Japan as a means of physical education, it changed so that it could be more easily taught to large groups in schools or university clubs. Understandably, much of the underlying application (in other words, the more dangerous waza and grappling moves) was set aside in favor of the physical movements themselves (reverse punch, front kick, and so on), since these movements supported the Japanese goals of large-group discipline and physical exercise. Ultimately, the original Okinawan Shorin-ryu was streamlined and reshaped into a new "Japanese" form of karate, with longer stances and bigger movements. In addition to being easier and safer to teach, this also made it more "dynamic" and attractive for sports competition. Eventually, a "jutsu" orientation was replaced by a "do" orientation, and much of the old Okinawan real-world application was lost.

Goju-ryu has a short syllabus of kata that retains quite a bit of its Chinese White Crane roots, including tight circles and techniques that are ideal for in-close, short-range fighting. Most Goju-ryu schools retain a focus on underlying techniques, and do a lot of two-person application drills based on their kata. They also practice specific breathing techniques which are pretty much absent from their Shorin-ryu and Shotokan cousins.

Please tell us a little about your relationship with your teachers Sensei Kuniba, Sensei Hayashi and Soke Kenzo Mabuni?

I first met Sensei Shogo Kuniba and Sensei Teruo Hayashi in Japan in early 1968. At the time, Sensei Kuniba was Soke of Motobu-ha Shito-ryu karate under the Seishinkai flag. His honbu dojo was in the Nishinari-ku section of Osaka. Sensei Hayashi was the kaicho, or president, of the Seishinkai. They co-led the association in the Kansai area of Japan, and had a few other dojo in the Kanto area around Tokyo. I was a member of the Seishinkai in the US, in a group headed by Richard Baillergeon who had been a student of Kuniba-sensei.

When I arrived in Japan, I was a shodan in Goju-ryu, and upon meeting Kuniba-sensei, I made the transition to Shito-ryu. Kuniba-sensei was young (36 years old) and a dynamic instructor with lightning-fast snappy kata and a love for the jutsu side of applying kata. I remember his favorite kata were Seipai and Shiho-Kosokun—interestingly, one from the Naha-te and one from the Shuri-te side of the Shito-ryu syllabus. He had begun his study of karate at a very early age under Kenwa Mabuni himself, and received his shodan from him at just twelve years old. Kuniba-sensei was also graded in aikido and other grappling arts, so his blocks almost always turned into wrist locks followed by throws or takedowns. Physically, he was small in stature and quite slender. At 5'3" tall and about 110 lbs, he loved to take us bigger American GIs down to the mat at the dojo that I had established at Fuchu Air Station. I didn't realize it at the time, but I'm probably one of the few Americans who actually taught at and ran his own dojo in Japan. The three main dojo in the Kansai-Tokyo area were Camp Zama (a US Army base), Johnson Air Base (made up of Japanese Self Defense Forces), and my own dojo at Fuchu Air Station, which was a US Air Force communications center. Kuniba-sensei was very knowledgeable and very willing to share the information he had. I spent hundreds of hours soaking up whatever he would teach me on his regular visits from Osaka. Once I figured out the train system, I would arrange for four or five days off in a row and go down to Osaka and train with him—working out all day and then sleeping on the dojo floor.

Soke Teruo Hayashi, as much of the traditional martial arts community already knows, was an outstanding martial artist. He was not only my primary instructor but also a dear friend and father figure with immeasurable influential on my life as well as my study of budo. Though a strict and exacting teacher, Soke Hayashi could also be warm and playful both on and off the mat—sides of himself that he often showed during our time together.

My first years training with Soke Teruo Hayashi (then Hayashi-kaicho) were in the many Seishinkai dojos scattered across the Osaka area as well as at my own Fuchu Air Station dojo in Higashi-Fuchu, near Tokyo. This was in Japan during the Vietnam era, 1968–1971. My first impression of Hayashi-sensei was of a martial artist with dynamic, strong, and precise technique--both exact and amazingly fast for a man of his years. He epitomized my mental picture of what a martial arts master could be, and I was humbled to be able to be in his presence and receive his precious instruction. For me, the opportunity to meet and learn from a true master in Japan was the fulfillment of a lifelong dream. I would dedi-

cate the rest of my life to honoring these experiences as I diligently worked to better my own karate and kobudo while handing down Soke's priceless knowledge to the next generation of traditional martial artists, both in the United States and around the world.

After training with Hayashi-sensei during my years in Japan, I brought him to the US several times during the mid-1970s for seminars and special private instruction. To my knowledge, 1975 was the first time that Soke had ever given a seminar in the United States—and certainly the martial arts camp I organized in 1976 at Sunrise Ski Lodge in Arizona was the first time he had ever taught kobudo outside of Japan. I remember fondly the countless hours that he and I spent in the dojo together, training morning until night and pausing only to grab a quick bite to eat. During a whirlwind of marathon instruction in 1975, Hayashi-sensei taught me over a dozen kata in the course of a single week. Of course it would be many, many years before I was finally able to fully assimilate this wealth of priceless information and truly call it my own. Soke Hayashi made his fourth trip to Arizona in 1979. During this visit, we held an in-dojo tournament at the Arizona Budokan, which was then located not far from downtown Phoenix. Sensei and I also traveled to a studio in Burbank, California to participate in an extensive photo shoot and interview for Black Belt Magazine.

In 1979, I took another trip to Japan for the All Japan Rengokai Championships. I served as the coach for the US team, which was competing in a friendship tournament with a Japanese group of martial artists. The team consisted of students from the Arizona Budokan as well as practitioners studying under Sensei Fumio Demura, Sensei Yamazaki, and Sensei Ken Rossen at their respective dojos in California. Following the tournament, I trained with Hayashi-sensei at numerous Hayashi-ha dojos

throughout the Osaka area. These intense training sessions were often followed by plenty of socializing and good times—during which I learned even more about Shito-ryu and traditional martial arts. I'm sure that anyone who has had a true sensei can relate to receiving these valuable off-the-mat lessons.

Soke Hayashi again visited Arizona for the fifth time later that year, and I went to Japan again in 1980 for the tenth anniversary of Hayashi-ha Shito-ryu karate and the first annual Hayashi-ha World Championships. Following the ceremony and fierce competition, martial artists from all over the world gathered for a weeklong marathon of training in both kobudo and karate. This offered practitioners of Hayashi-ha hailing from over 30 countries the opportunity to train side by side, sharing both camaraderie and technique. Soke was understandably delighted at this milestone, which in no uncertain terms announced to the world that he had arrived as the bona fide head of his own highly successful international Shito-ryu organization.

Soke Hayashi's made additional trips to the US in 1981 and again in 1985. It was during Soke Hayashi's 1985 trip to San Diego, I was able to test for my sixth dan ranking in karate. This was especially challenging as the testing was held in the open fields at Ski Beach, with no dojo walls or mirrors to orient myself during the performance of several complex upper-level kata. The year 1985 also marked the second annual World Hayashi-ha Championships in San Diego, where one of my female black belts took first place in kumite competition. The entire week following the tournament was packed with training sessions in both karate and kobudo, all led by Soke Hayashi.

During his 1986 trip to the US, Soke shared with a carefully selected handful of his top students a great deal of kama knowledge that he had not given to us freely before. I took this as a sign that he felt that our kobudo in the United States was maturing to the point that we were ready to receive this rare and priceless information. During his 1987 visit, I tested for my fourth dan ranking in kobudo. To my knowledge, this was the highest kobudo rank that Soke had ever granted anyone at the time, much less an American practitioner.

Soke Hayashi's 1988 trip to San Diego was the first time he had the heads of all five of his major US Hayashi-ha groups assembled for one event. This trip included a tournament in addition to the usual week of intensive training. This was the first time Soke taught some of the coveted Ryuei-ryu kata he had received from Nakaima-sensei, forms which he had previously guarded from even his top students.

In 1988 I was again able to return to Japan, and was pleased to be able to attend a special kobudo training session in Osaka with Soke Hayashi, Sensei Hashimoto, and Shigeki Uemura. I was surprised to see just how far kobudo in the United States had come--and to learn that in many cases it was quite a bit more advanced than what was being practiced in Japan. This was of course thanks to Soke Hayashi's many patient hours of instruction and our commitment to bringing him over to train with us each year. The trip was full of many memorable experiences, as I was fortunate enough to be able to train with a variety of senior instructors both in the Tokyo and in Osaka regions.

In 1989, Soke Hayashi visited Las Vegas for Sensei Ozawa's International Karate Championships and accompanying seminars. This three-day event featured master instructors from several disciplines in addition to the popular international tournament. The championships always afforded the Hayashi-ha members an opportunity to interact with a host of practitioners from many styles from all over the world. Our Hayashi-ha competitors dominated the events in all categories, which made us proud to be members of such an elite group headed by such a dynamic and dedicated living treasure of martial arts knowledge. I feel privileged to have had such a long and close relationship with Soke Teruo Hayashi and can only hope that my subsequent dedication to bettering myself as a traditional martial artist while passing on what he taught has honored his life and his memory. He was the dearest of mentors, and I continue do everything in my power to ensure that his legacy will never be forgotten.

Kenzo Mabuni-sensei was a small, soft-spoken man. He was the second of Kenwa Mabuni's sons. His karate was simpler, less complex, and less dynamic than either Kuniba-sensei's or Hayashi-sensei's. Unlike them, his one and only instructor was his father Kenwa. Of course he carried with him an important legacy in that his father founded the Shito-ryu style. I first met him first in Las Vegas in 1993 at sensei Ozawa's annual tournament. Despite his family history, he had remained out of limelight after his father's death, overshadowed by his older brother Kenei of the Shitokai. I was delighted to have an opportunity to ask him many questions about his father and what training was like when he was young. At the time, I had a student that was Japanese and his father served as translator both for our written communication and when I sponsored him to come to the USA to tour my several branch dojo. Committed to absorbing whatever he had to teach, I learned his complete syllabus of Seito Shito-ryu kata—which were somewhat different than I had learned from my previous instructors. Overall, his application concepts were simpler and featured far fewer jutsu-waza than what Kuniba-sensei or Hayashi-sensei had taught.

How do you remember them?

My instructors are a part of who I am. I carry photo albums in my brain of certain moments—moments that were poignant, intense, funny, instructive, or just part of knowing them. You never know when one of those special moments will happen. I could tell you a thousand stories of things that have happened over the five-plus decades that I have studied budo. Even as they were happening, I had a deep sense of how special time with Hayashi-sensei and Kuniba-sensei was, so I never wanted to miss an opportunity to experience training with them. This of course includes time on the floor, but also includes all of the lessons they shared over dinner or beer or just hanging around. I often share these off-the-mat lessons with my students as well. I think this is a special aspect of the teacher-student relationship in Japan. The respect of the student and the lessons from the teacher continue whenever they are together—whether training intensely or relaxing together in social situations.

I carry on their legacy by making sure I always tell my students who taught me the individual kata or waza we practice, and by perhaps sharing a story about some of those special moments. As practitioners and modern-day sensei, we are the sum total of off all of our training and experiences, just as our sensei were. You cannot put a value on it, and I think this value is lost on many students today. How often do we really consider what the masters had to go through to gain the knowledge that they share with us so freely and generously today? They all paid their dues, as have I. All of us that dedicate our lives to martial arts have endured a lot to acquire the knowledge that we have. And all we want to do is pass it on to the next generation with our hard-fought and deeply considered additions and personal insights. This, I think is what allows martial arts—budo—to keep living and evolving with each new generation while always honoring that precious knowledge that was given to us by our teachers, and theirs before them. Our students will never have to go through what we did to get this knowledge, just as we did not suffer to the extent our own teachers did. No amount of tuition from a student could ever match the value of the information they are being given. But I do hope that students can have the respect and awareness to appreciate that value and honor it by diligently studying it and passing it on to the next worthy student. This is the only way we can repay our teachers for the gifts they have given us and the sacrifices they have made.

Karate is nowadays often referred to as a sport... would you agree with this definition or is a martial art?

I think it depends on what your focus is. Some schools' entire reason for existence is to compete—even to the point that the trophies you take home determine your belt rank. If that is what you value, then obviously that becomes your focus and what you train for. In this case, the term "sport" certainly applies.

However, in most traditional dojo, competition is only one of many focuses of study—and typically, only a small percentage of the students want to participate in tournament-focused training and competition.

In my dojo, we practice the art of karate. That is to say, we are more focused on history, philosophy, good practical technique, and how it can best be applied in a real fighting situation. We train to establish good, strong basics and go into a lot of detail with even the most basic techniques. Our purpose is to fine-tune the toolbox of strikes, kicks, punches, and stances found in kata so that we can best apply them to the kata bunkai, develop them further in the kata oyo using additional locks and takedowns, and/or apply them in kumite.

Our students participate in tournaments two to four times a year. When we do, we have to shift the focus of our training to specifically work on "sport-oriented" karate for the event. Though tournaments are never our primary focus, our students always do well and come back with several medals each. Then we go back to our regular focus on precision basics and effective real-world application.

What are the most important qualities for a student to become proficient in karate?

First, you need a good, qualified instructor. If you are lucky enough to find one, you need the ability to listen closely to what is said and observe closely what is being done so that you can pick up not just the gross movements, but the finer detail as well. Finally, you need to keep asking questions and practice, practice, practice. Students need to make a commitment to themselves and be consistent in their training. A couple hours a week is fine for maintaining a certain level of proficiency and perhaps making some progress, but it takes more than that to really move forward and capture the richness and detail of effective karate technique. I can't stress it enough: practice, practice, practice. Practice what? Basics, basics, basics.

SHITO RYU MASTERS

When teaching the art of karate – what is the most important element; self-defense or sport?

As I mentioned earlier, it depends on your focus. For me it is self-defense.

And what that really means is, can you take this technique or series of movements and show me how it can actually be applied—how it can effectively function—against an opponent. This applies equally to empty hand techniques, traditional kobudo weapons, sword, or whatever it is you study.

Kihon, Kata and Kumite, what's the proper ratio in training?

Kihon is most important. If your basics are weak, your kata, your kumite, and your self defense will also be weak. So at least half of your time should be spent developing good stances, strikes, kicks, and blocks. Developing your basics also means practicing moving, timing, footwork, pivots, distance, angles of attack and defense, and so on. Once your basics are strong, you can then apply them to your kata, kumite, and self-defense training. You can't do everything in every class, so the best thing is to start by focusing on a particular set of basics and then take those into application in one or more of the categories (kata, self-defense, kumite) as time allows. Most of our classes are structured this way.

How has your personal expression karate has changed/developed over the years and what is it that keeps you motivated after all these years?

When I was a young black belt, I thought in black-and-white terms—meaning, there was only one right way to do a technique and anything else was just wrong. When I went to Japan, I was introduced time and again to the idea that "it's always done this way, except when…" This, I found, was a very typical Japanese way of thinking: lots of absolutes, with exceptions. Later as I matured with experience, I realized that the martial arts are very much like a fan. When you look at a closed fan it looks simple and straightforward. But when you begin to open it you realize that there are more and more possibilities, and you find a whole array of different ways that a technique may be justifiably executed or applied.

Years ago, I was a guest instructor at a seminar in Washington, DC. There were several senior instructors there, representing Shotokan, Shorin-ryu, Okinawan Kempo, and other arts. We decided to pick the kata Bassai Dai, since it was common to all the styles, and bunkai a piece of it. One by one, each instructor taught his interpretation of the same piece of the kata. Two and a half hours later, we were still on the same piece of kata! We explored many different applications, some of them inspired by watching one another, and all of them valid, workable interpretations. Given the vastness of the Shito-ryu kata syllabus, I'll sure I'll never discover all the possibilities.

How important is competition in the evolution of a karate practitioner?

I think competition has its place in training for several reasons. First of all, when you compete you must come out of your comfort zone. You are in a strange environment performing in front of unfamiliar faces. There are a lot of distractions—noises, emotions, pressure—that you must overcome in order to remain focused. In tournament kumite, you are typically facing an opponent that you don't know well, forcing you to try to read their movements and act or react accordingly. As a result, it is one of the best ways to simulate aspects of a real fight.

In short, I think tournaments can help practitioners can evolve into more confident individuals as they work to overcome their inner fears and the emotions associated with the experience of competition.

What really means "Ikken Hissatsu" and how it applies when used in Karate?

To me, the concept of a single killing blow means that one must be prepared to face an opponent or a difficult life situation with total readiness and determination—and then to deal with it intelligently, swiftly, and decisively.

However, your one killing blow may be to avoid the conflict masterfully.

How do you see the art of Karate evolve in the future?

I'm sure that the sports aspect of karate will continue to be developed. The danger is that in an effort to make things uniform, we may end up losing our identity. This is what happened to Tae Kwon Do, where instead of Tang Soo Do, Mu Do Kwan, and other distinct styles, we have a generic, watered-down version of them all. Judo started out as a gentler version of ju-jutsu, but still was considered part of the budo arts. After a few decades of Olympic involvement, it has become a pure sport and lost almost all of its traditional Japanese heritage. I would hate to see that happen to traditional Japanese karate.

On a positive note, during my recent visit to Japan I did see signs of traditional Shito-ryu and Goju-ryu groups making an effort to go back to their roots in Okinawa and China. I think evolution is important, but it is especially interesting to see this evolution taking the form of going back to our roots. I see lots of positive developments stemming from this trend.

Certainly karate has evolved dramatically since the masters we revere so much started the process. You don't have to go back very far to see it. What was being taught and the skill level of the practitioners in the sixties and seventies has been dramatically advanced. Each generation takes what their teachers gave them and adds to it. So it gets broader and richer—more diverse.

I think we are at a point where karate is developing in two distinct directions, one traditional and one sport. A similar thing happened with Ju-jitsu and Judo. There are certainly some very good, serious and "dangerous" practitioners of old ju-jitsu styles today. And then there are the judo "players" that do Olympic sport Judo. The longer time goes on, the more the two separate.

For my part, I'm a traditionalist. I teach my students that historically all the "do" arts, such as Judo, Kendo, Aikido, and Karate-do, originally descended from a "jitsu" art, like ju-jitsu, kenjitsu, aikijitsu, karate-jitsu. The jitsu part was and is the "martial" in martial arts. When we move into the do forms, we are moving to a less fighting-oriented, or truly "martial" art, and more into a physical/mental exercise or sport application. So I hope to make my contribution and pay respect to my teachers by better understanding the history of what was handed down to me and how the techniques can be practically applied

SHITO RYU MASTERS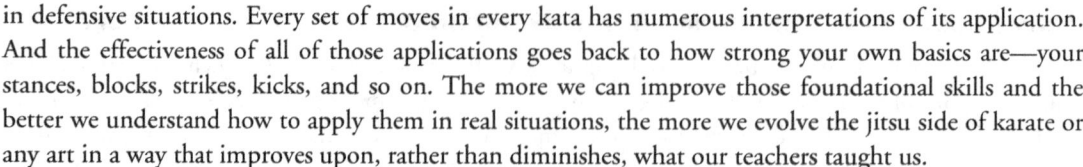

in defensive situations. Every set of moves in every kata has numerous interpretations of its application. And the effectiveness of all of those applications goes back to how strong your own basics are—your stances, blocks, strikes, kicks, and so on. The more we can improve those foundational skills and the better we understand how to apply them in real situations, the more we evolve the jitsu side of karate or any art in a way that improves upon, rather than diminishes, what our teachers taught us.

Do you feel that you still have further to go in your studies?

Recently I went to Japan for three weeks of training. I guess just the fact that I did that with fifty-plus years of experience speaks to your question. I still have a desire to gain a deeper understanding of the techniques and history of the arts I practice.

Anyway, one day while I was there, I was sitting with a group of master-level instructors and they asked me how old I was. When I told them, they responded, "Oh, you're just getting started. You need at least another ten years of training—then you'll start to understand where we're coming from. When you hit 70, things really start to make sense." So I guess I just need to keep learning!

What advice would you give to students on the question of supplementary training?

Supplementary aerobic and weight training can be a good thing. And for some students, stretching classes like yoga are a good idea. You have to look at your dojo workouts and ask yourself what would be a good complement for you personally. From the standpoint of broadening your punching and kicking skills, I think weapons training and grappling add whole new dimensions to your karate. Seminars with good qualified instructors can offer practitioners an opportunity to gain value-added ideas and knowledge to their base art.

What advice would you give to an instructor who is struggling with his or her won development?

It all depends on what they are struggling with. We all hit plateaus, and those you just have to work through. In those moments, you are not where you were and not where you want to be. Basically you just have to keep training through it, and one day your brain and body get in sync and it just clicks. I remember as a brown belt I was struggling with trying to do a proper side snap kick. I could see it in my head but my body just wasn't doing it. So I went to the dojo early and started kicking the bag all alone. Gradually it started to connect. One day my sensei walked in and watched me for a moment before crying out, "Yes, that! That's it!" Perseverance can be the key when you're stuck—whether you're at brown belt or eighth dan.

Have been times when you felt fear in your training?

I think we all feel fear at some point in our training—fear of failing the belt exam, fear of sparring the big guy, the higher-belt guy, the better-than-me guy. Fear of not performing your kata properly—in spite of the many times you have practiced it. It's overcoming those fears that builds character and is part of what karate is all about.

I remember a time when I was a green belt in James Cheatam's dojo in Newark, New Jersey. It was a Saturday class and I got paired with this burly marine-type man who was really intense. I was a skinny teenager with no meat on my bones at all, and I looked down at my partner's arms and thought, "My god, his arm is as big as my leg!" I can still see his huge sweaty forearm in a down block and his intense eyes. He charged and knocked me over several times. I eventually figured out that I should move to the side and not go straight in. Though I started out in a place of fear, the experience ended up being a valuable lesson for me. I think we all have those lessons in our training, and overcoming fear can bring tremendous gifts.

Do you think that Olympics will be positive for the art of karate-do?

No. As I expressed earlier, I think it will undermine traditional Japanese karate and has the potential to homogenize the rich stylistic traditions we have. Certainly this has been the case with Judo. And historically, we have already seen how a movement towards broad standardization, as happened in the development of Shotokan, can cause us to lose touch with the underlying real-world applications that make traditional martial arts so multifaceted and effective in true self-defense situations.

What are your views on kata bunkai? Is it bunkai really important?

Kata bunkai is absolutely essential if you are to truly understand kata. Bunkai and oyo applications are a gold mine of self-defense techniques. Students that only do kata without application practice may as well do aerobics—you might get a good workout, but beyond that it is of of no practical use.

How important is for a Shito Ryu practitioner to know all the Kata of the style?

One of the benefits of studying Shito-ryu karate is that it has such a rich array of technique to offer anyone that choses the style. Thanks to the broad roots of our style, there is something for every body type. There will always be certain kata that suit your body and become "your" kata. You will find certain kata that you will "own" in a way.

Knowing all the kata is certainly required if you intend teach the style—a kata that does not suit your own body may be just right for someone you are teaching, and as a sensei you need to be able to look at your students and choose kata that fit them. The other reason to learn more kata is that as I've said before, every move in every kata has an application—or several applications—that can be useful in self defense. In Shito-ryu especially, each kata is performed according to its own unique rhythm and timing,

which makes them harder to master. As I often tell my students, Shito-ryu does not have any "vanilla," or cookie-cutter kata. All of them have their own unique character and feel, and these features along with their applications must be accurately mastered if you are to truly understand the richness of kata.

How do you like to train yourself? Has this changed over the years?

I typically do my own practice in the dojo before the students arrive. Since I practice several arts, the type training changes with the art I'm doing—but they all have kata. I like to work on things like timing, balance, and posture. I also like to practice kicking on the target dummies for accuracy, distance, and penetration. Anything that requires a partner, I can do in class with my black belts. I used to do a lot of makiwara training when I was younger, but not anymore. Now I work on hitting faster, softer, and with greater accuracy—though my students sometimes think I'm not getting anywhere with the "softer" part.

Shotokan, Shito Ryu, Goju, Ryu etc...How do you think the different styles affect the art of Karate?

Having studied several styles earlier in my career and three schools of Shito-ryu, I can say from experience that they all have their strengths and weaknesses. Having a variety of styles does offer students the opportunity to choose what fits their own body type, their athletic ability, or simply their own sensibilities or personal tastes For example, if you are into grappling applications, you wouldn't want to study Shotokan, but you may be interested in Goju-ryu or Shito-ryu. If you loved kicking and had the athletic ability to do it well, you may gravitate towards Tae Kwon Do. There is really something for everyone, if they take the time to look and compare.

The different styles or different schools of the same style are really a reflection of some sensei's interpretation of what they learned from someone else. Karate, as with other martial arts, has evolved over the decades. What we are doing now is based on what has been passed down to us and then further developed by long-time practitioners like myself. After fifty or sixty years of training, you are entitled to have an opinion. Mabuni-sensei carried on the legacy of his teachers Itosu and Higaonna, along with others as he felt was best. Funakoshi did the same with what he learned from Azato and Itosu, and Miyagi did the same with Higaonna. But in all cases, they changed or added or expanded upon what they had been given from their teachers. That is natural and in most cases a good thing. As time goes on, we all hope to take karate to a higher level in terms of effectiveness and efficiency. Students are now free to pick and choose the style or technique that suits them best. I think in general, karate has gotten broader and deeper with each new generation. I hope I can make a positive contribution to the history of Shito-ryu, and in doing so both honor my teachers and add to what was handed down to me.

Do you think Kobudo training is beneficial for a Karate practitioner?

Yes, absolutely. In my dojo, we practice Kobudo regularly in separate classes from day one. Studying weapons adds several things to your training. It changes your whole understanding of distance and adds dexterity skills, coordination, and a different sense of combat—especially if you practice weapons sparring. From a practical standpoint, bo techniques for example can be applied using a broom stick, pool cue, or some other readily available everyday object for self-defense. Sword techniques can be applied using a golf club or fireplace tool. The tonfa is quite similar to a police baton. So there certainly is a practical side to becoming familiar with the ancient weapons. Also, if you know how to use a weapon, you always have a better understanding of how to defend against it—even if you are unarmed. Since a good percentage of street attackers have some sort of tool or weapon, kobudo can be ultimately practical and a great way to enrich your empty-hand training.

From the standpoint of "what does your dojo offer differently from the guy down the street," we teach three arts under one roof, whereas most dojos only offer one thing. Not to mention that the kids love it. It gives them diversity and a fresh challenge, so they stay interested and motivated to move on to the next kata or the next weapon. And of course the weapons sparring or even fixed kumi exercises are also fun.

What is your opinion about the "Shobu Ippon" division in Karate competition?

From the standpoint of efficiency, it's a great challenge. You must be first. You have to choose your attack well because there is no second chance. And much like a real fight situation, you don't have time to get comfortable with your opponent before you have to react decisively. We do one-point matches in our dojo regularly. If you know that your first mistake may mean the end of the match, you will fight differently. In contrast, if you are using the new eight-point rule system you can be down two, score a head kick for three points, and be winning again. So again the question is: what do you value? Is it efficiency and decisiveness that mimic a real-world situation? Is it entertaining an audience with longer matches that promote kicking techniques through a higher point structure? Once you have determined your priorities, they will determine what and how you train.

What are the most important points in your teaching methods today?

I get into the application of techniques almost immediately. We regularly spend time on basics, but I always show the student how the basic technique functions by giving them a partner to work with right away. When I was a younger instructor, my students spent a long time practicing basics up and down the floor before they ever got to try them out with a partner. What I eventually discovered was even if students couldn't do the technique correctly, once they understood the application concept, they now had a reason to try to do it better so it would work better in application.

I also give students space to practice and explore on their own—particularly once they reach the brown or black belt level. I'll introduce something, explain it, and then say, "OK, work on that," and leave the floor. After a few minutes I'll come back to see how they are doing and make adjustments. If you are constantly hovering over your students, they don't think for themselves—they just blindly follow the leader.

Another thing I always make a point to include in my classes is some history—whether it's the history of Shito-ryu as a whole, the lineage of a certain kata, or even a story about the specific instructor that taught me a particular technique or application idea. I have a strong belief in the value of knowing your roots and where you come from—not just as interesting information, but as a means to gaining a deeper awareness of your art and how to execute it. Knowing whether a certain Shito-ryu kata has its roots in Naha-te or Shuri-te, for example, helps students further the define timing, body language, and "feel" of that particular kata. If we are to truly call ourselves traditional martial artists, I believe that passing down history and the stories of our teachers is important as replicating the physical techniques that they taught.

Finally, you have to interject a little humor in the class instead of barking commands constantly. Getting students emotionally involved in the lessons always makes them stick better, but you can't just stick with a single note—always the joker or always the drill sergeant. Changing things up keeps it fresh and engaging.

What karate can offer to the individual in these troubled times we are living in?

Karate has always been my anchor. Whatever stressful situation was going on in my life—my job, my relationships, my finances, my family, whatever—I could always go to the dojo to work out and regain some balance. Karate works your body and your mind. They both have to be engaged to do it right. So with karate you get the benefits of staying in shape and the benefits of maintaining a healthy mental outlook. Meeting and overcoming obstacles in our training better prepares us to overcome the obstacles in our lives outside of the dojo.

After so many years of training, what is it for you that is so appealing in this style of karate and why?

Earlier in my training, I studied several schools that came out of the Shuri-te/Shorin-ryu line of Okinawan karate. Later I studied the Naha-te/Goju-ryu side. Both had a different focus, and when I trained in one, I didn't have access to the other. If I tried to mix them, the sensei would say, "We don't do that in our style." I found that frustrating because I could see the value of the techniques that I knew from one side that were not included in the other side. I was forced to choose and omit. I found Shito-ryu in 1968 when I went to Japan, and I thought wow, this is great. I don't have to give up anything because it's all included in one style. I never looked back.

Shito-ryu karate has such a diverse syllabus that you can never get bored. My Okinawan kobudo is the same. I've studied several styles with many great sensei, and even now I'm finding out new things about the particular weapons and how they may apply to another weapon. Our weapons kata syllabus includes many older, obscure forms, each with their own personality and rich variations of technique. And within my study of Japanese sword as well, the combination of several instructors and schools, including Toyama-ryu Iaido and Shinkendo, gives me access to an incredibly broad base to draw from when I'm

looking to apply weapons like sai or tonfa. Between Shito-ryu karate, dozens of kobudo weapons, and Japanese sword, I'll need another fifty years to digest it all and truly know it properly.

Finally, what advice would you like to give to all Karate practitioners?

Find a good, qualified sensei. Watch a class. Talk to the students. Get a sense of the dojo. You want to train in a dojo, not a studio. A studio is where they teach dance—and that's often about the depth of what you're going to get in terms of traditional technique. A dojo is where they teach the "do" or the way. It's multifaceted, it's complex, it's rich and rewarding—and it takes a lifetime to master.

Next, make a commitment to train regularly—at least two or three days a week. Regularly means consistently. No excuses. Then practice at home between classes at the dojo. Even ten or fifteen minutes here and there helps to compliment your training and solidify what you learn on the mat. When you go to the dojo, you mostly take in information. At home is where you can practice what you learned and make it yours.

Third, study the history of your style. Read books, find videos, check on YouTube for old footage. Get to know more than the physical aspects of what you study.

With your sensei's permission, go to occasional seminars—even if they are in a different art or style. This will broaden your horizons and compliment your training.

Have patience and determination and you will persevere. Karate can be a way of life. It builds character, promotes physical and mental strength, and arms you with effective self-defense skills. All of these are of great benefit as we work to overcome the many opponents we meet in life—from physical attackers to challenging and stressful situations, to the most important of all: ourselves.

DEL SAITO

A JOURNEY OF WISDOM

HE IS ONE OF THE MOST HIGHLY RESPECTED KARATE-DO INSTRUCTORS AND OFFICIALS IN THE WORLD. HIS EXPERTISE IN THE ART OF KARATE HAS MADE A GREAT IMPACT NOT ONLY IN THE UNITED STATES BUT ALSO BEYOND THE AMERICAN FRONTIER. BORN AND RAISED IN HAWAII, HANSHI DEL SAITO BEGAN HIS MARTIAL ARTS TRAINING AT THE AGE OF 11. HE RECEIVED HIS KARATE TRAINING FROM TWO OF THE MOST OUTSTANDING INSTRUCTORS IN THE SHITO RYU STYLE, CHUZO KOTAKA SENSEI AND SOKE MABUNI KENZO, SON AND HEIR OF THE GREAT MABUNI KENWA.

MORE THAN THREE DECADES OF TEACHING KARATE HAS LED TO A STRONG TRADITIONAL APPROACH, COMBINED WITH AN OPENNESS TO NEW IDEAS AND CONCEPTS FOR GROWTH. TEACHING KARATE FOR MORE THAN TECHNIQUE, HE ATTEMPTS TO HELP PEOPLE TO FIND THEMSELVES, TO DISCOVER THEIR CREATIVITY AND THEIR CAPACITY FOR OVERALL GROWTH THROUGH THE ARTS OF BUDO. HIS GOAL NEVER HAS BEEN TO GLORIFY HIMSELF, BUT RATHER TO PRESERVE ALL THE KNOWLEDGE PASSED DOWN TO HIM BY HIS TEACHERS IN ORDER TO PERPETUATE THE ART OF KARATE.

AS THE NATIONAL EXECUTIVE DIRECTOR FOR THE AAU KARATE, HANSHI DEL SAITO BELIEVES THAT A MORAL AND ETHICAL BASE SHOULD BE TAUGHT IN ALL THE DOJOS: "KARATE IS A SYSTEM WITH DEEP TRADITIONAL ROOTS. OUR SPIRITUAL NEEDS, OUR MORALITY, AND OUR BELIEFS HAVE SLIPPED INTO AN ABYSS," HE SAYS. "IT IS IMPORTANT TO ACT TO INVOLVE OURSELVES WITH PROPER ATTITUDES AND TO FIND OUT MORE ABOUT THE ABSOLUTE TRUTH. THIS IS THE TRUE BASIS OF THE ART OF KARATE-DO."

How long have you been practicing the martial arts and why did you start karate training?

Back in my childhood, I watched a lot of Chambara (samurai) movies, but karate and other martial arts were still mysterious to me. I knew more about sword fighting than any other martial art. My introduction to martial arts as a practitioner came when I was eleven years old, in 1961. I had convinced my parents to sign me up for Judo in Kahuku, a nearby sugar plantation town, and I can still remember the vigorous formal exercises that we were put through, as the sound and smell of the sugar mill also were a part of the dojo. I was just a skinny kid and many of my partners were on the chubby side and had a few pounds advantage over me. I hadn't yet figured out the throwing techniques and depended a lot on strength, which I also lacked. Needless to say, I cleaned the mat on many occasions and would go home frustrated. I wouldn't dare complain, however, because I knew my dad would lecture me on commitment and not feel sorry for me one bit. After a year of that "abuse," I was fortunate to meet

SHITO RYU MASTERS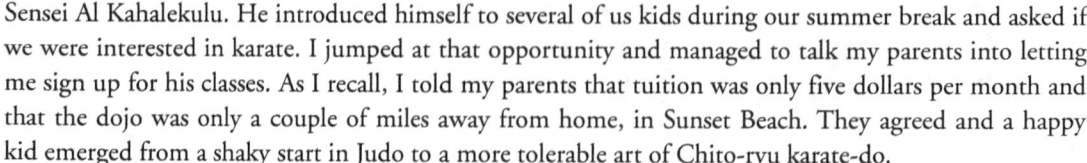

Sensei Al Kahalekulu. He introduced himself to several of us kids during our summer break and asked if we were interested in karate. I jumped at that opportunity and managed to talk my parents into letting me sign up for his classes. As I recall, I told my parents that tuition was only five dollars per month and that the dojo was only a couple of miles away from home, in Sunset Beach. They agreed and a happy kid emerged from a shaky start in Judo to a more tolerable art of Chito-ryu karate-do.

What was most interesting or challenging to you as a youngster?

In karate, I would have to say that it was how to break boards and cinder blocks. My friends and I would meet after school or on the weekends to challenge each other on who could break the most boards or bricks. We would constantly be toughening our hands and feet by striking hard rubber targets or jury-rigged makiwara pads. Our knuckles would get all callused and that was our trademark for karate excellence. No one would mess with you if you had those calluses. Fortunately for me, that period did not last for more than a few months. The pain we suffered when the board or brick proved harder gave us a lot of laughs as well as tears.

Aside from karate, sand surfing had a great appeal to me. As the waves would swipe the sand and leave a slick surface, I would run, throw my flat smooth board in front of me, and jump on it for a thrilling ride into the oncoming surf. If my timing was less than perfect, the board would stick in the sand or would be enjoying the ride without a rider.

For lessons in life, the most interesting as well as challenging thing would have to be the Christian education I was exposed to since I was five years old. My parents were leaning towards the Buddhist religion back then, but never hesitated in placing me in a Christian School. We were taught strict principles and our teachers and pastor would even frown upon dancing. Yet the biblical stories and lessons were interesting and made a lot of sense. A lot of positive seeds were planted in my mind in those early years and it was always a challenge to stay on the straight and narrow path. I can say, though, that a sound spiritual base has been vital in steering me through much stormy weather and many of life's challenges.

How many styles of karate or other martial arts methods have you trained in?

Kodokan Judo, Chito-ryu Karate-do, shito-ryu Karate-do, and Muso Jikiden Eishin-ryu Iaijutsu.

Who were your teachers during all these years?

I had several. When I met Sensei Palimo (Judo), I was only eleven and don't remember too much about him, other than his emphasis on mat work, proper methods of grappling, footwork, throwing, and submission techniques. Later he allowed randori (sparring) and I certainly had my share of cleaning the mat.

Al Kahalekulu Sensei was a gentle yet tough sensei and he was the saving grace for me to exit from judo training. He introduced karate to me, and for that I will always be grateful. His training was tough and he always reminded us to polish our character. He made his monthly home visits to check how we were behaving and was a big asset for our parents, as they could keep us in check when we would get a bit testy. His Chito-ryu instructions helped me develop confidence.

Chuzo Kotaka Sensei was my first shito-ryu instructor. He emphasized the kihons and that in itself solidified my overall karate foundation. His vision was directed more into competition, and many of us did quite well in that arena. He still maintains that focus and his students continue to be very successful, winning at all levels of competition.

Kenzo Mabuni Soke was my second shito-ryu instructor and I came to know him as a sincere and good man, a friend, and a sensei who wanted to pass on his father's legacy as best he could. He had a clear vision as to what he wanted to accomplish. He wasn't interested in subjecting me to doing things exactly as he had his students do in Japan. Rather, while instructing me in kihon, kata, and kumite, he would point out things that seito shito-ryu emphasized. One of the major difference from his ryu-ha and my last shito-ryu experience was keeping all the preparatory positions closer and less exaggerated. Once I accomplished this, he was very pleased.

Masayuki Shimabukuro Sensei is my iai-jutsu teacher. I am always fascinated with his stories of the samurai, their strict code, and their ability to use the sword. Sensei Shimabukuro has helped me understand how to make the sword come alive through perfection of technique and spirit.

What was you first impression of Al Kahalekulu?

A very powerful man who you did not want to mess with. Yet, you could sense compassion and kindness that kept you from avoiding him. Sensei Kahalekulu was a big Hawaiian man whose arms were larger than both of my thighs, and yet he could move very quickly and gracefully, which really impressed me. He taught me many lessons on life and his encouragement made it possible for me to improve my leadership skills. In the dojo, he would bark out commands, and because he gained our utmost respect, we poured everything we had in every class. In those days, we could not even scratch an itch or look around while we were in training. If you did anything that was unacceptable, a quick sting of the shinai reminded you to maintain total awareness on the task at hand. Our dojo was in an old house that someone had let us use, and the screenless windows invited many mosquitoes that we used as our excuse for getting swatted by the shinai. After each class, our dogi would be soaked from the workout, and walking home afterward in the cool offshore breeze made everything worthwhile.

Have there been times when you felt fear in your training?

I never felt fear in my training but needed lots of encouragement in teaching classes. I was very shy and had difficulty getting in front of people. The karate environment changed all that, as no one teased

or commented negatively when I first began assisting in class. Unlike giving a book report in school, everyone in the dojo was respectful and understanding.

What did your father do for a living?

My dad was a carpenter and worked for my uncle Fred Shimote for many years. He then joined the union and began to work on some larger projects like the Del Webb Kuilima Hotel, now the Turtle Bay Hilton, on the North Shore of Oahu. My parents were born on Maui and were second-generation Japanese. During summers of my younger years, my dad would take me to work with him and would teach me how not to hit my thumbs with a hammer. I learned how a finish carpenter had to have lots of patience and carpentry skills to produce a finished product with excellence.

Who were some of the karate notables when you first began karate training?

Well, there were quite a few names that I kept hearing back then, the first being Dr. Tsuyoshi Chitose, the Grandmaster and founder of the Chito-ryu karate-do group, who had his headquarters in Kumamoto City, Japan. Then there was Sensei Tommy Morita, who was the chief instructor of that style in Hawaii. I also would hear about other instructors, whom I eventually met later, such as Sensei Bobby Lowe of the Kyokushinkai group, Walter Nishioka from the Statewide Karate League, James Miyaji from the Butokukai, Kenneth Funakoshi from the Shotokan group, and Chuzo Kotaka from the IKF, whom I eventually trained with. There also were other instructors in other disciplines that were heading strong organizations in Hawaii as well as on the mainland, such as Professor Okazaki, a massage therapist and Jujitsu expert, Professor William Chow from the Kempo group, and Sonny and Adrian Emperado of the Kajukenbo group. As there were many ethnic groups in Hawaii, so were there diverse karate styles. This led to a strong martial arts base that eventually would make a great impact for the growth of karate in the United States as well as abroad.

In the late sixties and early seventies, I was fortunate to meet several influential instructors who helped expose karate to many people throughout the country, if not throughout the world. One of them was Ray Dalke Sensei. He was one of the top JKA American instructors who trained directly under Hidetaka Nishiyama. I came to know Ray as a friend and respected him for his courage to accept me, a non-JKA (shotokan) practitioner, as his peer, rather than his adversary. We would practice together and help each other with the tournaments we held.

About that same period, I was introduced to Sensei Dan Ivan. I remember him as a considerate, kind, and very knowledgeable martial artist. He shared his interesting stories while he lived in Japan. He always helped me arrange demonstrations for my tournaments with his popular Japanese Village demonstration team. He reminded me of David Krieger, who helped Kotaka Sensei establish the International Karate Federation. Dan did the same for Sensei Fumio Demura, as they established the Japan Karate Federation in this country.

It was about 1971 that I met Sensei Chuzo Kotaka, and after several meetings, he accepted me into his organization. He impressed me with his strong techniques and beautiful form. He appointed me National Director for the IKF and I carried that position until 1999, when I decided to establish my own organization.

It was also in the 1970s that I met Sensei David Krieger. He was an exceptional man with a gentle heart. His karate was good and we had lots of great times together, both in Hawaii and in Santa Barbara, where he presently resides.

Why do you think you and your friends were able to keep out of trouble?

Many of us were poor compared to those who lived in the city. Parents lived paycheck to paycheck, and that taught us to share, to be creative, and to enjoy the outdoors. We all had gardens to manage and from that came many of our meals. We learned to work together and oftentimes we would all congregate at one of our buddies' homes to help him finish his chores in order for him to play with us. Most of the moms were at home, and they all made sure we behaved. Whenever anyone of us failed to measure up to what was expected of us, our parents were informed and the belts didn't feel so good when our dads came home. Parents also took the time to teach us skills and lessons in life. They made sure we addressed the adults as Mr., Mrs., Miss, and Sir or name. Whenever we made a promise, they made sure we followed through. We also had supper together and I think that kept a tight family. We would never want to do anything that would shame our families or let our parents down.

How long did it take you to really "get" karate?

Not until many years of study of not only its technical aspect but also the challenges that solidified my understanding of character. The mental training was very trying and difficult to accept at times, but after hours of repetition, things started to connect and made sense. The clarity of the philosophy at times would become very cloudy, but that was because the underlying agendas of the karate leaders made it almost impossible to grasp the full concept of this art. Interestingly, the politics, personal goals, and organizational strategies of the leaders had a great deal of influence on the standards of karate. Some organizations were like fraternities, and if you endured their initiation and oftentimes humiliation, then you were considered one of the boys. Many traditional instructors prohibited their students from learning from other instructors and would ostracize those who did. It was all of those kinds of things that caused me to understand karate-do, and it was from then on that I felt it was my mission to help maintain karate-do in the spirit it was meant to be.

What was your biggest frustration in training?

From the technical point of view, at first the movements were very foreign and it took many months of training for them to sink in. In my early days of training, I was unable to reference books, video, or television. Everything was totally new and many aspects of karate were missing. It was like putting a puzzle together with many of the pieces missing. However, through time, I began to understand the principles that allowed me to execute the movements properly without being too stiff or overly zealous to be the best in my class.

The dojos of yesteryear usually were at community centers, churches, or classrooms shared by other groups, and supervised training was limited to only a few days per week. I wanted more direct instructions from the sensei, especially in the beginning stages, and I was frustrated when formal training was limited to only a few hours per week. My biggest frustration, however, was due to instructors who thought that their style was the only one that had any merit. Their tunnel vision caused many students to eventually abandon the traditional styles and to form their own open or "eclectic" styles. Perhaps that trend would have occurred anyway, but I would argue that it was because of these earlier instructor's attitudes that karate was revolutionized in this country.

Another frustration is how many instructors still hang onto the coattails of past martial artists who seem to have no one equal or better. If all that they still advocate and teach holds true, why is it that no one has yet achieved such a level of excellence. I know that in my style of karate, we have many outstanding teachers, students, and athletes. Even my students now have surpassed me in many areas, and I am grateful that I was able to teach them.

Are any of the students you grew up with still active in karate?

I don't think so, not from the original group of guys and gals that started with me. However, a good friend, John Isabelo, who began training with me a few years later, still works out with Sensei Walter Nishioka in Honolulu. He earned a Medal of Valor while serving with the Honolulu Police Department and was one of their outstanding homicide detectives. He now works as an investigator for the Attorney General's office for the State of Hawaii.

Who were your biggest role models?

Definitely my mom and dad. They both were loving and kind and always taught me life skills that I have learned and accepted. Mom was a housewife and always was home to care for me and my five brothers. She was always washing clothes, sewing, or cooking, and kept everyone of us in line. We had to learn how to wash, cook, iron, and clean house. My dad was a carpenter and worked constantly. Even after returning from his job, he would be working in the garden or doing something that he managed to involve us in. We would do everything the old-fashioned way, which was never easy, and he made sure that we did it right. He would even make his own bows and arrows and I would be the one to turn the handle for his makeshift lathe. I sure did my share of grumbling but little did I realize at that time that dad was teaching us how not to be afraid of work, which would have positive results both outwardly as well as inwardly. My parents never used profanity and always seemed to make ends meet.

My dad was interned right after the attack on Pearl Harbor. He was placed in a camp at Tule Lake, California, for about four years. Eventually, I began to ask my dad all kinds of questions about his ordeal, which I thought was totally unfair. He never once had anything negative to say about our country, even though he had to endure those troubling times. He would remind me however, that in order to prove that we (the Japanese people in Hawaii) are good citizens, we needed to move on to become productive and hard workers. I always remembered those words of wisdom and respected him even more.

Aside from my parents, my first instructor had a lot of influence on me. His concern on my well being also helped me at home. Sensei Kahalekulu would make periodic visits to my home and would check to see if I was practicing my karate, by-laws, and resolutions. My parents also would remind me whenever I became too testy, that their report to sensei would not be taken favorably. I would immediately straighten up, as even the slightest thought of upsetting him was too embarrassing.

I attended Sunset Beach Christian School on the North Shore of Oahu from Kindergarten to eighth grade. One of my favorite teachers was Miss Aileen Miller. She was a sweet educator who had lots of patience, and her love for her students was very apparent. Her close relationship to the Lord, total commitment to her mission work and daily instructions, provided me with an abundance of hope in the years of challenges that would come my way.

David Krieger was another great man whom I admired, and was in many ways a role model for me. He was well-educated and the person responsible for getting the IKF started with Kotaka Sensei. He held a Ph.D. in Political Science and headed the Peace Now Foundation (a nuclear disarmament program)

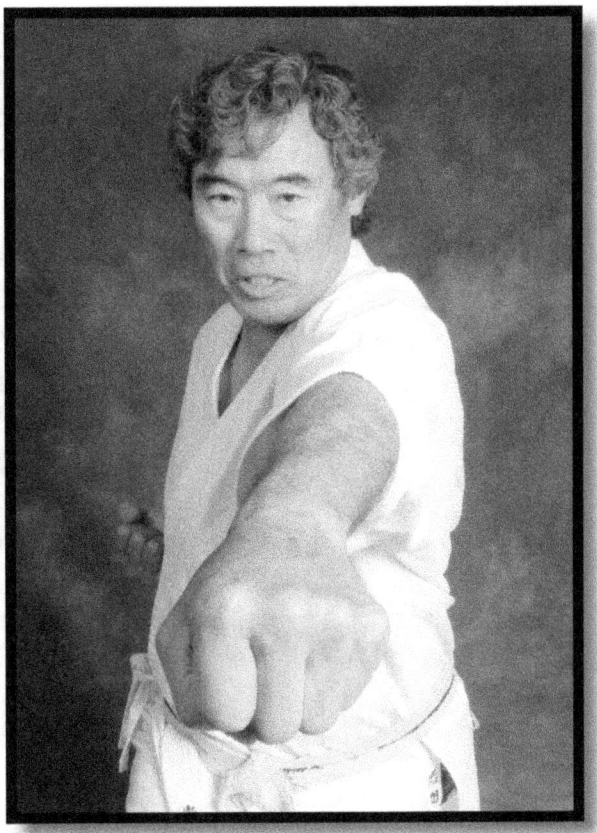

based out of Santa Barbara, California. Since then, he has also completed law school and obtained his real estate broker's license. He also is a very accomplished Shito-ryu sensei and founded the Pacific Karate-do Institute. David Krieger was a gentle man who would find good in people and did not dwell on the negative. Although very intellectual, he would not even remotely talk down to anyone, even if they were quite ignorant. I admired all he stood for.

Another role model was my late friend, Mr. Henry Takaki. He was the local postman, and would take time on the weekends to gather a few of us kids to treat us to a movie. He would teach us how to communicate and think, and would do so by cleverly asking us things that would spark our interest. He always was involved with community organizations, and spent countless hours in keeping the North Shore community alive and educated. He was instrumental in guiding me to be involved with community projects and taught me about volunteerism.

Did you prefer kata or kumite?

I preferred kumite at first because we were not allowed to spar until several months after signing up for classes. We would watch the adults spar and then, on the way home from the dojo, stop at Ehukai Park at the Bansai Pipeline and mimic the moves. We made sparring very dramatic as we would announce to our opponents what technique we were about to do. As I recall, the "Shooting Star" was one of our favorites; it was a glorified jump kick that was prepped by Kung Fu-like hand gestures. We

had a blast and thought that was the ultimate in karate. It was not until my senior year in high school that I became more interested in kata. I guess I came to realize that the kata held more information and learning tools that I could gather with more acceptance and seriousness of its practice. That realization came from my personal development and maturing. As I'm getting older, I enjoy kata more than ever. The bunkai-oyo, or practical application, and kakushite (hidden techniques) are fascinating, and the wealth of information kata holds always amazes me. I still enjoy kumite as well, as it pushes me to maintain my agility and stamina while maintaining my distance and timing practice. It also is more enjoyable sparring with my friends as we have come to learn how to train with it rather than to prove our strength by hurting each other.

Did you compete a lot in Hawaii?

Not a lot. When I first started training, my instructor was not into competition. It was not until the late 60s that I began to compete in Hawaii, and I competed in only a handful of events there. By the seventies, I had already moved to Southern California and was more interested in preparing my students for competition. The last tournament that I competed in was in Hawaii in the early 80s, where I was fortunate to win first in all my events.

Most of the tournaments I competed in were in California. Kumite in those days were all shobu-ippon or one-point matches. You could be preparing for a tournament for months only to be beaten in a couple of seconds. There were only a few round-robin or double elimination tournaments. And repechage was not even heard of. Athletes back then did not want to win by contact penalties, either. If your nose was broken, you would hold the bleeding with toilet paper and be ready to fight on. We were tough then but perhaps our young impressionable age made us a bit foolish. But how much fun it was just to survive. I just hope that the abuse we put our bodies through doesn't come back to haunt us.

The most enjoyable and memorable competitions and events were those at the Japanese Village and Deer Park presented by Senseis Fumio Demura and Dan Ivan. Not only was the Japanese Park setting ideal, but there were always players from Japan who kept the competition interesting. One year, after winning the Black Belt Kata division, I met a stocky Japanese in the finals. After several exchanges, I landed a front kick to his stomach that nearly tore my toes off. The pain was excruciating but the win made it bearable. Until this day, I am reminded of that match every time I look at my crooked toe.

Who were your greatest rivals and what were they like?

I guess I would have to say the players from Japan. In those days, all you heard about in competition was how tough the Japanese Nationals were. They were the ones that ruled. So whenever I had the opportunity to face one of them, I was very prepared. Fortunately I was able to beat every one of them. Aside from competition, our greatest rivals were students and instructors from other dojos. Oftentimes, they would appear unannounced to challenge you to a kumite match just to test your worthiness. Some of those fights would get pretty rough, but if you emerged victorious, you would be left alone. Those that didn't fare well eventually closed their dojos.

What are your favorite techniques?

I have managed very well with keeping my arsenal simple. I rely on foot sweeps, thrusts and front kicks for success. The magic is in the timing, distancing, and confident execution of the techniques; and of course, strategy has an important role in packaging my delivery. Some have said that I have a mean look about me when I'm in the ring which causes my opponents to be intimidated. If that works, I guess I won't be needing the services of a plastic surgeon.

How has your personal expression karate developed over the years?

One of the positive changes I see is that more traditionalists are allowing their students to mingle and to train with other instructors in the form of clinics. It would seem a given that an instructor would see to it that his students have accomplished instructors. As an example, parents who think they can teach their children everything, and not allow them to be exposed to others to be taught or mentored, are surely stunting their potential to grow. As for development of the karateka, I believe today's students are stronger, have more technical savvy and develop quicker than those when I first began training. The understanding of nutrition, stretching, muscle development, psychology, plyometrics, et cetera, plus easy access to information, gives the modern karate warrior access to many more pieces of this fascinating puzzle. Of course the old timers who are still active also have progressed and can hold their own. They still possess courage and confidence that equal or oftentimes surpass the younger martial artists.

We definitely were tougher back in the old days. We never wore any protective gear, and if you got hurt, other than very severe injuries, you kept on going. Much of the kumite training was to survive. It was that kind of dojo climate we all endured, and you had to be prepared for outsiders who would come to your dojo to basically challenge you (dojo yaburi).

The important point of my teaching is to utilize karate-do as a vehicle to develop good character, healthy minds and bodies, and assist in directing those who I serve to learn to be of service to others. Students, on the other hand need, to understand and practice commitment. Students who are committed to learning correctly and training for the long haul provide me with the opportunity to expose them to all the necessary tools to build a solid foundation. From strong roots and with healthy spirits, students will be able to keep a healthy attitude to preserve the style for others to learn and enjoy.

I don't think that it is healthy or even reasonable to cling to things that have no room for improvement. Changes and adjustments are necessary as long as they don't wander too far from the original source. Can you imagine where medicine would be today if we kept it "pure" as of yesteryear?

Do you think different 'styles' are truly important in the art of karate?

I think it is good to maintain the various styles, as each has many unique qualities and flavor. Styles offer healthy choices for students. Once they have come to understand their style, they can better appreciate other styles while maintaining their unique characteristics and integrity.

What is your opinion of fighting events such as the UFC and Mixed Martial Arts?

I imagine there is a following for that type of fighting. Perhaps there is even a need for those who feel that they have to constantly prove that they can whip others into submission. It should be kept away from the impressionable eyes of our youngsters.

Karate nowadays often is referred to as a sport... would you agree with this definition, or is a martial art?

There is definitely "sport karate." In fact, many athletes only practice kumite if they wish to excel in sparring, or practice only kata if they wish to perform well in that arena. True karatekas learn how to defend themselves internally and externally. The delicate balance to practice correctly is definitely a part of the martial aspect of karate. Senseis need to sculpt a landscape that all students, young and old, can appreciate. Too often, I see older students retire and put to pasture because the interests of their teachers have waned. A healthy dojo would have many seniors practicing eagerly for the love of the art, nothing more.

How do you think karate has most influenced you?

By teaching me from a young age to be disciplined, focused, and balanced. By doing so, I became confident and overcame my shyness. What the public schools lacked in fulfilling my shortcomings, my karate school provided. Throughout the years, karate has opened the door to many opportunities to serve in a leadership capacity, such as my present position as National Executive Director for the AAU karate Program. Karate also has led me to meet many outstanding practitioners of the martial arts, and has provided me the opportunity to help others overcome their obstacles. Karate has become a part of my life and, as life unfolds countless lessons, so does karate. I am always searching for ways to keep students healthy and active, in order to provide me with enough time to teach them adequately. As the new-age approach of teaching has invaded many circles, I want to maintain the disciplined dojo atmosphere without negative reactions from students or parents. Without the proper discipline and respect, teaching becomes almost a chore rather than a blessing.

When did you get involved with the AAU Karate?

In the mid 80s, I met Sensei Joe Mirza, another Shotokan practitioner, at one of Dalke sensei's tournaments in Riverside, California. He was a man of good character and his love for karate became very apparent to me. Soon after that first meeting, Joe Mirza convinced me that I should become active in the AAU National Karate Program, which he was chairman of. I guess he sensed that I was looking for an organization that I could really sink my teeth into, to make a difference in strengthening classical Karate-do in the U.S. My hat goes off to him as he has accomplished so many things that our earlier pioneers pursued but came up short on. His passion and dream to take Karate-do to greater heights of excellence also has made me partner with him to make that a reality.

How do you see karate in the U.S. at the present time?

Confused. Instructors who have used martial arts as a business are winging the approaches of successful operators who make a hefty income from their dojos. I say more power to those who have been financially successful. I'm sure they are not losing any sleep at night, despite the fact that their students

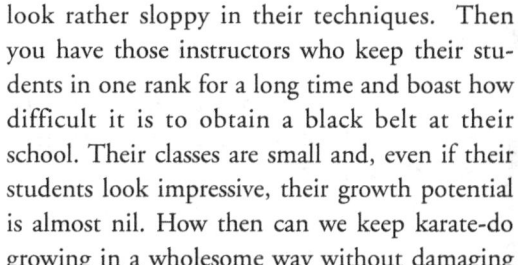

look rather sloppy in their techniques. Then you have those instructors who keep their students in one rank for a long time and boast how difficult it is to obtain a black belt at their school. Their classes are small and, even if their students look impressive, their growth potential is almost nil. How then can we keep karate-do growing in a wholesome way without damaging the integrity of our precious treasure? All true senseis need to be finding a sane and wholesome solution.

How does the karate style differ from other martial arts methods when applying the techniques in a self-defense situation?

I would hope that karatekas would defend themselves wisely, quickly and effectively. By utilizing self-defense techniques of awareness, confidence, and positive body language, karate students will be able to defend themselves before actually being attacked. Some of the other martial arts provoke one to attack just to test his or her abilities. I recall a martial art school in Hawaii that did just that. The instructor taught his students how to fight, and after training they would go to the local bar and stir up trouble with the GIs so they could test their techniques. Technically, karate incorporates grappling, throwing, submission maneuvers, and non-tournament applications that are very effective. Regardless of the techniques applied, karatekas understand the need for control and not abuse their right to defend themselves.

Self-defense is a very important element in the art of karate-do. And self-defense is not only physical but mental and emotional as well. Sport karate also should be urged as a learning tool for competition. Life is competitive in many ways and, despite all the necessary preparations, there are winners and those that have to wait for other opportunities.

Forms and sparring: what's the proper ratio in training?

In the beginning the ratio should be 90 percent kata. After the kihon is solid, sparring and forms should then be equal. Then, for those who reach the autumn of their lives, I feel the ratio to be 70–80 percent kata and a slower pace of sparring. Kata is very important in the budo aspect of karate-do. By practicing kata, one can fulfill physical and mental training and learn how to become victorious over oneself; that is, to destroy the enemy within. So many times, students, especially adults, are hesitant in performing kata in front of an audience due to their insecurities. Yet, by practice and encouragement, they learn to push that aside and come to enjoy the opportunity to share the movement of their body with the proper components with others. Kata also is a very ingenious way of transmitting information

from teacher to student in order to preserve the style and self-defense techniques.

Do you have any general advice you would care to pass on to the practitioners?

Seek out the right sensei. One of the most important phases of training is the beginning. Correct application of techniques, healthy attitude, wholesome philosophy, and a clean and safe environment are important considerations to hold in your quest for karate excellence.

Train regularly. Hold yourselves accountable to your trusted dojo mates and keep karate a healthy attitude that nourishes your mind, body and spirit.

For senseis, learn to communicate effectively. It is an ongoing process that needs to be understood in depth in order for positive learning to take place. Instructors and students alike have a built-in basis, such as culture, religion, politics, and age. For example in many circles, physical contact is taught to be kept within the immediate family. As a result, when a teacher corrects a student's technique by touching him or her, it may not be taken as the teacher intended, but rather cause a negative reaction because it may be in direct violation of the parent's rules. Religions that advocate that one should not bow to anyone but God bring questions of bowing to others in the dojo. And then there are those who teach their children to always question authority because many who are placed in superior positions have abused their power and taken advantage of those in their care. These are some of the filters that need to be addressed to maintain an open line of communication. Compared to the World War I veterans, who were totally committed to honor, respect, duty, and sacrifice, the Baby Boomers believe that honor is based on their personal ideals, duty is formulated with teamwork and not independent hard work, respect may come after authority is questioned, and respect is embraced only if it encompasses diversity.

What do you consider to be the major changes in the art since you began training?

More networking with other instructors and students is tolerated. The earlier pioneers were myopic and hard-headed in many ways, and considered themselves to be the authorities of karate-do, when in reality, they were young, adjusting to a different culture, and building a reputation for themselves. They frowned upon mingling with practitioners of other styles not their own, and made those who came from

Japan achieve higher status no matter if they were juniors to those who were their sen-pai here in the States. This resulted in a major meltdown and the beginning of the American revolution of the martial arts. I don't know if we can bring the extreme right wing martial artist to some happy medium with the left, but those of us who understand karate-do must work together to preserve what we have.

Who would you like to have trained with that you have not?

Chojun Miyagi and Kenwa Mabuni. Miyamoto Musashi for Iaijutsu. Miyagi Sensei knew that many trappings, such as belt color and titles, would allow karate teachers to be judged by their belt and rank, rather than their character.

What can you tell us about the late Soke Mabuni Kenzo?

I came to know him as a dear friend and I respected him greatly. He supported me when many of his own instructors first had doubts about me, especially when they were unclear as to my real motives in karate-do. Soke Mabuni also recognized my TKO organization and the AAU as important organizations of Karate-do. He made it possible for me to run my organization without having to interrupt our day-to-day operations by joining another organization. He provided me with a direct line to him. He trusted me with making wise decisions that would enhance the betterment of Shito-ryu in this country as well as abroad. When he stayed in my home, it was a treat to hear his stories of his dad and of what karate meant to him. It was also a joy to go outside with him to practice kata. I was also very honored when Soke allowed me to direct the 4th International Shito Cup in Grants Pass. I admired him for being able to be a great leader, orchestrating as well as challenging all the leaders in his organization. I also saw the special joy he had seeing children performing kata. The smiles and twinkle in his eyes clearly told me what karate is about. The autumn of his life began to wear on him; yet, although very frail, he managed to be a part of our AAU Nationals. He loved karate for the right reasons and I will always remember that.

What keeps you motivated after all these years?

Students who have grown to be outstanding citizens and continue to be of service to others. Students who have overcome adversities thanks to their karate training. My good friends and colleagues who continue to strive to maintain a sane and useful art. Younger students of karate-do, such as Cyndi-Yu Robinson, Ophira Bergman, Linda Donner, Brandon Arashiro, Kate Roin, Tony Mendonca, Justin Wilson, as well as others, impress me with their karate performance and sincerity. By their involvement, I know that karate is in good hands and keep me motivated as well as hopeful.

What is the philosophical basis for your karate training?

Train with what you are able to accomplish without injuring yourself. Always try your best but don't beat yourself down in the trying.

After all these years of training and experience, could you explain the meaning of the practice of karate?

If you are talking about keiko and not renshu (training), I believe it goes hand-in-hand with shu-ha-ri (the stages of learning and mastery). Drawing from the past to identify the core of karate-do is important. Once a level of mastery is present, the journey then requires improvement to better the path of those who preceded us. Incorporate the infinite wisdom of old with modern concepts. This kind of understanding will keep the art improving with each generation. That is and should be the practice of karate-do.

How do you think karate practitioners can increase their understanding of the spiritual aspect of the art?

I believe that as one becomes more in harmony with oneself and with others, a deep spirited manifestation to seek truth becomes apparent. God has planted seeds in each one of us to grow and to seek Him. He has provided an internal compass to find Him. Through practice, one needs to understand what is God's will as opposed to man's will. In the dojo, we are constantly appraised to determine our self-worth. Unlike buying a car or property, where the worth is based on the blue book or appraiser, our worth should not be left to the sole appraisal of the sensei. We need a higher source to keep our character value high. For example, there are instructors who keep students who make them look good on a pedestal and allow their shortcomings to be overlooked. Then, there are those who will keep promoting students, not keeping them at a high standard, fearful that they may quit and reduce their financial bottom line. That self-interest equates to selfishness and ultimately results in disappointments. Senseis and students need to look for the interests of others. This will result in humility. Spiritually, then, we should all keep God as the captain of our ship and allow Him to direct us in our karate mission in order that we may all stay the course.

Is anything lacking in the way martial arts are taught today compared to how they were you began?

I would have to say seriousness. We worked hard and learned karate to experience the unexpected. It was survival. If you were not serious, you paid for it. For many these days, karate is just another seasonal extracurricular activity.

Could I ask you what you consider the most important qualities of a successful karate practitioner?

Trustworthiness, humility, and sincerity, augmented with the willingness to train hard on a regular basis. Learning karate-do to improve one's well-being and applying it in one's daily life in order to be a productive and outstanding citizen. To apply karate lessons which have been rooted in one's moral values and overall conduct that defends one from negative peer pressures.

What advice would you give to students on the question of supplementary training (running, weights, et cetera)?

I recommend wind sprints, correct weight training, stretching, (cross-training), plyometrics, and balancing it with healthy reading, fishing, and golf.

Why do you think that a lot of students start falling away after two or three years of training?

I blame lack of enthusiasm, too many extracurricular activities that fog the vision, classes that become boring and lack motivation, and phases of their lives that need more tending to. Also, lack of commitment; disciplined environment (the dojo) not readily accepted by today's youths; other activities such as soccer; computer games; parents who don't take the time to teach their children commitment; and the relaxed overall attitude that becomes a conflict with a structured and disciplined dojo.

And the old methods of instructing need to be modified in order to keep students long enough to be able to teach them the true benefits of karate-do. With all the extra fun curricular activities available, instructors need to reevaluate their teaching methods in order to maintain a good student enrollment. The fact is that many technically unqualified karate instructors, as judged by the traditional masters, pack their schools with hundreds of students. Their modern methods of teaching fits in perfectly with the times, and their marketing and business savvy puts many of these masters to shame in that department.

For other disciplines, one marketing strategy is to make the black belt easily attainable, much easier than at the classical dojos. Once achieved, this new black belt will always elevate their status and spread the greatness of their style, school and instructor. Traditional instructors, on the other hand, relish how hard it is for their students to achieve the black belt. It becomes a no-brainer when a

parent asks how many students have achieved their black belt this year and you say five, compared to 100 in a non-traditional school. I'm not advocating that we all begin teaching that way or begin handing out black belts, but we certainly need to re-think how we can preserve our art.

What led you to become the Director for the Traditional Karate-Do Organization?

I would have to say that all the interesting chapters of my life led to my present position with the TKO. In the late 60s, Sensei Al Kahelekulu retired completely from karate. He gave me the authority to continue teaching Chitose-ryu and promoted me to Godan. I then formed the Goshinjutsu Organization and was unattached to any other organization at that time. My dad had heard the name Goshinjutsu and said that it was a good name so I agreed. I had Sensei Kahalekulu sign each certificate and operated the independent organization until the early 70s, when I joined Kotaka sensei's IKF. In 1998, Sensei Jo Mirza, who had already established the TKO, invited me to head the Shito-Ryu Division. I told him that I would perhaps consider it one day, not knowing that I would accept the offer the very next year. Sensei Kotaka had made a few changes in his organizational operations, which led to my resignation from the IKF. I informed all of my branch instructors of my decision and gave them my blessing if they wished to remain attached with the IKF. Fortunately for me, they all decided to trailblaze with me, and as they say, the rest is history.

SHITO RYU MASTERS

What leadership roles do you presently have?

I presently am the owner and operator of Del Saito's Martial Arts Training Center, Executive Director for the AAU National Karate Program, Director of AAU Karate Regional 12, Chairman of Oregon AAU Karate, Governor of Oregon AAU (all sports), President of the Grants Pass Asian Cultural Society, and Director of the Traditional Karate-do Organization, and recently elected to the National AAU Board of Directors for all sports.

What would be your ideal for karate in the USA?

That karate would be incorporated into every junior and high school. I think there is a definite need in the school system for this kind of training, which could benefit everyone involved. I believe that ingredients of discipline, respect, honor, awareness, motivation, accountability, and responsibility provided in a dojo atmosphere would definitely extend into the classroom. I see so many good kids who have too much unsupervised time that gets them in trouble. If we could only figure out a way to minimize that problem and get them involved in a wholesome yearly activity, the lessons they would reap will keep them from learning the hard way.

To what do you attribute the success of your program?

Honesty, fairness, and my autocratic methods of running my program have been the keys to the success of our schools and organization. Karate sensei, students, and parents need to be assured that what we provide is a sound program that will be of benefit to them. I always make sure that each person has ample time to research our program before admitting him or her to our school or organization. I go over what is expected of them and what they can expect from me. My leadership in the dojo is not democratic because, throughout all the years of teaching, I have found it to be ineffectual, that it leads to wasted time, confusion, and at times even corruption. Those who understand what our service provides for them will stay and become a vital force in keeping the positive training spirit alive. Those who choose not to embrace our philosophy will fade away and not harm the prestige or integrity of our program. As for training, I still demand the utmost respect and discipline from every student. They do not leave the mat as they wish, and I expect them to give their best effort. Their achievements are based on their own hard work and diligence, and once they figure that out, they have learned the formula for success. I also end each class with a brief discussion on lessons of life, which include nutrition, behavior, dating, community service, and drugs, to name a few.

Who do you think are the top karate athletes these days?

The notables in the United States are George Kotaka, Elisa Au, Barbara Chinen, John Fonseca, Kenny Inami, and Alfonso Gomez Jr., to name a few. Others whom the AAU has groomed are Shannon Nishi, Kate Roin and Brandon Arashiro. I've enjoyed watching these athletes mature not only in the competition arena but in life as well. They are awesome technicians and skilled in martial arts, and most of all, they are well-mannered, respectful, and great role models. For the more senior athletes, I would have to say the list would include Linda Donner.

Do you think that Olympics will be positive for the art of karate-do in case that happens one day?

I don't know about the art of karate, but it may be for the sport if it maintains many of the classical principles that we now embrace. If the international sports leaders constantly change the composition of karate just to satisfy the sport aspect, then the UFC type of fighting may seem to be more appropriate for the IOC. It would certainly be clearer who the winners are.

What are your thoughts on the future of karate?

I am very optimistic. Although many of the pioneers of karate in this country had their shortcomings, those who made a sincere attempt to teach and preserve what they knew with passion and conviction can be appreciated and respected for their efforts. Likewise, today's instructors must teach wholesomely and seize every opportunity to keep karate-do from eroding, and to maintain its integrity for future generations to enjoy.

FUMIO DEMURA

LEADING BY EXAMPLE

ALTHOUGH FUMIO DEMURA HAS BEEN A MARTIAL ARTS SUPERSTAR FOR MORE THAN THREE DECADES, HE HAS MANAGED TO KEEP TRADITIONAL KARATE VALUES IN HIS LIFE, AND LOYALTY AND RESPECT IN HIS PERSONAL AND PROFESSIONAL RELATIONSHIPS. HE IS A SUPERB TECHNICIAN, A GREAT MARTIAL ARTIST, AND ONE OF THE FINEST PERFORMERS AND WEAPONS EXPERTS IN THE WORLD. HE IS CREDITED WITH BEING THE FIRST PROFESSIONAL KARATE PERFORMER TO INCORPORATE LIGHTS, MUSIC, COSTUMES, AND MARTIAL ARTS INTO THE SAME ROUTINE. HIS TECHNICAL PROWESS IS BREATHTAKING — AS IS THE TRADEMARK PRECISION OF HIS PUNCHES AND KICKS. EASY-GOING AND AFFABLE, HE IS ONE OF THE MOST ACCESSIBLE KARATE MASTERS TO LEARN FROM. AUTHOR OF SEVERAL BOOKS ON KARATE AND KOBUDO, SENSEI DEMURA IS KNOWN WORLDWIDE FOR HIS MOVIE WORK IN FILMS AS THE KARATE KID, RISING SUN, AND THE ISLAND OF DR. MOREAU.

THE ALL-JAPAN KARATE CHAMPION IN 1961, DEMURA CAME TO UNITED STATES IN 1965 TO SHARE HIS KNOWLEDGE AND SPREAD HIS TEACHINGS IN HIS OWN UNIQUE EXUBERANT WAY. IN SO DOING, HE MANAGED THE DIFFICULT TASK OF PRESERVING THE OLD VALUES PASSED TO HIM BY HIS JAPANESE MASTER, WITHOUT COMPROMISING HIS TRADITIONAL BELIEFS. LIVING IN SOUTHERN CALIFORNIA SINCE HIS ARRIVAL, DEMURA WAS A CLOSE FRIEND OF MARTIAL ARTS LEGEND DONN F. DRAEGER, WHO ALSO KNEW ACCLAIMED AUTHORITY DAN IVAN, THE MAN WHO BROUGHT DEMURA FROM JAPAN IN MID-60S. SIMPLY SAID, FUMIO DEMURA IS THE TYPE OF PERSON THAT PEOPLE NATURALLY FOLLOW AS A LEADER.

What's your rank in karate-do?

Rank is something I really don't care about, but because you asked I hold a 7th Dan in shito ryu itosu kai karate-do. I still consider myself a 5th degree, though, like most traditionalists. I was a 5th degree for over 25 years until my teacher told me that my own students were going to outrank me, and then gave me the 7th degree black belt.

Why don't you dwell on rank?

Basically, because I consider myself a Master Ryusho Sakagami student. I don't look at myself as a master at all. Today everybody wants recognition; everybody wants to be called "master." They say, "They don't give credit to me." I really feel embarrassed by all this for the sake of karate.

SHITO RYU MASTERS

What did Sensei Sakagami mean to you?

Everything. Master Sakagami had a big influence on my life and was like a second father to me. While he didn't physically train me so much, I learned a lot from him in other ways. Sincerely, I would say that he "created" me in many different ways. I really liked his personality and his way of doing things.

Did you study other arts?

Yes, I did. But because of my attitude towards rank, I never tested for belts in them.

When did you start training in karate?

It was a long time ago! I started training because of illness. As a child I got a severe infection in my tonsils which left me very weak. The doctor said I should exercise. When I was 8 years old I started taking kendo lessons under Sensei Asano. When he had to move away, he gave me a letter of recommendation for Ryusho Sakagami to begin karate training. But in fact I didn't take it seriously until I was around 12. I also studied aikido, kyudo, and judo during my high school days. I went to high school to study drama because I wanted to be an actor. But once I finished school, my father disapproved so I had to go to the university to study economics because that's what my father wanted.

How did you come to study kobudo?

Thanks to Sensei Sakagami, I was able to receive my training from Kenshin Taira, a kongou ryu kobudo master who died in 1973. Master Sakagami invited him to become a teacher in our dojo and he accepted the position and came to live in Master Sakagami's house. Master Taira influenced a lot of people because he was moving around all the time in order to teach. Due to his age, Sensei Taira was a little hard to communicate with – but his skill and teaching abilities were fantastic. He was a typical "old style" sensei and taught just one way, which never ever changed. He was very, very special. Master Sakagami was also a kendo and iaido teacher. I took iaido and kendo classes from him, but I also trained kendo under Sensei Taisaburo Nakamura.

Were you outgoing as a child?

My personality was very different from now. I was born in Yokohama and I had four brothers and two sisters. I was very bashful and it was almost impossible for me to go in front of people. From the physi-

cal point of view I was very weak, I had a problem with my tonsils. Fortunately, martial arts changed all that!

How was the training during the old days?

Very difficult! The training was harder and very demanding. We used to train the basics everyday for hours. Just basics!

It is true that you failed your first test for white belt?

Yes, I did! In fact, that made me realize a lot of things. That embarrassed me so much that I decided to set goals and put more time into training. Since them, I have always believed that failures can make you grow and improve if you know how to make a stepping-stone out of them.

How hard was it to win the All Japan Karate Championship in 1961?

That tournament was very hard because every style, association, and school was there – goju ryu, shotokan, shito ryu, wado ryu, and more. It was very difficult to win because the best fighters in Japan were competing in it. I was very nervous. I had fought in other small tournaments but never in a big one like that.

When did you decide to come to the United States?

The final decision was in 1965, but in 1963 I was helping Sensei Sakagami with a lot of demonstrations and I met Donn F. Draeger. Mr. Draeger was assisting his jiujitsu teacher, Takaji Shimizu, and I was helping Sensei Sakagami. I had no idea that meeting Donn would change the course of my life. We became good friends and he later introduced me to Dan Ivan. I remember that when I arrived in the States, I had to fight a great battle against frustration because of my poor English. I recall crying in bed for more than two days because I couldn't communicate. It was very difficult for me to adapt to a new culture and language. But Ed Parker gave a great opportunity to demonstrate my art publicly at the 1965 Long Beach International Karate Championships, and that boosted my confidence and self-image.

Who was your first connection in California?

Dan Ivan. He used to travel to Japan a lot and we became friends. He brought me over and later on offered me a partnership that

SHITO RYU MASTERS

lasted for a long time – not only in martial arts but in other different businesses such as real state. I would say that Mr. Ivan, along with Mr. Parker and Mr. Curtis Wong, helped me very, very much.

Did you ever meet Bruce Lee?

Yes. He was very nice to me. Bruce had a very strong sense for everything related to martial arts. He always wanted to learn more and was never satisfied with what he had. I remember that after my book on nunchaku came out, he would call me up with questions about the weapon, which he was studying at that time.

Dan Ivan is a shotokan stylist and you are a shito ryu practitioner. How did you combine those two styles?

Well, out of respect for him I learned all the shotokan kata and taught them so the school would have the same curriculum. Once we separated our schools, I went back to teaching strictly traditional shito ryu and kobudo. I don't recommend mixing styles. I tried to do it with shotokan and shito ryu and it was impossible – it just didn't work. If you really understand both styles' principles, they don't mix. There are a lot of reasons why many of today's modern innovators are going back to the traditional systems.

You were one of the first to use music to display traditional karate in a modern way. Were you criticized by your peers in Japan?

Very much. Even my own instructor criticized me for using music and giving demonstrations in a park. I was really upset. I kept asking myself if I was doing something wrong. Then my mother, Masu, whom I consider to be the greatest inspiration in my life, came to the United States and saw me perform. That gave me a lot of power and strength. She basically said that everyone was jealous because of my new position. She told me that people were paying for watching the demonstrations and that I had to give them a great show. The final turning point was at the WUKO World Championships in Long Beach, California in 1975. I gave a great demonstration in front of all the great masters from Japan, including the President of the WUKO, Mr. Sasakawa. I received a standing ovation, the biggest of the whole tournament. I guess that day they understood that I was not prostituting the art but drawing more attention to it. That's why I didn't understand the initial criticism at all. I really like the feeling of history and respect that the traditional approach provides.

What are shito ryu's strong points?

The founder, Kenwa Mabuni, studied under two major teachers, Yasutsune Itosu (Shuri te) and Kanryo Higaonna (Naha te). He combined the soft and circular approach of Naha with the hard and more linear techniques from the Shuri system. He also added part of tomari te, creating a very versatile karate method. You see, style does not matter; it's the instruction that counts.

Would you recommend the multi-style training approach?

No, not for beginners since this can be very confusing. At an advanced level I think it is very positive to learn something from other arts; the more you know about something, the more you can appreciate it. It doesn't mean that you have to like everything but at least understand it and have some respect for it.

Do you think traditional kata has to be changed to adapt to modern times?

Kata should not change at all. It is the traditional part of karate. Karate is an art. In the past it was used for combat and fighting. Perhaps a master altered part of the kata for certain reasons, according to his practical combat experience. To me, though, the kata has to be kept intact in modern times. Training methods and sparring techniques may change, but not kata.

How do you perceive the modern approach to karate?

I think that people want too much too quickly. They want to run before knowing how to walk; or learn advanced techniques without mastering the basics. You can't have a strong house without a strong foundation. The stronger the basics, the stronger the house – it's as simple as that. Unfortunately a lot of practitioners don't understand. Competition has a good and a bad side. The worst thing is losing sight of your training just to win a trophy. Sometimes, the trophy gets to be the most important thing and that's not right. The student loses so much when they think like that.

On the other hand, the good part is that competition can help the student learn about goal-setting. This allows the student to go through a learning process which includes a viable system of performance grading at the end of the process. I know that the end doesn't always seem to work, but what is important is that the student went through the process by increasing their training, focused their minds, et cetera. I would like to see all karate practitioners understand that competition is just an small aspect of their total training – it is not the ultimate aim.

As a karate sensei and kobudo teacher, do you feel both arts are related?

Of course they are! I always say that they are like the two wheels of a bicycle. They work under the same principles. A full study of kobudo is not for everyone but I strongly recommend some weapons training to everyone. My approach to kobudo is different from that of my instructors, though; in the beginning I use it more for supplemental training.

Which do you consider to be the best kobudo weapon?

I don't think there is a "best" weapon. They help you to develop different things. In fact, the kobudo weaponry is divided into three different categories; long weapons like the bo; short weapons like the kama, sai, and tonfa; and hiding weapons such as the nunchaku.

But you always felt very comfortable with the nunchaku?

Yes. I consider the nunchaku to be a very good weapon. Unfortunately a lot of people misunderstand its use – maybe because of Bruce Lee's movies. They think you really need that much movement and swinging, when in real life situations one simple swing is all it takes. There is no traditional kata in nunchaku training, but people made their own for practice and to structure the techniques – which I feel is very acceptable.

You've have been involved in the movie industry, working with celebrities such as Sean Connery, Burt Lancaster, Wesley Snipes, and many more. But you received the majority of your recognition for your work in The Karate Kid.

I've been very fortunate. But as result of all that work and seminars, and videos, I had a heart attack. That made me take a look at my lifestyle. I used to leave the dojo for long periods of time on travel, but now I try to focus more on school and doing a little bit of movie work. That's it and I'm happy. I like to help people. Sometimes people think that I'm doing great things for others, but in fact that's what a martial artist is supposed to be doing – helping others. That's what martial arts are all about.

What is your personal training like now?

I guess everybody goes through the same process. When we are young we try to show how tough we are and we do a lot of kumite. When we get older and our body start to hurt, then we start to appreciate kata. I emphasize more kata and kihon in my personal training. Sensei Sakagami always told me that the original Okinawan kata were easier on the body, because they put less stress on the joints. I didn't appreciate the truth of this until years later.

What's your message for all martial artists?

Never give up. Martial arts training is not easy, but if you believe strongly enough in yourself, you can achieve anything. For me, that's the greatest part of being an instructor. I don't care about the money. If I help my students to become better human beings, that is the greatest reward.

TERUO HAYASHI

IN PURSUIT OF EXCELLENCE

Hayashi Sensei was one of the world's most respected and admired karate masters. Born in Naha, on the island of Honshu, on October 1924, Hayashi Teruo started in judo and earned his black belt at age 16. He reached his 3rd dan in judo at 23 years of age and was considered one of the most promising young black belts of that generation. However, once he watched karate, he became so impressed that he gave up everything to study it full time. Today he is the Chief Instructor of Japan Karate-Do Hayashi-ha Shito Ryu.

Sensei Hayashi started his karate training in Osaka, Japan, under Kosei Kuniba, an original Shito-Ryu Karate-Do student of Kenwa Mabuni, who also received instruction from Choki Motobu and Funakoshi Gichin. Later on, Hayashi went to study under the great master of the Goju Gyu system, Seko Higa, from whom he learnt a great deal of practical knowledge of the Naha-te methods and was inspired to travel to Okinawa for further studies.

In Okinawa, he practiced Shorin Ryu with Chosin Chibana and then another Shorin Ryu method under Chojin Nagamine and Master Naga. He also studied kobudo under Master Hohan Soken, Shinken Taira and Kenko Nakaima, who not only taught him kobudo, but also a karate method called "Ryuei-Ryu." Sensei Hayashi decided to name his kobudo method "Kenshin-Ryu," which means "heart," and is another way of saying "Ryuei-Ryu."

He was known internationally as the "weapons man," because of his immense skill and knowledge and he became responsible for refereeing tournaments of the World Union Karate-Do Organizations, or WUKO. Sensei Hayashi was recognized as a great master who devoted most of his life to a selfless dedication in pursuit of karate excellence.

How did you start training in martial arts?

I remember that I was strongly attracted to martial arts at a very young age. I began training in judo and I got my black belt at 16. I was 20 when I went to the military service and I served as a co-pilot in the Air Force during the war. For a long time I could not train openly since all martial arts systems were

SHITO RYU MASTERS

prohibited by the Americans - but nobody could prevent me from training privately with my friends. When I reached 3rd dan, many people considered me one of the most promising students of my generation. Almost three years later I was introduced to an unknown martial art called karate. After training for a while, I fell in love with the art and I gave up everything else. I decided that I wanted to be a full-time karate student.

Who was your first teacher?

When I was 18 I went to live in Osaka. I started with Master Kosei Kuniba and then I studied the goju-ryu style under Master Seko Higa. He taught a great deal and I progressed very consistently for a long time. But then I decided to go to Okinawa to train. The main reason I did this is because I believed Okinawa to be the cradle of the martial arts, and I wanted strongly to go to the source of the knowledge. Now I know I was right because I was astonished by the amount of knowledge that I received there. I studied shorin-ryu under Choshin Nagamine, and I was formally introduced to the art of kobudo which I studied under Hohan Soken, Shiken Taira, and Nakaima Kenko, who also was a karate master of a method called "ryuei-ryu."

Did Nakaima Kenko train you in empty-hand karate methods?

Yes, he did. As a matter of fact, it was very difficult for me to be accepted into his dojo. Ryuei-ryu is a family art imported from Southern China over three generations before I went to Okinawa. The reason I went to him was because I was looking for a kobudo teacher. At the time, it was almost impossible to find a master who would teach an outsider, which is what I was. When I found Nakaima Kenko, his only student was his son and he had no intention of breaking that tradition. I sat in front of his house for many hours and begged for months until he decided to accept me as a disciple.

What method did you study under him?

Well, he taught me mostly the kama and the sai, and the empty-hand method of karate. In fact, I incorporated much of the ryuei-ryu theory into my own style. My other two kobudo teachers were Hohan Soken, from whom I studied the bo and kama, and Shiken Taira who gave me a lot of knowledge in several other kobudo weapons.

Why did you study under so many masters?

Well, this is a very complicated question. To begin with, each master only knew two weapons perfectly, and it was mostly in the form of kata. Each master had his own specialty since they were transmitting the knowledge in the same way they had received it from their instructors. When I arrived in Okinawa I realized that if the students of karate didn't do something, all these systems were going to die. So I committed myself to perpetuate these arts and when I returned back to Japan I kept all the information intact, but I updated some things and I tried to evolve a more practical and realistic way of training. Unfortunately, kobudo practice has degenerated around the world. You can find people who just took a couple of classes and became self-proclaimed masters. Then they teach and give certification and ranking! Some of them just take a short trip to Okinawa and return as a 5th dan. I think this is really a shame and personally I just don't want to have anything to do with that.

Do you think that training in different disciplines is beneficial?

Let me put it this way: it is very important to go deeply into one art and study everything related to it such as body movement, mechanism in the delivery of the techniques and body awareness, and to educate your body about the finer points, applying the proper energy, et cetera. When you truly understand your art after many years of practice and research, then you can look into something else and immediately have a greater appreciation of it because of your level of understanding. If you practice many styles without a base and without going deeply in one, you'll become a "jack of all trades, master of none." It is only after many years of training that you can research other methods effectively.

You have a great reputation as a fighter. In fact, it is well known that you used to travel and challenge other teachers.

Yes, but let me explain this. Let me start by saying that no modern martial artist should ever degrade his art by trying the techniques out in the street or by going to challenge any other school master or martial arts method. Times are very different now. What I used to do, some say was brave, others foolish, but in fact it was an honored tradition known as dojo yaburi. You fight against the lowest rank until you defeat the dojo's senpai. Then and only then, do you have the right to challenge the sensei himself. Probably, because of this practice, I became infamous and very good at kumite. Some didn't accept my challenge and would not let me get inside the door. Others, of course did. Anyway, upon reflection I realized the reasons for my street-fighting were wrong.

Did you ever get seriously injured during any of these matches?

Yes. Numerous broken ribs, a broken leg, a broken jaw, knee injuries, et cetera. But I always thought that if I was injured it was my fault for not being skilful enough to block or avoid the attacks properly. Every time I got hurt, I used to go back and train much harder; so by the time I'd fight again I'd be able to win. Please, don't assume that all my matches were against one person. On one occasion I fought ten men. I suffered head cuts but I was happy to find out that karate was and is a very good self-defense method.

Did you defeat all of them?

No! I laid most of them out - but then I ran away!

Is it true that Kuniba Kosei asked you to be his successor?

Well, he asked me on his deathbed to lead his organization until his son, Shogo Kuniba, reached a level of maturity sufficient to assume the leadership. So I did. I became the president of seishin kai until 1970. After that, I passed Sensei Shogo Kuniba the mantle of leadership and decided to go on my own with Hayashi-ha shito-ryu kai.

How do you keep yourself in such a good shape?

I train hard every day. I've seen very good martial artists that stopped training after the 40-year-old mark. The secret is to keep training hard. Of course, you're going to lose some speed and power in your technique but you can make it up with superior experience and knowledge about both the mental aspects and the real way the techniques work. You must focus on developing what I call "fighting soul." On the other hand, there is no way of bypassing the basic school of learning the technique; there is no way around it.

In order to achieve this there is something every practitioner has to understand - your body changes and your karate changes with your body. You become softer as you grow older. Some young practitioners don't understand that everybody's karate has to be different, must be different, as the karateka gets older. It would be stupid for a 50-year-old practitioner to try to keep doing the same karate that he did when he was 25. It's against nature and common sense. For instance, take the principle of kime; it takes more time for a young practitioner to achieve the correct kime in the physical motion. For an older and more experienced karateka the time for the right kime in shorter. Some techniques can be very effective for young people, but they are impossible for an older practitioner to make work.

There are other kinds of skill the real karateka should aim for when he gets older. Many people ask me if I have changed my karate. Well, sometimes the question is confusing so I have to be very careful when I answer. I did change my karate because I have changed myself both physically and mentally. I'm more experienced now than 20 years ago and have a broader perspective of things. My perception of life, of the world has evolved, therefore, yes, I have changed and these changes definitely affect the art I'm teaching. On the other hand, I don't teach karate to please the student. I teach the art the way I think it should be taught. Period. But as a teacher, I need to find better ways to communicate and pass the knowledge depending of whom I'm teaching at that time. Students have different backgrounds, education levels, understanding, et cetera and you have to adapt accordingly.

What's your opinion about grading?

Well, in the old days the whole purpose was increasing one's own skill. We cared about karate training, not about rank. Belt ranking came from judo. We used to train hard and if we got a dan along the way, fine, but it was never the goal of the training. I'm totally against the concept of selling grades as is happening all over the world. I think this is a shame for the karate world. Students get advancement in grading because the monetary connotations of what they represent.

Do you believe in the use of ki?

Well, we all have the energy but I don't like to spend time theorizing about it. I try to steer clear of that "mysterious" approach to karate training. The real skills come from correct training methods, strong conditioning and endless repetition. Too many stories have been around the art for too long; this master used to puncture an oil drum with his toes, that master's dojo had footprints on the ceiling, et cetera. I think it is more important to develop a fighting spirit which allows us to keep fighting against all the odds in life. That's why my classes are very hard. Good, hard training is what I consider important. If you develop a proper understanding of the art with correct technique, timing, and kime, using your body accordingly, you'll be able to not only cope with different opponents, but also different situations in life. I do believe that a student must be strong, not only physically but also morally. I don't accept lazy people or those who lack willpower as students. It is important for the student to learn the true budo mind and spirit. I understand that this is very difficult since the description of budo is very confusing.

What is your best advice for karate practitioners?

Always train in the basics. This is something I noticed during all the past years; some top-competitors have very weak basics, they lack kihon. And after the competition years, it is very hard for them to progress in the true art of karate-do. There is nothing wrong with training these basic competition techniques and become a champion, but the art of karate is not a sport, it deals with self-defense and this is another subject altogether. You can't build a house with just two or three tools, you need a variety of tools to accomplish that goal. On the other hand, training should not stop once you remove your gi. Without the right spirit your karate will be of little use.

I would recommend striving to be intelligent. I'm talking about the proper attitude towards learning. One person can be intellectual and not intelligent. Of course, the academic aspects help in karate training but it is not absolutely necessary. In the same way that a high education doesn't imply that the person has a high IQ, being academic in the art doesn't mean that you truly understand what you're doing. I understand that after many years of training the trick is how to get motivated to do the same things that you have been doing for so long. Fortunately, there are a lot of methods to achieve this. What is important is the understanding of how to achieve more with less training. This stage is reserved for those who have trained for many years. After a long time practicing, less training can bring more results than more training at an earlier stage. Nevertheless, the main point is to keep training and keep constantly seeking the right attitude.

Are you against sport competition?

No, not at all. To a certain extent, competition helps to improve your fighting ability - but in my time karate was full-contact karate; it was knockout karate. I like contact karate because it is a very good method of making you cautious and forces you to have your eyes open. The competition system is improving but there is still a long way to go in order to achieve the right scoring system that encompasses both the budo and the sport aspects.

For instance, the ippon shobu system makes a fighter very careful, they have to be more precise and the technique more powerful. This is more realistic because when you fight for your life you fight more carefully, too. Competitive kumite has changed a few things - for instance, the concept of mai or "critical distance." In the past we used to fight each other from further away. The idea was to make the opponent enter into our mai to deliver a decisive blow. These days, the fighting distance in competition is shorter because they know that even if they get hit they're not going to die from it. The real dimension of danger has disappeared. Nevertheless, and at least to me, both aspects are very closely linked and constitute what we call "modern karate."

In Okinawa, the art is practiced as a method of self-exploration, as an internal research, without focusing on fighting. And this is perfect for those who look for that particular goal but for those who look at karate as a fighting art, competition is necessary. On the other hand, the real purpose of karate training in not to get dan or compete against your fellow student but self-improvement as individual, finding your own way in the martial arts. Karate doesn't have to be your whole life but a major part of it. The philosophy and the training will help the practitioner to cope not only with difficult situations but also to show the proper respect to every human being. And that is tremendously important.

What do you feel is wrong with karate today?

There are too many so-called self-promoted karate-do schools who will issue certification and rankings to non-qualified instructors. This practice not only dilutes the quality of the art but actually degrades karate-do to the public. Karate-do training should constantly pursue higher technical perfection. The practitioner should reflect how their achievements have enhanced society as a whole. Karate-do should be a lifelong endeavor which is enjoyable and beneficial, and not seen as a personal burden.

JAMES HERDON

FORWARD THINKING

Hanshi James Herndon has practiced Japanese martial arts for more than 50 years, beginning in 1962. He met Soke Shogo Kuniba in 1971 and followed his teachings until 1992, when Kuniba-Soke passed away and Hanshi Herndon moved to Florida to take a new job as a police psychologist. Now retired after more than 3 decades as a psychologist, Dr. Herndon is sharing his experience and insight to help Kuniba-inspired organizations grow. Call it an attempt to repay Soke Shogo Kuniba for his teachings and inspiration.

Hanshi Herndon served as the Kenshin Kai USA Honbucho from 1973-1976, the Seishin-Kai USA Honbucho from 1980-1982, formed Kensei Kai in 1987, and served in a variety of roles in Seishin Kai Martial Arts, Inc. (SKMA) during the late 1990s. He operated Kensei-Kan Dojo in Chesapeake, VA from 1979-1990. He is the author of A Primer of Kuniba-ha Karate-do. Stepping up to assist Shogo Kuniba's sons (Kosuke and Kozo), he served as Kaicho Daiko for Kuniba Kai International from 2009-2011. He founded Shogo Kai in 2011 to further the goal of passing on the Kuniba legacy.

Hanshi Herndon's professional training is in human resources management (M.A., Pepperdine University), industrial/organizational psychology (Ph.D., Old Dominion University), and counseling psychology (Ed.D., University of Sarasota). He has earned five Diplomates in areas of Board Certification, to include Police Psychology, Forensic Examination, Psychological Assessment, Evaluation and Testing. Currently, he teaches at six colleges in Florida and online and dreams of Wekiva Budokan. He is a USAF Vietnam-era veteran.

When you began your training and how many styles have you trained in and who were your teachers? Do you practice any other art in conjunction with karate?

I began training in September 1962. As a 15 year old, I began dabbling in backyard Taekwon Do with Chico Rivera. Upon entering the USAF in 1966, I began training in Nippon Shorin-ryu Karate-do Kenshin-kai under Dennis Hollembeak and Shihan Shigenobu Nakano (1926-2012) of Fukuoka, Japan.

SHITO RYU MASTERS

I met Soke Shogo Kuniba in 1971 and began a gradual transition to Motobu-ha Shito-ryu Karate-do Seishin-kai. I trained with Kuniba-soke until his passing in 1992. Under him I learned not only Shito-ryu, but also Taira-ha Kobudo, Goshin Budo, and a little Mugai-ryu Iaido.

Would you tell us about your early days in karate with Shogo Kuniba Sensei?

Sensei Shogo Kuniba was not my first instructor; but, he had the biggest influence on me. That was because of his style and charisma. I had not seen anyone perform Kata like he did. He personified Kata. I trained with Shogo Kuniba throughout the 1970s and 1980s in the U.S. and in Japan. Those were the early days for me with him, and the early days of Kuniba in America.

In Japan, I trained at the Seishin Kai So Hombu Dojo in Osaka, as well as at Osaka Budo Center (Ikuo Yamada & Goichi Kobayashi) and Osaka Prefectural University (Masuake Minamide & Shuho Yamanaka). My Godan was awarded in Osaka in 1980.

Influenced by Shogo Kuniba, I opened a Dojo in Chesapeake, VA that became the Seishin Kai USA Hombu Dojo in 1980. Kuniba Soke would come to my Dojo weekly, beginning in 1979 and continuing well into the late 1980s, even though he opened his own Dojo in Portsmouth, VA in 1984. Our classes were demanding and at the black belt level. Many great students of my Dojo became students of Shogo Kuniba as time passed.

Were you a 'natural' at karate – did the movements come easily to you?

I would say, no. But, I did not find it too difficult to learn the basic movements. Being small, I found that technique worked better than strength. Kuniba Soke taught me that. It's not how big one is; it's how effective the technique is.

Please, explain for us the main points of your style and its differences with other styles like Shotokan or Goju Ryu and even with other Shito Ryu branches?

Most karateka are aware of the origin of Shito-ryu. Motobu-ha Shito-ryu was Kuniba's blending of kihon and kumite techniques learned from his father (Kosei Kokuba) that came from Choki Motobu in the 1920s and 1930s, and kata learned from Ryusei Tomoyori of Mabuni-ha Shito-ryu. As early as 1956, Shogo Kuniba called his blended style Motobu-ha Shito-ryu Karate-do. But, as he adapted his style to Americans, he called it Kuniba-ha to differentiate it from what was still being practiced in Japan,

Kuniba-ha is unique in its rich kata bunkai. That is because Shogo Kuniba had studied Aikido and Judo as a young man, and those arts influenced how he developed Karate bunkai. Woven throughout his style are fundamental principles, such as "foot first, hip twist," "elbow down, wrist twist," "blocks crossing and cutting," the notion of Sashite, and the importance of "eyes first, then movement (stance), followed by application of technique." Kuniba believed and demonstrated that power (Chikara) was not important; Ki and Kime could be more effective, as well as more efficient. He also believed in "weak point" and "much pain soon coming."

Please tell us a little about the origin and evolution of the Kuniba-ha Shito Ryu?

Well as I mentioned before, Motobu-ha Shito-ryu is a blended style that combined the old Ryukyu Karate of Choki Motobu with the Japanese kata of Kenwa Mabuni. In the mid-1980s, Shogo Kuniba began to realize that things needed to be done differently in America; Kuniba-ha Karate-do became his name for what was taught outside of Japan. More emphasis on kata bunkai and the development of Goshin Do separated West (U.S.) from East (Japan).

How did you meet Sensei Shogo Kuniba and what can you tell us about him?

I met Shogo Kuniba on his first visit to the U.S. in Mobile, AL, March 13, 1971, at the Dixie National Karate Association Championship. There was a Seishin Kai instructors meeting the night before and we all had a chance to meet him. He was the chief official and put on a superb demonstration (where I saw the kata 'Seipai' performed by a master technician). My eyes were opened.

Shogo Kuniba was a gentle man, a gentleman. He had a quick smile and a good sense of joie-de-vivre. He liked people and people liked him. He was non-confrontational and fun to be around. But, on the Dojo floor he was a task master. He delighted in using big guys as an example of technique effectiveness. With a twinkle in his eyes, and a touch of his moustache, he'd bring instant pain to the non-believer. He could, and often did, perform any kata on demand. He had beautiful penmanship and his calligraphy is distinctive. He also was a good artist.

SHITO RYU MASTERS

What are the most important qualities for a student to become proficient in karate?

Patience, persistence, perseverance, practice. These 4 Ps lead to the fifth P: Proficiency.

When Sensei Kuniba was teaching the art of karate – what was the most important element; self-defense or sport?

Self-defense, no doubt. Sport was not emphasized. Shogo Kuniba taught Goshin Budo and kata bunkai. Practical applications were emphasized. Even in kumite, basics were stressed at all times.

How is the current situation of Kuniba-ha Shito Ryu method in the US and around the world?

Kuniba-ha is practiced and taught in the U.S. I am the main proponent of Kuniba-ha Karate-do, as I wrote the book on it in 1984. Bill Price became the Nidai Soke of Kuniba-ryu Goshin Do and what was then called Kuniba-ryu Karate-do in 1992. While he and I were both direct students of Shogo Kuniba, we emphasize different aspects of his arts.

Motobu-ha Shito-ryu is still practiced in Japan and brothers Kosuke and Kozo Kuniba run Kuniba-Kai. Those who follow the Kuniba brothers adhere to the Motobu-Ha Shito-ryu brand.

There are others around the world that follow students of Shogo Kuniba who have not kept up with style changes and/or remain unaffiliated with Kuniba Kai, Chikubu Kai, or Shogo Kai. Seishin Kai has many spin-off organizations.

How has your personal expression of karate developed over the years and what is it that keeps you motivated after all these years?

I have tried to remain true to what I learned from Shogo Kuniba. What motivates me is the desire to keep his legacy alive and to dispel myths and misinformation about his style. Those who barely came in contact with him have made exaggerated claims and have really missed the mark on what he taught.

What really means Ikken-Hissatsu and how does it apply when used in Karate?

"One strike, one kill" is a motto that has been adopted by military snipers, as well as Budoka. It is the principle of efficiency. Minimum effort; maximum results. Karate is not a game. Playing Karate, as in tournament sparring, is inefficient and contrary to the aim of doing what needs to be done; no more, no less.

How do you see the art of Karate in general evolve in the future and Kuniba-ha in particular?

I hope to see a return to tradition; back to the fundamentals of style. But, I realize that change is constant. People seek the new and the novel. We live in a throw-away society where people get bored easily. Karate training takes patience and persistence. These qualities seem to be scarce in most people.

Kuniba-ha will change as newer Sensei carry on the legacy of Shogo Kuniba. What I see some of the younger Sensei teach bears little resemblance to what I learned from Shogo Kuniba. Memory fades, people learn and retain different aspects of the art, and some improvise. But, I hope all will never forget the fundamental principles of the style.

Do you feel that you still have further to go in your studies of karate?

The path (Do) is endless. Whenever someone concludes they know it all, they demonstrate that they know very little. I will follow the Do for as long as I live. Karate-do is but one way.

What advice would you give to students on the question of additional training?

It depends on their goal. I am a purest, so I stick to one art. Mixed martial arts, in my mind, are a misnomer. "Jack of all trades, master of none." Speed, strength, power, etc. can be enhanced many ways. But, what is the purpose? Competition, fame, fortune, ego? Karate-do is about humility and character development. I'd say to examine the goal of the journey.

What advice would you give to an instructor who is struggling with his or her own development?

Stop teaching; become a student again. In America, many think that a Shodan can teach. Shodan is a beginner level. Only at the Sandan level, or above, with proper instructor training, should one dare to teach.

Have there been times when you felt fear in your training?

No. A Dojo has always been a safe place in my experience. If otherwise, perhaps the Sensei has watched too many movies about Karate.

Do you think that Olympics will be positive for the art of karate-do?

No. In my mind, the notion of competition misses the point of self-development to the extent that the focus becomes one of external validation; being a winner in someone else's opinion. Testing one's skills may be part of the growth process. Gaudy trophies fool the ego. Better to test in the Dojo. I know others disagree with me on this. That's OK.

With Taekwon Do already in the Olympics, how can Karate-do offer something substantially different? JKF recognizes some 46 Ryu/Ha. How would it be decided which style should represent Karate-do? There are many issues and hurdles to overcome. The art of Karate-do would hardly be helped.

What are your views on kata bunkai? Is it bunkai really important?

Without bunkai, Kata are just dance. What's on the surface is easy to copy. What lies beneath are the hidden treasures of the art in application. Kata are learning devices, a means of encoding to pass along the elements of style. Decoding occurs when bunkai are taught.

How important is it for a Kuniba-ha Shito Ryu practitioner to know all the Kata of the style?

Not important. There are more than 50 Kata in Shito-ryu. Kenwa Mabuni was a Kata encyclopedia. Shogo Kuniba was also quite knowledgeable about many Kata. He taught most of the Kata syllabus to many Sensei; but not all to everyone. Some, I never learned. I did not worry about that. I am not the Soke; that was his job.

If one applied the maxim "Hito Kata San Nen" to our style, it would take 150 years to master all the Kata. In kata I like to practice mainly kata Seipai, Tomari No Bassai, and Rohai.

How do you like to train yourself? Has this changed over the years?

My training has changed over the years. When I was younger, I trained hard. Now, I train smart.

One can train in a small space. One can perform a Kata anywhere. I sneak in training in daily activities, while working, walking, waiting, or worrying. I use mental imagery and go through Kata in my mind quite often. I use mental rehearsal. I also use the principles of Shin (Shoshin; Isshin; Fudoshin; Mushin; Zanshin) in my everyday life; the psychology of Budo works in dealing with life's challenges. As a police psychologist, the martial arts can be applied in crisis negotiation and many other conflict situations. I teach police officers how to deflect and defuse. Karate-do teaches resilience.

Shotokan, Shito Ryu, Goju, Ryu, etc.... How do you think the different branches and styles affect the art of Karate?

Fragmentation causes discord. Too many people claim one style is better than another. What matters is that a style fits the individual, not vice versa. Karate-do is Karate-do. If we focus on the art, the style is only an expression thereof. We should not lose sight of that.

Do you think Kobudo training is beneficial for a Karate practitioner? Did Sensei Kuniba enforce its practice amongst his students?

Yes, Kobudo is beneficial from the standpoint of expanding one's martial competence. Without getting too fancy or too flashy, the weapons of Kobudo can be used to augment the empty hand.

Kuniba-soke learned Kobudo from Shinken Taira and Kenko Nakaima. He passed that along to us.

What is your opinion about the "Shobu Ippon" division in Karate competition?

Not particularly important to me. Maybe the younger generation likes it. Tournament kumite usually degenerates into sloppy technique and excessive power without adequate control. Control is the essence of skill. Kumite brings out the animal instincts. Whatever happened to not fighting as a goal? In real self-defense, there are no kumite rules; there are no referees. Reality principle number one: avoid the fight, if at all possible. If it cannot be avoided, get it over with quickly and efficiently.

What are the most important points in your teaching methods today?

Basics count. It's not how much you know; it's how well you do what you know. Hara, Kokoro, Kime seem lacking in many of today's crop of martial artists. In the West, flash trumps substance. Ego overrides personal development. The way to build character is to strip away hubris.

What can karate offer to the individual in these troubled times we are living in?

If approached for the right reasons, Karate-do can teach humility and personal discipline. Both of the attributes can take one a long way in life.

After so many years of training, what is it for you that is so appealing in this style of karate and why?

Kuniba-ha is beautiful and efficient. It works for me. I am a scholar-warrior, believing the pen and sword are one: Bun Bu Ryo Do. I have pursued Budo for more than 50 years and attained two doctoral degrees (PhD and EdD) along the way. Body and mind together developed.

Finally, what advice would you like to give to all Karate practitioners, regardless of style?

Stick to the fundamentals. Avoid the MMA madness. Take your art to heart.

YOSHIMI INOUE

RETURNING TO THE SOURCE

THIS QUIET AND REVERENT SENSEI WAS ONE OF THE MOST IMPORTANT SHITO RYU INSTRUCTORS IN THE WORLD. HIS POSITION AS DIRECTOR OF JKF "INOUE-HA SHITO RYU KEISHI-KAI" DEMANDED OF HIM A CONSTANT TRAVELING SCHEDULE. WITH AN EXCEPTIONAL LEVEL OF SKILL SECOND TO NONE, SENSEI INOUE DISPLAYED ALL THE MAJOR PRINCIPLES OF THE SHITO RYU-HA DEVELOPED BY THE GREAT TERUO HAYASHI.

HE TAUGHT EXTENSIVELY IN JAPAN AND EUROPE AND IN THE U.S., AND TRAINED PRIVATELY SOME KATA WORLD CHAMPIONS WHO LOOKED FOR IMPROVING THEIR TECHNICAL PERFORMANCE IN COMPETITION. YOSHIMI INOUE SENSEI WAS ALWAYS GENEROUS WITH HIS TIME AND AGREED TO SPEAK FREELY ABOUT THE PRESENT STATE OF KARATE-DO. HE WALKED THE PATH OF BUDO FOR MANY DECADES AND WAS ONE OF THE FEW MASTERS IN THE WORLD WHO TRANSCENDED STYLE AND POLITICS. IF SOME MEN POSSESS A PHILOSOPHICAL APPROACH TO LIFE AND CAN SUFFER IN AGONIZING PAIN AND STILL FIND SOME GREAT INSTRUCTION FROM THE LESSON LEARNED, INOUE SENSEI WAS WITHOUT DOUBT ONE OF THEM. "THE GOAL OF KARATE SHOULD NOT ONLY BE SELF-DEFENSE," EXPLAINED INOUE. "THE ART SHOULD PROVIDE A GUIDE FOR LIVING AND THIS ENCOMPASSES THE STRIVING FOR SELF-CONTROL THROUGH THE DISCIPLINE OF DEDICATED PRACTICE."

IN AN AGE OF MEANINGLESS SUPERLATIVES, IT IS DIFFICULT TO DESCRIBE THE DEBT OF GRATITUDE KARATE OWES TO SENSEI YOSHIMI INOUE.

Sensei, how does Hayashi-ha Shito Ryu differ from other karate styles?

Hayashi Teruo Sensei trained in different styles {including Kobudo] and finally decided what was the best approach to combat. He developed a series of principles that should be used in combat, and his main idea was not to face strength with pure strength. His approach was substantially different from other masters who emphasized more kata over kumite. Hayashi Sensei realized the limitation of some traditional techniques in actual combat and began to modify the technical structure of the techniques to better fit into a realistic fighting situation. He studied with great masters to learn new things and eventually to mold what it would be his creation: the Hayashi-ha style of Shito Ryu karate.

What can you tell us about the balance of the opposites [soft and hard]?

In the universe, all is based on the balance of opposites: day and night, cold and hot, etc. Karate is the same: relaxation and tension, hard and soft, body and mind ... it is all in there. No Karate style is "hard" or "soft" per se if you truly understand Karate. Some people say Goju is "soft," Shotokan is "hard," etc... that makes no sense. All Karate styles use the principle of balancing the "hard" and "soft". It is just a matter of the level of understanding and knowledge of the person or karateka who is talking.

What is your opinion about trying to make [in Kata] the external technique perfect from a visual point of view?

With the possibility of including Karate in the Olympics, there has been an attempt to standardize not only the actual kata but also make the physical movements "prettier," to say at least. The idea of a perfect "outside" visual form has become the goal. But there is a big problem here because Karate kata is not gymnastics. Kata is not about the external technique only but about the "philosophy" and "meaning" of the actual technique. If we change the outside form to make it look better but lose elements that "show" the real meaning of the technique, we are losing a great deal of understanding. If we don't maintain the "function" of the technical movement, then it is no longer kata. It's gymnastics. Once kata is only visual (as we see these days), it has no point. The visual of the kata must represent technically the "bunkai application" of the movement. We have to consider the "bunkai" when we do kata.

Can you give us an example?

For instance, in some kata when performed in competition, the karateka jumps higher than what the actual technique requires; they slow down the techniques breaking the actual rhythm of the form, etc. Why? To impress judges. Every movement can be used and it has to be performed as it works. That is a choice you have to make: perform kata for looks or for true Karate. Real Karate kata may not be more beautiful but certainly is way more meaningful.

What about Kihon training?

Kihon training, although it may be boring is extremely important. If the foundations of a house are weak, as the house gets older, problems will arise. This is the same for all Karate styles, no matter their origins. A lot of people spend many years training to realize later on, after 30 years of karate practice, that they don't have a solid foundation and their technique is not "polished" at all – that they lack solid basic, clean Karate technique and they feel embarrassed because they have a high rank. You find this situation mainly among karateka who have devoted their training mainly to kumite. Don't misunderstand my words; kumite is not easy but it is not what makes a good karateka. Kihon and kata are the foundation for Karate. Kumite is a "personalized" way of using Karate technique. But you should get that [technique] first. Unfortunately, you see high ranks who lack good Karate basics and they try to cover it up focusing on kumite. This shows what kind of "attitude" and "personality" these practitioners have.

How can these practitioners who focus mainly on kumite correct that?

Well, that is a little bit difficult. They will realize this problem later on in their Karate training; they may be 5th, 6th or 7th Dan already. They have a reputation at stake [some may be Asian, European, American or world champions] and it is hard for them to acknowledge what they truly lack in their Karate. They never had the motivation, patience, and sense of detail to begin with and that is why their Karate is like it is. So, it is very hard for them to accept that fact and go back and do thousands of basics to catch up with the deficiencies of their past Karate training. Karate's basic movements are incredibly difficult to perform correctly and it takes a certain attitude and personality to focus on details. Kata is kumite at its most complex form. All the techniques and strategies used in kumite and also in self-defense are contained in the fundamental kata. You just need to know "where" to look and "how" to uncode them. In traditional Karate, kata equals kumite but kumite doesn't equal kata.

Some people may argue that good technique is alright...but Karate is about "if you can fight or not." What do you have to say about that?

Very simple; that show how little these people know Karate and their level of understanding. That mentality shows why they lack technique. And no, Karate is not about "if you can fight or not." Mike Tyson at his best could probably have knocked down 90% or more of the karate practitioners around the world, but that doesn't mean he knows Karate. Fighting is a part of Karate but it is not Karate. People use this excuse to justify they own inabilities. MMA champions can really fight, but it has nothing to do with Karate or true Martial Arts. So, if these people only are interested in fighting, why do they do Karate and not MMA?

What can you tell us about kumite?

Kumite is based on two principles: distance and timing. Without these two, nothing else matters. Not matter how good your primary elements (techniques) are, they will be useless. But even with a lousy technique, if you have developed a decent amount of ability in using distance and timing, you can be very good in sparring. You won't have a "good" Karate but you can win competitions, even world championships.

Would you elaborate, please?

If you don't have the right distance, your attacks will fail and your defenses will be useless. The right technique without the right [delivery] distance is useless. Then, if you have the right distance but the technique (attack or defense) is not delivered at the right time, it will either fall short in execution or won't be done to its fullest potential. The "when" to move is at least as important as the "how." It is useless to have a powerful technique if your body movement can't put you in exactly the right place and at the right time to use it effectively.

How we can develop the "right" distance?

Let me begin by saying that there is no one "right" distance. It is true that the "basic" kumite distance is the one that is slightly farther than the reach of the rear leg of the opponent. For instance, if you opponent is facing you, he won't be able to reach you with a kick from the back leg without taking a preliminary step toward you. That is your basic "safety" or "critical" distance. During a kumite match, the distance alters constantly so the key to obtain the right distance is "correct footwork." If you don't have the right kind of footwork, you won't be able to attain the right distance efficiently during the match.

What do you mean by the right kind of footwork?

You need to know what kind of footwork you should use to defend, to attack, to intercept, to shorten the distance, to create distance when defending, or to create distance in order to simply create space, etc. Not all footwork patterns are the same and shouldn't be used randomly. Right footwork "gets" you there and gets you "out."

What about timing?

Timing is a very complex element because it requires a sense of rhythm – not only of the correct [intrinsic] rhythm of how the technique must be used and works but also of the rhythm of the fight. Then, you need to have an understanding of the opponent's rhythm and the tempo and cadence of his movements. Distance can be drilled and developed by Sanbon and Gohon kumite but timing only through actual jyu-kumite.

And ...?

Then, it is when you can actually find a certain pattern in your opponent's rhythm and find out how to break it. You can create it, too, and force it into your opponent, but that is more complex. You can read the opponent's rhythm and then break it to hit efficiently.

You mentioned Sanbon and Gohon Kumite but some modern practitioners might argue that attacking someone with Oi Tsuki is not "realistic." What do you say?

That they don't know what they are talking about. Oi Tsuki as a technique in itself shows a lot about the practitioner's technical level. If you can actually hit somebody with a full Oi Tsuki, that tells a lot about us as karateka. But let me say that for prearranged kumite drills like Sanbon and Gohon Kumite, many people don't actually do it right. The right starting distance is when you place yourself with your fist actually touching the partner's face. Then, you take one leg back to Zenkutsu-dachi. From there, you initiate the Oi Tsuki. It is not a long distance but an actual "striking distance." Your intention is to "hit" the training partner, not just pose the punch. The fact that Oi Tsuki is more "visible" allows the trainee to coordinate his reaction and timing better. This is a training process; it is not a fighting drill, but a training drill to learn how to time the defense, the counterattack, and the tempo of the response. If you don't understand the actual use of the drill, then you may make nonsense statements because of lack of understanding on what you are talking about.

It is believed by many that the power comes from the hip but studies proved different. What can you tell us about this?

It is true that people say that the power in Karate "comes from the hip." Let's start using the words correctly. Power comes from the ground up. It doesn't come or originate from the hip. This is pure physics. A Karate punch [or kick] does not begin with the hip rotation. It passes cleanly through the hips into the torso, but it is not the hips that cause the power or the turn. The power that starts/originates or comes from the ground is transmitted to the upper body [and eventually to the punch or kick] by the correct use of the hip and then directed to the target via the arm or the leg. Our hips will impede the progress of the leg force/thrust if we don't know how to open them loosely as pivot points. Why the legs? Because if you have no base, you have no power. Once again, pure physics. Your connection with the ground is the base for the power. Studies have been made in universities where professional boxers and karateka have been placed in the air hanging, with no base or contact to the ground whatsoever. The result? Their punching power was gone, decreased to the simple arm power. Why? Because they had no base. Those studies proved that the power originates from the ground up, not from the hips. It is impossible to deliver a powerful punch without a strong stance to launch it from, as

you cannot use the rotation of your hips without being rooted to the ground. This is the right way to express it. What is important to the body mass and the way the hip is used.

Body mass?

Yes. The real driver behind power in any punch or kick is the amount of mass behind the movement and the direction of that mass. Check all the physics equations for force, momentum, and impulse. The way to maximize the amount of mass behind your attack is to get as much of your body moving in the direction of your attack as possible.

So what is the role of the hip?

As I said, the hip is the transmitter of the power that originates from the ground and from your "rooted" stance. Hip rotation is an accelerator that adds speed, and of course, increasing the speed of your body mass will increase the amount of power. But hip rotation is only one way of increasing the speed of your body mass and never is a substitute for proper application of your body mass to your techniques – which involves the whole body. You alos need to know how to use the counter-rotation of the joint and when to use it properly. Hips are where the body's center of gravity is located; our center point of mass is at the hip level and we should learn how to use our hips to increase velocity of the body mass – not necessarily speed. The right use of the hips helps to keep posture, balance, and stability for every move, but at the same time, being used incorrectly may shut off the powerful thrust of the legs. Hip

rotation – not hip shifting – is used for adding speed to the body mass and therefore develop maximum power in karate techniques. That is why we say that in karate we always try to punch with the hips and kick with the hips, etc.

One more thing, the hips can't generate power. Power is generated by the muscles around the hip. Two of the largest muscle groups in the body are the buttocks and the abdominal muscles; therefore, utilizing their strength, as well as rotating or shifting the hips, will add power to any techniques. As the hips turn, the torso and buttocks are added to the force of the technique. The hips are part of the bone/skeletal structure. A bone does not generate power .... muscles do. The real power comes from the buttock and the abdomen muscles. But a tight hip with no flexibility will decrease the potential power that you can use from your body mass and technique.

What about hip shifting? What is the difference from hip rotating?

These are two different things and should be used in different ways. Shifting is the movement of the entire body from one point to another in a straight line. Shifting includes both stepping and sliding the feet. And this is how the hips should be used because if you don't move, you simply can't hit your opponent. So shifting your hips is the real key.

Shifting the hips and not rotating the hips is the method which allows the karate-ka to develop the greatest amount of force. This is possible because we use the maximum amount of body mass by using the legs driving against the floor [origin of the power] to push forward against the hips.

The rotation is developed by the circular motion of the body mass. Control of rotation is centered on the use of the hips. The outside hip joint moves forward and backward, while the inside hip acts as a hinge. This can be practiced without technique, and then with techniques added. It is very important that the knees remain locked in place without moving. The pivot point in hip rotation changes depending upon the situation. It is always either one hip joint or the other, never the center of the body. Rotating on the center of the body would mean that one leg is retreating while the other is moving forward, eliminating the effect of the rotation. With the use of hip rotation, it is possible to create very powerful techniques in a small space.

Another important aspect is to fully understand the hip rotation around a central axis and the application of the hip shifting in the same motion. This is a completely different concept and a more realistic way of using body torque to use the technique effectively. One aspect we should be aware of is that dif-

ferent styles tend to use or move the hips differently, although they are based on the same principles. Shotokan uses a very "wide" application of hanmi and shomen and Shito Ryu, Goju, and Wado use the same principle but with more emphasis on shifting.

Why you think people explain it incorrectly?

They are misinformed. Hip shifting and hip rotating are both important. Hip rotating by itself won't do anything to your punch unless you are punching a stationary object and your distance is already there. It is like rotating the tap of a bottle ... it doesn't move/shift forward to reach the target. You need to use hip shifting and body mass, and then you finalize the movement with full hip rotation that concludes at the moment of impact, not before. And this has to be syncronized and not divided in parts or different movement sections.

What do you mean by "divided in parts"?

You see many people snapping the hips back and forth. They really get good at "hitting" and snapping the hips but this is useless in real Karate. It is just showing off. When they punch, you see clearly when the hip movement (rotating) starts and when it ends. You can actually see the "separation" between the hips and the rest of the body movement. Well, this is wrong. The hip movement or rotating should be "hidden" along with the punch [or kick]. It should be "one" with the punch [or kick]. These people snap the hips and then punch. This is ridiculous. The hip movement should be coordinated with the rest of the body and not be visible. It is like the separate parts of a whip ... when snapped in the air, you see just one single action, not several segments moving one after the other. Only one single perfectly coordinated movement, that is what a karate technique should be. So drop that hip snap. It may look "impressive" to a beginner and fellow karateka's, but not to someone who knows and understands Karate.

What would be your final advice for the readers?

In Karate you never stand still. You always have to try to move forward, to get better and improve what you are doing. When you go to train every day, you have to go far beyond the idea of simply "training" and use your mind when you train. That is the only way to really progress.

YASHUNARI ISHIMI

THE INTERNAL SERENITY

THE PRECISION OF HIS MOVEMENTS IS OUTSTANDING. RHYTHM, POWER AND TIMING SYNCHRONIZED PERFECTLY IN THE FORM OF A HUMAN BODY. ISHIMI SENSEI HAS DEVOTED HIMSELF TO DISCOVER NEW LEVELS OF UNDERSTANDING IN KARATE SINCE HIS FIRST DAYS OF TRAINING. A DISTINCTLY UNORTHODOX PERSON IN SOME RESPECTS, THIS SHITO-RYU EXPONENT HAS LEFT HIS MARK FOR GENERATIONS TO COME. EXTREMELY POLITE AND FRIENDLY, HE WALKS WITH THE POSTURE AND BEARING OF A WELL TRAINED BUT RELAXED MILITARY MAN. DESPITE HIS SUPERLATIVE EMPTY-HAND TECHNIQUES, HE SHUNS THE TITLES OF MASTER AND TRIES TO STAY AT THE LEVEL OF A STUDENT. HE ALSO CRITICIZES THOSE WHO PLACE SUCH A STRONG EMPHASIS ON TITLES AND CERTIFICATES. AN ADVOCATE OF INTERNAL SERENITY, ISHIMI SENSEI REMINDS US THAT PHYSICAL ACTION IS MASTERED BY THE MIND AND THE FORM IS THE OUTWARD REFLECTION OF INNER QUIETNESS. "THE ART STEMS FROM A CALM MIND, FOR ONLY WITH A CALM MIND CAN INTELLIGENCE ENTER THE MOVEMENT AND STABILITY BE MAINTAINED PHYSICALLY." THIS IS YASHUNARI ISHIMI, A KARATE-KA WHO MANY HAVE DESCRIBED AS THE CLOSEST MAN TO A TRUE MAN OF BUDO.

Did anyone in your family practice any martial art before you started?

Yes. My father was a kendo practitioner, and my brother was training in judo. I began training in kendo because of my father's influence, but I stopped when I was 15 because I didn't like the fact that he had imposed the training on me. Looking back, I truly think all that hard training was extremely valuable for my future education, not only in the arts of Budo but for my life, as well. Now I understand. I decided to practice karate because I thought it matched better with my personality. Before getting into Kobe University, I used to train three times per week. Once I got into the university karate club, karate became my life. I was training every single day. My teacher was Tsujikawa Sensei, and he is a direct student of shito-ryu founder, Kenwa Mabuni.

SHITO RYU MASTERS

You also trained under Mabuni Kenei, right?

Correct. After hours of training under Tsujikawa Sensei at the University, I used to go to Mabuni Sensei's dojo and train some more. That was the perfect combination of training because they were both excellent teachers and great Budoka. The lessons I received from them are priceless.

What is your opinion of how the teachings of karate-do have been passed down onto the new generation of practitioners?

Much of what is taught in the Western world is based on techniques and information passed down from one person to the next. A lot of the verbal transmissions are translations from the old texts. Unfortunately, these translations are incorrect. Someone translates ancient information incorrectly and then teaches this to his students. Then, the students transmit this information to the next generation. Already something has been changed and lost. Then, the next generation gets a different version of the same facts. When you look at the end of the chain, the facts are totally different from what they were originally. That's why I think it is important to be familiar with the terminology and language of the original Budo arts. It helps to understand things in a clearer way.

What do you think of all the technical differences in kata?

It is true that today there are many differences in kata, and I honestly think that they are irrelevant because they display only the personal flavor incorporated by the teacher. A lot of the time the arguments are simply nonsense. It is true that some specific movements should be performed in a certain way and no modification should be done. But then, there are other movements that are not that important, and the way you express them is not that relevant. There is a certain idiosyncrasy or temperament to it. You can personalize the movement, but you have to be aware of the essential meaning and principle behind the technique. And this shouldn't be altered at all. A traditional master teaches his students according to the student's capabilities, dedication, understanding and trustworthiness. All these elements may affect the way the student receives the knowledge. The problems arise when the student tries to copy the "teacher's idiosyncrasy," and he believes that this is the only way. This will create a problem in the future. The master taught the teacher in a very personal way, so the teacher performs karate in a very individualized way. That's the all-traditional format of transmitting the knowledge. He modifies things to adapt the movements to his body, but he never changes the essential meaning of the form. And this is the point that many people don't understand; there is no one correct way of doing a kata. What we need

to keep constant is the principle of the kata and not necessarily the specific details of the minor technical movements.

In the old traditional way of teaching, after a student asks a technical question, an instructor has him repeat a technique over and over. Do you like this method?

It is the traditional way. The "old" teacher used to send the student to a corner and ask him to repeat the movement 10,000 times. Then his questions would evaporate. I know this is not an acceptable way of teaching in the Western world. In the West, when a student asks you a question, you simply answer. There is a downside to this. The student will go back to training thinking and believing that he knows [the answer], but he doesn't. He just listened to the answer, but he doesn't know it. By doing the technique, the student needs to feel [the technique] and understand why the movement is performed that way. He needs to go inside for the answer. The problem lies in the fact that this method requires a lot of time because the answer is not learned immediately. This method [teaching yourself] is very good for those students who have a strong will and are dedicated. But let me warn you here ... many instructors with very limited knowledge use this approach to avoid answering a student's questions when they don't know the answer. The student's passion to know becomes a threat to the instructor.

It's always difficult to find the right dojo. What are your suggestions for a prospective student?

This is a tough question, and it requires many different answers. First, if a person gets involved in karate simply because he wants to exercise, I don't think he really knows or cares about the important things that should be known before entering a dojo. [In this case], the dojo where he ends up will [strictly] be an accident ... mostly because the school is conveniently located near his work, home or school.

If the individual has at least a little idea of what the art of karate-do is and represents, then let me explain few things here. The art of karate-do includes a vast spectrum of styles and each one has a special orientation and characteristic. It is not the same to train in shito-ryu as it is to train in kyokushin-kai. This is obvious. The important thing here is to match your needs with the right instructor and style. If you are not interested in sport competition because of your age or orientation, don't enter a school that mainly focuses on entering tournaments. Ask questions when you visit the dojo. Don't be afraid. Once you know the kind of karate you want to do, then you have to find the right teacher. Visit several classes imparted by the same instructor. Make sure that he is consistent with the classes and he really cares for the students. It is very sad to spend not only money but also time with the wrong individual. You can make more money [if you throw it away on the wrong instructor], but you can't get the years back. Time is priceless. The problem for the inexperienced student is how to evaluate the authenticity and skill of the instructor. It is here where many so-called masters take advantage of good people. Try to learn as much as possible about the teacher's background. Nowadays we have the Internet and although there is a lot of incorrect information there, it can be also beneficial to verify and confirm some specific details. This process can be tedious and usually very few people follow it before enrolling in a martial arts school. Once you have found the right dojo and teacher, however, put yourself into it with heart and soul. Trust your teacher and make sure you receive the proper respect. Only then you'll be able to achieve your goals.

Do you think traditional forms and techniques are really useful for modern self-defense?

First, let me remind you that traditional arts were taught by invitation. You couldn't step into a dojo and ask the instructor to teach you. The instructor knew the student's personality, physical capability and limitations when he decided to teach him. The art was taught to the student in a tailor-made format. The teacher had the time and motivation to make the art or style fit perfectly with the student's physical make-up and qualities.

Second, any physical movement performed as a reflex — which is the very basic essence of the self-defense — must be extensively trained to become a natural reaction. This only can be accomplished through tedious repetitive training of the basic movements of your style. Once you have these movements in your system like a reflex, you need to have the strength and knowledge to use these techniques. The body must support your technique; otherwise, your technical knowledge is useless.

The final aspect of self-defense is [developing] the right fighting spirit or decisions to get you through a fight. This last aspect is the most important.

But don't fool yourself. Doing sanchin up and down a dojo floor won't be useful to defend yourself in a serious situation in the street in which your physical integrity is at stake. You have to take everything for what it really is and then you'll be at peace with yourself and happy doing whatever it is you are doing. And this applies to everything in life.

You seem to be very traditional in your approach to kata. Why?

You can look at this from the perspective of karate-do and what you do in a competition. The art of karate and kata — as part of it — shouldn't be altered to the point that the essence of what the art is all about gets lost. As I said before, the global meaning of kata is what counts, and I am talking about real and true traditional karate now ... not sport karate.

You have to focus on keeping the real essence of the form with the proper global rhythm and pace. That's what you should keep in mind. If you do that, then a little modification on the speed of a hand movement or sequence won't matter at all. What is wrong is when someone alters the essence of the form, which includes changing movements to make them more spectacular for competition, increasing or decreasing the general pace of the kata to look better when doing it, creating additional and unnecessary movements that are incorporated into the form to compensate for a lack of training and skill or spicing up a segment that doesn't seem too flashy. You can practice a traditional kata and perform it beautifully in a tournament without having to alter and modify the original form to look better in front of the judges.

If a karate-ka knows a large amount of kata, does that reflect the amount of his technical knowledge?

Definitely not. Having five cars in your garage does not make you a better driver. Karate is not about quantity ... it is about quality. Those who think that a karate-ka is better than another because he knows a larger number of forms should re-evaluate his thinking. Old masters like Funakoshi Gichin, Miyagi Chojun and many of their predecessors never tried to learn or teach great amounts of kata. Shito-ryu founder Mabuni Kenwa Sensei, who was determined to accumulate many of the old forms to prevent them from being lost, is the only exception to this, but he never pushed his students to learn 60 kata either. The student has to go deeper into the meaning and application of every single movement and principle found in the forms. And this is a lifetime study because many of the real techniques are hidden in onyo bunkai.

Do you believe that shito-ryu has a more natural "flavor" to express kata than other karate styles?

Maybe. Shito-ryu has a strong influence from Okinawa's culture, and they [Okinawans] tried to make the practice of karate very natural for the human body. Karate is a part of the practitioner's life, and the Okinawans approach it like something that you will be doing for the rest of your life. Therefore, they don't train in karate like it is something you do when you are young but quit when you get older. This mentality influences the techniques of the art. If you practice a kata in which you have to jump 360 degree in the air and land flat on your hands, are you planning to do that when you are 60? You have to be logical in your approach to karate. Using logic, you can practice the art for the rest of your life.

What is your opinion of kumite in modern competitions?

Shiai kumite is not real kumite as it is understood in traditional karate. In a sporting event, the main thing organizers need to provide is a safe environment, and this is always based on rules and regulations. Shiai kumite is controlled sparring under safe sportive regulations. And that is what it is. To stay close to the true essence of traditional karate-do, the requirements to score a point should reflect the important points of any given karate technique. Otherwise, competitors will score with anything. Unfortunately, this is what is happening these days. A scoring technique should have the basic technical elements required by the art; a tsuki is always a tsuki and a keri always a keri, but a competitor needs to deliver the scoring technique with balance, the right ma-ai (distance), kime, control, body mechanics and the correct fighting spirit. And finally, a perfect zanchin should be shown after the technique has been delivered and scored. If we ask the competitors to maintain these qualities and the referees strongly reward these technical elements, then sport kumite represents the true idea of fighting in traditional karate, which means displaying Budo attitude. The problem arises when anything that touches, regardless of the way the technique has been delivered, is counted as a point. Then, it becomes a matter of touching the opponent instead of delivering a powerful, well-controlled technique.

SHITO RYU MASTERS

Let's not forget that shiai kumite is an aspect of the whole kumite side in karate-do. It has regulations and many effective techniques have to be eliminated to prevent major injuries. Karate has many fighting techniques as eye attacks, elbow and knee strikes in close-range, kicks to the legs and knee, et cetera. These are highly efficient and powerful. Sport karate is good if we keep the essence of what the right attitude and real technique should be in a life-and-death situation. This is as close as we can get to Budo.

What is your opinion of the various forms of full-contact karate and fighting events practiced these days?

Full-contact karate, kickboxing and other types of sport fighting events are good for young people if they feel inclined to do them. [However], these kinds of activities are [only] good up until a certain age. If a practitioner has only focused on fighting, he has nothing left. That's why karate is for life. You can always train because the art will always have something for you.

How should supplementary training such as running, weightlifting and other sports be balanced with pure technical karate sessions?

Runners run, weightlifters lift weights and karate-ka do karate. Now that I have said this, let me elaborate a little. Everything a karate-ka does — besides practicing the art of karate-do — should be specifically designed to supplement and help the technical element of the skill training. Don't lift weights like a bodybuilder does and don't run like a marathon runner because it won't help. Instead, a karate-ka should do intervals (sprints combined with recovery) because they duplicate the change of rhythm found in kumite and kata. The karate-ka should lift weights to balance the less-worked muscles in his body because this will strengthen and support those, as well as the ones used all the time in karate training. He shouldn't, however, try to develop huge mass, plus he should work on flexibility. In essence, he should be strong and supple.

If any additional training doesn't help the karate-ka improve his karate, why is he doing it? I have seen many practitioners run, lift weights and do other things because they think these activities will help them in karate. The truth is they don't do them to fit into the structure of the martial arts. Instead, they do them as an addition, and this prevents them from spending more time on the technical aspects that they really need to [focus on to] progress in their chosen art.

How important is self-defense?

Very important. Karate is a self-defense method. Not only does it teach you how to use your body to protect yourself from an aggressor, but it also gives you the moral and ethical code to avoid confronta-

tions. In combat, the highest level of skill is the ability to read and neutralize your opponent's actions before he moves. Similarly, the highest level of [skill in] self-defense is [the ability] to prevent a dangerous situation before it arises. You should be able to foresee how an irrelevant incident may escalate before it becomes a difficult situation. Feel it, see it before it becomes bigger and abort it. This is true mastery.

Do you believe there are advantages to studying in Japan?

I really do, and it's not for the technical and mechanical aspects of the art. Instead, training in Japan will teach you a lot of the feeling of the land where karate was developed. The atmosphere, the ambiance, the etiquette, et cetera feels different if you train in Japan than if you follow the same rituals in another country. Of course, this is true for those who are interested in going deeper into the traditional and cultural aspects of Budo and Japan. If you practice karate simply as a sport, then I don't think it is necessary. You can learn, perform and become a world champion without ever going there.

Sensei, on a personal level, you had cancer and went through an extremely dangerous surgery. Nevertheless, you came out on top and you continue training in karate as you used to do. What is the secret?

There is no secret. When you face death with the true attitude of Bushido, there is nothing to lose and everything to win. Karate-do helped me to maintain the warrior spirit and be ready for whatever came into my life ... good or bad. I have learned to simplify my life and stay close to my good friend and loyal students who have been training with me for more than three decades.

Finally, what does it mean to you to practice the art of karate-do?

The martial arts and karate-do are a vehicle and a prescription for personal growth. They provide a useful tool to greater understanding and acceptance of many things in life. It is a perfect learning environment to test ourselves to the limit, deal with certain issues that can bring us closer to the life-and-death situations of the old Samurai and stretch our conception of reality until the only impossibility is lack of change in what we are doing. Karate helps you to understand how simple life should be: strive to happy. Life is very simple, but we [human beings] tend to make it very complicated. Budo is a way to find life in the midst of death. In combat, we need mindlessness and acceptance of what is; therefore, we learn to be in peace with the outside world. In dealing with this paradox of life-and-death, and peace in the midst of violence, we teach our minds to accept the duality of existence and focus on the now rather than trying to evaluate everything and try to find a reason behind it. Karate-do is a valid vehicle to reach the higher levels of human existence.

GENZO IWATA

THE SHITO KAI LEGACY

When you meet Sensei Genzo Iwata – the Technical Director of the "World Shito Kai Federation', you will feel nothing less than the energy of someone seriously devoted to the study of karate-do. Although Genzo Iwata started his training a very early age, he is extremely understanding, approachable and respectful – not only as a karate instructor but as a human being as well. His long years of experience and training under the guide of his father, the legendary Manzo iwata, have allowed him to internalize the important moral aspects of the art and use them in his daily life. Internationally recognized as a Shito Kai authority, he found a way of life in karate and became obsessed with sharing his knowledge and experiences with students both young and old, regardless of their ability. What sets him apart is that he is ready and willing to not only train hardcore karatekas, but also individuals interested in personal development as well. He is a knowledgeable and fascinating man, full of interesting stories, and brimming with a positive attitude towards teaching and to life.

What was your father Manzo Iwata Sensei as an instructor?

He was very serious. He trained us very hard and always encouraged us to not only train hard, but to intellectually study what we were training as well. He always stressed understanding ourselves as human beings and to strive to be productive not only as karatekas but also as members of our society. Karate is not only about the Martial Art. Karate is also about the relationship between the Sensei and the student, which is similar to the relationship between a father and child. But children cannot choose their father, but in Budo, a student can choose his teacher (father).

Did you have any other Sensei?

Obviously I had the chance of receiving knowledge from my Sen-pai but I would only call my father my "sensei". By being able to see with my own eyes and experience with my own body so many great teachers and sempai capable of such a high level of Karate represents a huge source of wealth and experience for me.

Do you think that Sport Karate is destroying the spirit of Karate-Do?

It's important to have a balance. The true path lies in a balance between Training Karate for health, Training Karate for Sport and Recreation and Training Karate for Budo (Karate for a life and death self-

defense situation). Technically these things are very different. You must not mistake the true path as being only one of these aspects of Karate. Training Karate for health will allow your body to defend against illness and you will live a longer higher quality life. Real Budo Karate training for self-defense will have ramifications of serious injuries to you and your training partners. You must be very careful in Budo training. Besides, you should never have an occasion to use Karate in a real situation anyway. You should develop the intuition, character and ability to avoid a fight. Training Karate as Budo has little to no application in our society. Avoiding a fight is the best self-defense. If you lived in a time of war where real combat would be used, your training would be drastically different.

Sport Karate Training allows you to develop without serious injury, to a physical level not possible before. The attitude in your training is most important. If the spirit of Karate-Do is being destroyed, it is happening because of people and attitudes, not because of sport competition. No matter what you are training, you should always train with the idea of becoming a better human being. Train to understand your strengths and weaknesses. Train to be a good, honest and trustworthy human being. Train to perfect your character. This is the spirit of Karate-Do.

What were Iwata Sensei's feelings about Sport Karate?

He understood that our Karate would grow and change. He understood that it would be influenced by many people and many things. The perfection of one's character was the most important thing. I think this should be our concern and more important goal in training.

Do you think that fear in the Dojo is positive or negative?

Every instructor creates different level of "fear" or "tension" in the Dojo and every student feel different level of fear in the dojo. Fear could make the mind focused and enhance the development of mental strength. Fear is not always good and it could make people weaker. But when you overcome the fear, you develop the confidence and turning it into strength Training makes you physically stronger. When the body gets stronger you feel more confidence and also mentally you get stronger. When you mentally get stronger, you can push more and work harder. And it will relate to you life style. It will relate and affect your relationship with your family or at work. When you work at the edge of your limit, your mind and mental strength at the time changes your performance. From an instructor point of view it is important to make a class where students can focus on what they do during the class.

What is your opinion about "Ippon Shobu?

"Ippon Shobu" teaches the karateka to maintain a heightened awareness and superior concentration because there are no second chances when your life is on the line. We need that intense mental and emotional pressure to remain in the correct frame of mind. Traditional "Ippon Shobu" also helps to promote and maintain a high standard of technique. We should keep the traditional approach of the idea of making our Karate effective in a real situation. Training with this intent raises your spiritual awareness and appreciation of life. Modern day Karate has lost the "Ikken Hisatsu Spirit."

Would the different principles of the different styles promote confusion or conflict in the student?

If a Martial Art is being taught properly, all the essential principles should be the same and compliment each other. There is only one human body. When I say become familiar with many arts, I don't mean to practice Shotokan on Monday, Goju on Tuesday, Jujutsu on Wednesday, etc... I mean that you should have an open mind to exploring principles, techniques and training methods taught in other styles. Study the Budo with an open mind.

Would you recommend that Shito Ryu karateka study some of the original Okinawan versions of our Katas and some other Okinawan Katas that are not found in the style?

Shito Ryu has a great number of katas within the style but any additional study is positive. The study of old Okinawan Katas is a must for the advanced only. It will allow you to see and better understand the evolution of our modern day Kata. The Katas were originally designed for Budo. Kata was a library of techniques to incapacitate and even kill the opponents. Remember, the origin of many Kata and techniques were Chinese. These fighting methods eventually found their way to Okinawa and Okinawa was involved in wars. These fights were all hand-to-hand combat. Killing was face to face.

This developed a mental focus in the warrior that is indescribable and most probably unattainable unless you were in the terrifying reality of hand-to-hand, face to face warfare. The techniques found in Kata came from actual battlefield experience where killing and killing quickly was necessary.

Modern masters modified the Katas to be more physically demanding and more focused on body dynamics and beauty. This allows the student to focus on defeating his most dangerous modern day opponent, himself.

Are there philosophical lessons taught and represented by the physical techniques of Kata?

Yes. The deep practice of Kata is linked to interpreting opponents and reading and understanding human beings. You must also understand the relationship between Kihon, Kata and Kumite. The mental focus and image training taught in serious Kata training will help you to anticipate the thoughts and movements of others and will bring a greater focus to your life in general. You must study this very hard for a very long time.

Shito Kai is known for the natural high stances, how this approach fit into the regular kihon training?

We practice moving from a high stance when we do drills that require you to begin from a Shizen Tai, then shift into a stance to block and counter. In this training you start from a high stance. You don't really need to practice a high stance because it's much easier than a low stance. Everything depends on the situation. You should use the appropriate stance for what is happening at the moment. In a fight, height will naturally vary. Tai Sabaki (Body Shifting) is better from a high stance because higher stances provide more mobility than low stances. Lower stances provide more stability because of their shape and the low center of gravity.

Because the situation should dictate the height of the stance, a karateka must be able to generate power from a stance of any height. Power only comes after a person is an expert at generating power from body rotation. We must understand how they make power. One can generate great power if they understand proper body dynamics. One of the most important things emphasize is pushing from the hips and to keep the rotation of the hips smoothly, always keeping the direction of the rotation parallel to the floor. The ideal training to develop instant or instantaneous power comes through training the body with slow movements. In order to be able to develop the body so that it can accelerate, you must be able to understand how the body moves, and this understanding can be developed through slow motion training.

Would you please describe the concept of Kime?

Kime is the same as control; some say focus, but it is the same as control. When we punch, some muscles are for pushing and some are for pulling. If they are working at the same time, then you cannot punch. So, when punching, the pulling muscles should be relaxed to allow you to punch. If the muscles work together, then the technique will be more efficient. For me, Kime is when the muscles, tendons, ligaments and spirit, intention etc. locks for a split second. There is no waste.

When you are travelling it must be difficult to find time for your own training?

Even when I am teaching, I try to do the techniques as many times as possible, demonstrating them to the class. So, I must show strong techniques and do them correctly.

How has Shito Kai training changed in the years since you began training?

In my opinion karate has not changed a great deal but our approach has changed somewhat. Of course, having Manzo Iwata Sensei was a constant source of information. Also some of the training methods have changed. He also pointed out that we changed when better methods of training were introduced to us.

What was the primary focus under your father training?

The primary focus was to become the best instructor possible and be able to impart to our students what we have learned. That's the primary emphasis engendered by Manzo Iwata Sensei and it hasn't changed.

Do you have any advice to offer the current and future instructor?

With age we cannot train with the same vigor as when we were younger, and though strength and flexibility wane with age, we never stop growing mentally. Therefore, we must modify our method but continue to train for a lifetime. Persevere and continue to practice. The WSKF is an organization that is able to successfully continue, support and pursue Kenwa Mabuni Sensei's Karate in terms of technical, theoretical and spiritual aspects that his Karate embodies. I have a tremendous enthusiasm to pass our techniques to as many of the younger generation of karateka as possible all over the world.

SANAUOV JASTALAP

UNCOMMON WISDOM

SENSEI JASTALAP IS ONE MARTIAL ARTIST WHO HAS HAD A MOST UNUSUAL KARATE-DO CAREER. HIS INTEREST IN THE ART OF KARATE-DO AN THE JAPANESE CULTURE INTRINSIC TO THE ARTS OF BUDO AND THE TALENT AND ENERGY HE DEVOTED TO IT MADE HIM ONE OF THE LEADERS OF THE ART IN THE EASTERN EUROPE.

A MAN OF MANY TALENTS AND BROAD VISION, HE HAS A WARM, OUTGOING NATURE AND A SENSE OF HUMOR THAT ENDEARS HIM TO HIS FOLLOWERS. A FIRM BELIEVER OF HARD WORKOUTS, NOT ONLY FOR STUDENTS BUT FOR INSTRUCTORS AS WELL, SENSEI JASTALAP LIKE TO REMIND MODERN KARATE INSTRUCTORS THAT 'THE GI IS NOT A HOLY GARMENT, BUT A STRONG WORKING SUIT AND IS MEANT TO BE USED."

HIS WORK AS A KARATE INSTRUCTOR AND NATIONAL COACH IS RECOGNIZED ALL OVER THE WORLD AND HIS REPUTATION IN THE SHITO KAI COMMUNITY IS SECOND TO NONE. HIS LIFE AS A STUDENT HAS BEEN TO FIND THE MEANING HIDDEN IN THE ART AND AS A TEACHER HIS GOAL IS TO HELP STUDENTS TO FIND THE PURE PLEASURE IN PRACTICING SOMETHING SO SIMPLE AND YET SO COMPLEX. THE ULTIMATE GOAL, AS HE DESCRIBES IT, "IS PRESERVING THE TRADITION AND ENSURING THAT IT IS AVAILABLE FOR FUTURE GENERATIONS."

How long have you been practicing karate?

I was introduced to karate when I was 12 years old. My first Sensei was Alexander Hendrickson. When I started karate, there were very few opportunities and not too many choices for styles and schools of martial arts. We trained where we could and that was it. However, the feeling was extraordinary, the spirit was very unique and sincere. We wanted to learn everything, understand everything…we were ready to absorb any knowledge. There was passion and we were fanatical about the art of karate.

And the deeper we penetrate into the consciousness of the unknown the more our curiosity grew. I must admit, that this feeling is still with me. The result is karate has become my life.

How many styles (karate or other Martial Arts methods) have you trained in and who were your teachers? Do you practice any other art in conjunction with karate?

My journey in search of the preferred style took me through several methods. My first stop was Shotokan but I saw a certain lacking of depth in kata bunkai, I did perceive a lack of inner content. Then I trained in Goju Ryu under Sensei Higaonna and the bunkai was definitely there. Goju focuses a lot on close range techniques. I did reach the 'shodan' level in Goju in the old USSR.

Under the guidance of Sensei Sigiura, I did train in Wado Ryu. It has a very strong kumite, especially in exercises as "inashi" and "idori" but kata in this style does not play a big part. After a long search, I met Shito Ryu, which suited me in all areas. It contains kata from all three of the previous styles. Sensei Kenwa Mabuni, the founder, had set a goal to bring together kata and the creators of these forms were natives of Okinawa. And he succeeded. Moreover, he kept intact all their complexity, including bunkai, unlike the founder of Shotokan, Sensei Funakoshi, who brought great changes in kata as he learned it from Sensei Itosu.

In addition to karate there is one thing that is very present in my life. This is "Kylyshtasu" - national martial arts of fencing with swords... the Art of the ancient nomads.

Were you a 'natural' at karate – did the movements come easily to you?

To be honest, the physical techniques came very easily to me. Of course, I did experience difficulties in certain elements but in general, I felt pretty good when learning a new technique or kata.

Please, explain for us the main points of your style and its differences with other styles?

The style of Shito-ryu is different from other recognized traditional styles of karate-do in several ways.

I think we can come out with few aspects that make it different: a) the amount of kata information studying karate Shito-ryu, exceeds the amount of information being studied in other styles. For example, in Shito-ryu you have to study around 60 plus kata. The number of bunkai for one movement of any kata can be from two to five or more variations, and this number increases depending on the depth of knowledge and understanding of the movements in that particular kata.

The following point that is a fundamental difference from other styles is the preservation of the old Okinawan principles in teaching the art; you must learn to do well one thing, and then you are given new information. It is about refinement and not accumulation. Therefore, at the qualification exam even for the 10th Kyu, the performing of each movement is very strict, not only to show good external form, but also the internal content of the technical action, then there must be good speed, concentration, the distribution of effort and accuracy, etc. To learn physical movements is very simple, but to "fill it" with good content can only be achieved by dedicated students.

The third difference lies in the process of rank testing. For instance in testing for the 10th kyu, a student must show his training in kata and "rendosa-no-kata" and "teysiki-ippon kumite" assisted by other student.

The fourth difference is that traditionally, in Shito-ryu there is only six belts and to get the next color belt takes from two to five years of study. Many students because of the high requirements involved in the pursuit of colored belts moved to other schools of karate and get faster promotions.

Please tell us a little about the origin and evolution of Karate in Kazakhstan and its Federation?

During the existence of the old Soviet Union there was a period when karate was prohibited, from 1983 to 1989. After the abolition of the ban, almost on the edge of the collapse of the USSR and the emergence of new independent States, the history of Kazakhstan's karate began.

Established in 1992, the Federation of Kazakhstan originally included two styles - Shotokan and Goju-ryu, and later – Wado-ryu and Shito-ryu. Afterwards different branches of the Federation were opened all over Kazakhstan and the first domestic and international competition took place. The formation of teachers and Coaches happened quickly and without too much difficulty, largely that because Kazakhstan had many karate fans and enthusiasts.

How did you meet Sensei Antonio Oliva and what can you tell us about him?

Sensei Antonio Oliva is a name we have all heard for many years in the sport of karate. When we had the first opportunity we decided that we have to invite him. It happened in the beginning of 2000. This was a turning point in the evolution of the karate in Kazakhstan. He showed and taught us things that only a "Professor" knows.

I am sure that the success of the Kazakhstani athletes took place largely because of the knowledge that was obtained during meetings and training sessions with Sensei Oliva: he passed it onto us and we delivered. Since year 2000, he has been visiting us constantly and cooperates closely with our National Team

and other competitors. He is a very important piece in the development of karate in Kazakhstan.

What is the level of competition in Kazakhstan at this moment?

The level of Karate competition in Kazakhstan is high. Just look at the list of participants, among them you can find winners of the world championship WKF, champions of Asian Championships and other international tournaments. The same applies for the national tournament organization, management and marketing. The last five years the national championship of Kazakhstan was broadcasting on sports and national channels of Kazakhstan. This fact, says a lot about the promotion and expansion of the art of Karate in the country.

What are the most important qualities for a student to become proficient in karate?

I think it is very important to take part in sport competition, because it allows to expand the boundaries of our knowledge. The opportunity to be and compete with those who are strong, and at the same time to test ourselves, to learn our weaknesses. Only practice can achieve such understanding, through analysis and comparison. You need to use this competition experience to find your limitations and your strong points. This is a very personal journey. Test yourself constantly.

When you are teaching the art of karate – what was the most important element; self-defense or sport?

It all depends on your age. When a child comes to the dojo, it is important the technical components, gaining experience, learning to achieve success in competitions, i.e. Karate is more an sportive acitvity than a very strict art of fighting. Eventually - after mastering the basics of karate, including emotional, psychological, sportive aspects, the more important part of the art of karate, or self-defense, internal thinking and understanding of the essence of karate will take over.

How is the current situation of Karate in Kazakhstan?

Karate is very popular, there is a strong support from the Government. This contributed to successful performance of our athletes at the Asian Olympic Games and other competitions. As recognition for the high level of Kazakhstan's karate - we carried out of the first Cup of Champions of Asia, the first commercial tournament in the history of the Asian karate - in the capital of Kazakhstan, Astana.

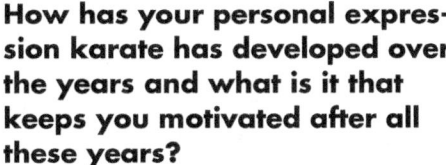

How has your personal expression karate has developed over the years and what is it that keeps you motivated after all these years?

The longer you train, the stronger the feeling of inability to comprehend all in karate gets inside of you. That makes you dig deeper in karate. The way the style of Shito Kai is organized, forces you to study more and more.

What advice would you give to students on the question of supplementary training?

If this applies to students who are competing, I would recommend to carefully studying the rules of the competition. This is necessary for the success in sport tournaments. Too often the defeated fighter asks for clarifications about why he has lost, and it is up to his/her Coach to explain. Competitors need to learn about the rules. This is a very important point.

What advice would you give to instructors whom are struggling with their own development?

It is important for teachers and Sensei to understand that when you are in the dojo, you are the one who set the rules but when you are in a tournament or sport competition the circumstances are completely different. All teachers and Sensei must obey the competition rules and regulations. They must respect those and set an example for their students and athletes. It is also the teacher's responsibility to know the competition rules and teach those to the students who will be competing.

Have been times when you felt fear in your training?

It was not fear but rather the doubt of knowing of what I was doing was right. Especially in the years when I had no direction from a Sensei. I was lucky that I found such a great teacher, thanks to who these doubts were resolved and resolved very quickly. His name is Sensei Yukihiro Nozawa, Technical Director of the "World Federation of Shito-Kai".

Do you think that Olympics will be positive for the art of karate-do?

The Olympic Games, undoubtedly, will have a positive effect for the art of karate. However, this coin has two sides. The first is positive: if karate becomes an Olympic sport, it will get more popular, and will increase the support from the Governments, and the athletes will have a better incentive. For any athlete competing, an Olympic medal is the most desirable goal.

The flip side is that in the pursuit of medals, there is a danger of losing the traditional karate; it will become more "sport". In any case, I think that the Olympic Games will be a great influence on the development of karate around the world.

How do you like to train yourself? Has this changed over the years?

Regarding the self-study of the technical side of karate, which is always present in my life with constant practice, now I have another professional interest: the scientific study of the practical skills and exercises. I hope one day I can put all these in a book format.

Shotokan, Shito Ryu, Goju, Ryu etc...How do you think the different branches and styles affect the art of Karate?

Those styles do the same things but differently. Like cooking...rice is rice but can be cooked differently. It is interesting to know how other styles do approach this or that kata or this or that kumite principle or technique.

Given the history of origin of each style, we can say that they all complement each other [in a way] and contribute to the enrichment of the art of karate. Each style has its pros and cons - and everyone who is really interested can find themselves engaged in a single style of their choice but also gain knowledge and information by studying others.

Jastalap

What karate can offer to the individual in these troubled times we are living in?

Karate gives the practitioner something different than other kind of exercises or physical activities. Some physical activities wear the body down but karate builds it up with energy. Karate is more than a simple exercise and provides a way of healing and recovering the body after a day of stress. It is a "way of life" and that is the reason why in Japan they hold the "Masters Cup" with participants of 70 years old. This is karate-do, this is the "way of life" of the art of the empty hand.

After so many years of training, what is it for you that is so appealing in this style of karate and why?

In general, we can say that Shito-ryu is an encyclopedia, collected works of all Okinawan Sensei kata and training, all of them are kata in their original form. And thanks to its specifications; there are close combat and long combat techniques. That is why this style is most suitable for sport Kumite. Studying kata and apply a smooth transition to Kumite.

Finally, what advise would you like to give to all Karate practitioners, regardless of style?

The main thing is to study, study and study; to broaden the horizons, to learn other styles, to keep moving forward. The most important thing is not to stop and get stagnant in our training. I like the philosophy of Yamamoto Tsunetomo, Samurai of clan "Nabeshima", the author of a collection of books on practical and spiritual guidance for warriors. He said: "Improve your mind, be humane and show courage" - I think that may well be the motto for sport karate and for Budo karate.

CHUZO KOTAKA

A LONG JOURNEY

Sensei Chuzo Kotaka, established the "International Karate Federation" (IKF) in 1966, in Honolulu, Hawaii. Born on November 11, 1941 in Hyogoken, Japan, he began his karate training at the age of seven under Sensei Genryu Kimura. Towards the end of his high school career, he also learned under a well-known master named Soke Shogo Kuniba.

In 1962, Sensei Kotaka won the "All Japan Karate Championship", the most prestigious karate tournament in Japan, even to this today. The All Japan Championship title was his most notable accomplishment but there were many other prestigious titles he accomplished. He won the West All Japan title from 1962-63 and the All Japan Seishinkai from 1960-62. He was also nominated as Co-MVP in 1960 along with Master Tetsuhiko Asai. This tournament had brought together the best fighters from each of the 4 major styles at the Osaka Namba Furitsu Taikai.

In 1965, Sensei Kotaka, at the age of 23, moved to Hawaii on a goodwill tour to teach karate around world. Master Chojiro Tani, founder of Shukokai, asked Sensei Kotaka if he would like to become a professional karate teacher. Kotaka Sensei went through a rigorous teaching and training schedule for over one year before he was allowed to travel abroad. His first stop was in Honolulu, Hawaii and then he had plans to go to Australia and South Africa in the years to come. Sensei Kotaka fell in love with the island of Oahu and decided to stay there permanently. After one year on Oahu, he decided to make Hawaii his home. In 1966, International Karate Federation (IKF) was established, and the style Kotaka-Ha Shito-Ryu was born.

Since the opening of IKF's first dojo, Kotaka-Ha Shito-Ryu has grown statewide, to the continental United States, Japan, and India.

Sensei, how karate has influenced your life?

I am sure I'd be a totally different person if the art of karate wasn't part of my life. It allowed me to have a better understanding of things and myself, it helped me to "grow" as human being. As times passes by, my karate has become "smaller" but way deeper than it was when I was younger. There were lessons hidden behind simple training sessions and those "lessons" are the ones that stayed with me throughout the years.

So, karate changed your life?

I don't think karate 'per se' can change a person. Karate doesn't make you better or worse, but the little things we learn in practice and the experiences we have to go through during training, definitely shape us inside. All the answers are inside of ourselves but through hard training we get to discover them if we look into the right places.

Do you think that we are losing the 'traditional' aspects of karate?

Tradition in the art of karate is found not in the punches, kicks, and kata but in the attitude we have when training and living the art. It is important that we live our lives based on the traditional values developed and taught by the old masters. That tradition is not about mimicking the same kata as Mabuni Sensei, or Funakoshi Sensei used to do, but in how we approach our lives and strive to be better individuals in everything we do.

You always mention to "go beyond the comfort zone". Why is that?

You always have to train outside your comfort zone as often and as long as you can…in every training session.

Comfort zone is the point where your mind and body say you can't go any harder and can't focus any longer. This is when you need to take control of your emotions, thoughts and actions to continue working past these barriers. Every time you break this barrier you become a little stronger, you expand your "comfort zone". The work you put in while outside your comfort zone is exponentially magnified when compared to work done inside it.

That means toward the end of training when you are facing a tough opponent and you don't feel like you can go any longer, but are able to muster up the strength to score with a solid punching or kicking technique, that technique is like drilling a punch or a kick a 1000 times under optimal conditions (estimate, but you get the point). If an athlete can do this on a regular basis their "comfort zone" is constantly expanding. This means they are constantly getting stronger, quicker, better technique, etc…

Every time you break through these barriers your confidence increases as well. The battles you win inside your head when you want to quit are what build confidence and the burning passion it takes to win close matches.

What kata represents in karate training?

Kata is a very important part of karate training because it doesn't teach you movements; it teaches you the way of learning the principles of movement. In many ways we can say that kata is our basics. It is the tool used to perfect all the techniques and movements. It provides a structure to learn and grow so our training is not meaningless: it is the element that ties of karate factors together.

What can you say to us about makiwara training?

Makiwara training is something many people don't want to do. It simply hurts. But traditionally, its training teaches many things, not only techniquewise. I believe it conditions our minds and not only our hands. If we don't have the right attitude when facing it, the makiwara will defeat us. Some people say the makiwara is not a realistic piece of training, but no opponent can take more punishment and still stand in front of you. You will give up before it does.

Do the students today have more knowledge than those from past generations?

The amount of information available to us nowadays is immense. An old "shodan" knew a certain and limited amount of information. The "shodan" today have [at their] fingertips all the information in the world. He or she may not have other aspects of what karate represents and means but the material and information, if taken correctly, can make them much more knowledgeable than the old generations. It is very important though that the new generation keeps the right karate spirit.

Sensei, what do you think is the main physical element in sport karate?

Well, there are aspects like "kime" and power that can't be assessed in a karate sport match. This leaves us with the attribute of "speed" like the most important. The problem that I see is that a competitor may have a bad basic technique and still score faster than his/her opponent. The technique may have an incorrect form but be fast enough to beat the opponent. We can't sacrifice the quality of the technique for its speed so we can score a point. If we do this, the main danger is we'll get caught in a game, a game of tag, in the case of a contest. We can't allow a competitor to win using a poor technique.

SHITO RYU MASTERS

I remember hearing you saying that 'many injuries are related to a lack of defensive skills'...

And it is true. We are seeing more and more, competitors that are disregarding the training of the defensive skills. They are focusing on attacking actions to score points and even use attacking techniques as answers to the opponent's offensive. This is wrong. The matches are turning into a "crashing of bodies". The competition system does not rewards the defensive skills so, for many, there is no reason to train them. Because of this, many competitors are being injured during the matches. The extreme emphasis on attacking techniques has resulted in a deficit of defensive maneuvers and actions in the sport of karate.

Your style, Shito Ryu, has a great number of kata: do you think it is necessary all these kata to master the style?

The number of kata found in a style of karate does not determine the level of mastery in the art. We need to look deeper in the kata and focus on improving the ones we are doing instead of trying to memorize more and more. Quality over quantity. I don't mean it is not good to learn several katas, but don't loose yourself in the "number" and pay attention to the quality of what you are doing.

Is Karate Budo or a sport?

Karate is essentially Budo, not just a sport, but it represents different things to different people. When an athlete wins a championship, he gets all the recognition and fame but we can't forget that this is a temporary thing and only based on athletic ability. As a budoka, we must strive for winning many 'championships' throughout whole life and become a person of value for our society.

I remember you saying 'there is a moral responsibility in winning a contest'. Would you please elaborate on that?

Yes. Every time a combat or fighting art becomes a sport, there are always moral consequences. When an athlete scores a point and celebrates it like an American football player celebrates a touchdown, there is a sense of being disrespectful to the opponent. Beating an opponent is not a thing to rejoice, but to reflect. We need to show a dignified behavior, good manners and restrain.

Is there any "secret" to reach excellence in karate?

There is no really a secret to become an exceptional karateka, but there are several basic guidelines to follow in becoming and maintaining yourself as a successful budoka. This is true whatever your goals may be, whether you want to become al tournament champion or whether you simply want to practice the art for your won health and well being. Be as it may, one thing you should never settle for is becoming "good". Instead shoot to be "great", the best in your field. And once you have accomplished this goal, keep your ideals high so that you will not fall backwards in your development.

Where do you see the art going in the future?

The sportive element of karate has grown tremendously in the last decades. The society is changing and the student's mentality has changed also. The old traditional training that many of us did in the past, it is not suitable for modern days. Karate training is a constant pattern of breaking old habits and forming new ones. We need to adapt. Karate is something that we have to be consistent on. Keep pushing. We can't stop or the "water will get cold". If you start slacking off, you will have just a "shadow" of what you had when you were training hard and consistently.

Sensei, what is your final advice to all practitioners?

In karate training there are many questions that we must ask constantly ourselves on a daily basis. We can't allow our training to become 'dry' and 'stagnant'. By asking those important questions everyday, we become better karatekas, better human beings, and that's what is really important. It is an endless quest for a perfection that we'll never achieve. There is where the real meaning of karate-do lives. I have to say that I am a lucky man, and grateful that my life in an art of Budo has been pleasant. I wish everyone could have the feeling of peace, friendship and brotherhood that this karate-do believer has found in his art.

KENEI MABUNI

THE POWER OF INNER STRENGTH

AN AWESOME KARATE MASTER WITH A UNIQUE CHARISMATIC PERSONALITY, HE WAS BORN ON FEBRUARY 13, 1918 IN SHURI, OKINAWA. THE OLDEST SON OF THE SHITO RYU FOUNDER KENWA MABUNI, HE STARTED TRAINING KARATE AT A VERY EARLY AGE AND OFTEN HELPED HIS FATHER GIVE DEMONSTRATIONS THROUGHOUT JAPAN DURING THE 1930S. WHEN THE DAI NIPPON BUTOKU KAI WAS FOUNDED, KENEI MABUNI HAD THE OPPORTUNITY TO TRAIN AND LEARN FROM THE NOTABLE VISITORS WHO CAME TO TRAIN AND LEARN FROM HIS FATHER. THIS INCLUDED SUCH LEGENDARY FIGURES AS KONISHI YASUHIRO, CHOKI MOTOBU, AND FUNAKOSHI GICHIN. SHORTLY AFTER THE DEATH OF HIS FATHER FROM A HEART ATTACK, KENEI MABUNI SUCCEEDED HIS FATHER AS THE SECOND SOKE OF THE STYLE AND ACCEPTED THE AWESOME RESPONSIBILITY OF MAINTAINING THE QUALITY OF SHITO RYU KARATE WORLDWIDE. HIS TECHNIQUE AND KNOWLEDGE COMPLEMENT HIS EXCELLENT PEDIGREE. ON JANUARY 15, 1984 HE WAS PRESENTED THE DISTINGUISHED SERVICE MEDAL FOR HIS CONTRIBUTION TO THE MARTIAL ARTS BY THE JAPAN MARTIAL ARTS COUNCIL. MABUNI KENEI ALSO ESTABLISHED THE WORLD SHITO KAI KARATE-DO FEDERATION, OF WHICH HE WAS NAMED GOVERNOR. HE PASSED AWAY ON DECEMBER 2015.

You were born in the dojo, so to speak, weren't you?

Yes. I began my karate training in Okinawa in 1925, when I was 7 years old. The dojo was part of the house my father owned so it was something very natural. He was a policeman at that time. My father, Kenwa Mabuni, trained extensively under two of the greatest karate teachers of that time - Anko Itosu of Shuri-te and Kanryo Higaonna of Naha-te. Later on, he develop his own method called "shito ryu," a name that uses the ideograms from "Itosu" (shi) and "Higaonna" (to). It was his way of paying respect and giving credit to his teachers.

What do you remember about training under your father?

Well, my father was a very strong man and very strict with me. He always gave me a sense of commitment in everything I did. As a boy I wanted to become stronger but later on I became fascinated with the philosophy and spirit of budo. My father's teaching was based on the principles of "shin," "gi" and "tai." "Shin" means heart, "gi" means technique, and "tai" means body. The practitioner should look for a perfect balance among these three aspects. Unfortunately, many of today's karateka fail to balance these elements properly. Technique-wise, the movements from Shuri-te are faster and they use a lot open hand techniques. Naha-te is based on the idea of power - the strength coming from the hara as the kata

"sanchin" proves. The main idea is to keep your center of gravity low and use your hara along the proper breathing patterns. At the time my father was teaching there was a rivalry between both schools of karate and, in fact, challenges weren't an uncommon thing. Don't forget that many other karateka came to train under my father and did not always easily accept my father as their teacher. He had to prove himself to them!

Was your father ever concerned about the use and development of ki?

Of course! Not in a mystical sense, but in a very real and practical one. He was aware of the energy we all have and he knew how to properly use it for karate training. He studied the Bubishi and he knew how to attack the vital points.

How important is bunkai for you?

Bunkai is a very important aspect if we are interested in learning the right form of karate-do. We have to notice though, that bunkai varies depending of the style that you practice and does not always indicate the skill level of the practitioner. For instance, shotokan styles favor more long range techniques as compared to shito ryu or goju ryu. Therefore, the application of the physical techniques is based on a different conceptual approach. At short distance, you need to use your limbs and shoulders in a different way. One problem I have perceived in the understanding and development of bunkai is that many practitioners try to explain the kata techniques, or bunkai, and how they apply to a real situation, as they are performing the actual form. This is alright at a basic level but not for the advanced karateka. If you think about how kata techniques are applied to combat then you're thinking that fighting and combat will give you a different mentality. If you understand this point you'll realize that your mind needs to be in a very different state, which give a very different flavor to the kata technique. You can't try to put that into a real situation and squeeze the physical into the form of the kata. If you do that then you can come out with a very weird and unrealistic application of kata movements. The classical or the traditional movement found in kata is one thing and the way you directly apply them in a real situation is another. The body mechanics may be the same but the flavor of the combat application is different because your state of mind is different. Only if you know what you're looking for will you find the karate behind a real confrontation. Curiously enough, bunkai doesn't make you a good karateka - kihon, kata practice, and kumite do. Don't be mistaken.

Is kata truly the essence of karate?

There is a very high number of practitioners all around the world who are interested in what we call "old" or traditional karate-do - thus using kata as the center of their training. And this is good because it helps them to understand the roots of the art. Proper kata training is not as easy as it looks. Let's assume the practitioner has a good technical level in kihon, remember "No kihon, no karate." The first stage is to learn the pattern, to learn the actual form, and memorize the movement in the proper order. You have to make your body fit into the form. Then you start to add speed and power to each technique. Your body knows the movements so you can put more into it. The next step is to learn and develop the right timing and rhythm in the kata. This is a difficult part since now the practitioner controls the kata and the way the form is performed. Once the karateka has a kata with good technique and rhythm, the next stage is to introduce more advanced principles such as mental control and concentration. His mind is the important point now. He can only focus on this once he already has the physical control over the movements and the rhythm of the sequences. Your mind has to be in control before, during and after the execution of the form. This is a very difficult part of karate training where kata becomes a kind of meditation. Reaching this level is extremely difficult and only then can you say "the kata is mine." Your mind takes control over everything else.

What's your opinion on the evolution of kumite in competition?

Kumite is a misunderstood aspect these days. Kumite is not sport competition. Sport is one aspect of kumite. I would say that on the physical level, the most important principle in kumite is ma (distance). Interestingly enough, ma not only applies to kumite but also to kata training. Anyway, if a practitioner understands and is able to control ma he can control his opponent in a fight without delivering a single technique. Whoever controls the distance controls the fight. Other important aspects such as mushin, sen no sen, go no sen, et cetera, are only possible when the karateka has reached a certain level of technical proficiency and skill. He doesn't need to think about certain things so he can develop the higher principles of karate-do. He can feel his opponent's actions almost instinctively and is in perfect synchronization with every movement during the fight. His body is not in control, his mind is. He is able to read actions and react with no wasted movement or energy. This level of skill is very hard to reach and only comes after many years of intensive and dedicated practice and training. It's a kind of sixth sense.

SHITO RYU MASTERS

Do you see any differences between Western and Eastern practitioners?

It's hard to say, but I feel there are differences between an American or European practitioner and a Japanese karateka - and not only physically. The Japanese student will follow the sensei's instructions and try to think and figure out by himself why things are done the way they are done. The Westerner will ask "why" almost immediately, and even if he doesn't, his logical approach requires a reason why. Orientals more readily accept and understand the idea of training mind and body at the same time, whereas Westerners do not think about the mind that much but focus more on the body. Of course, there is a downside to this approach - the student will grow old like everybody else and then what? What happen when you can not rely just on strength and physical abilities? That's the reason karate should be approached as a long-term goal. It's for the rest of your life, not just something you do while you are young. If you start training your mind from the very beginning, by the time you're old your mind will be strong and your body won't go down. If you're strong mentally and physically I believe you can face any problem in your life and come out victorious. In short, the instruction then must be adapted to fit into the mentality and culture of the place where the instructor is sharing his knowledge. The teacher doesn't have to change the art, just adapt the way he's transmitting the information. But the information has to be correct.

How does karate apply to the practitioner's life outside the training hall?

Alexander Pope said, "Some people will never learn anything because they understand everything too quickly." Karate can't be understood quickly. Karate training doesn't stop when you remove your karate gi. Karate is for life. It is true that there is a time for hard training and a time for soft training - but always the focus should be time for training. In fact, and in a traditional sense, the student has to know how to "steal" knowledge from the teacher. And in order to do this persistence is the keyword. Training alone won't make you a good karateka, but correct training and right attitude will. Keep training in the right way and in the right direction and the rewards will come. Some practitioners set unrealistic goals and they become disillusioned after a while. Karate is not about winning or losing but about character development. The character of the karateka is what is really important. Aim to develop the spirit and the higher self. It's important, through karate-do, to develop a philosophy of life that helps you.

Kenei Mabuni

Is shito kai in constant evolution?

My father never thought karate-do was perfect and finished. He knew the art was meant to grow and evolve, that's why at shito kai we have studied and built-up the karate technique. Shito kai contains a lot of techniques such as locking and throwing that are not so obvious at first sight. I'm constantly searching and learning. Karate is sometimes difficult to understand; you may train for a long time, day after day, and find nothing. All of a sudden, one day, you find out that you have truly improved not only in karate technique but also in karate spirit. As a teacher, in order to improve yourself and teach properly, you must speak to people and have experiences in life. It seems that in martial arts it is common to break with tradition - but there must be an understanding of what tradition really means to begin with.

Do you think that the different styles of karate are something important, or the should the art should be unified like Kodokan judo?

I think each is definitely important. Every style or ryu is a tradition, and the heritage of the different masters has to be preserved. I agree that sometimes the technical differences are strictly based on a personal preference of doing things a certain way, but these personal preferences provide us with a very unique and different point of view. I truly believe that we should maintain the ryu -they bring different flavors. It is like painting - there are many schools of painting that were developed over the centuries, but all of them are art.

Did you train in kobudo?

Yes, I studied kobudo. This art helps the karateka to understand certain karate principles on a different level. The use of tai-sabaki, ashi-sabaki, et cetera is very useful in both arts. Also, it is a great training tool to develop a keen sense of distance and focus. Don't forget that kime is different if you have a bo in your hands, than if you're punching with your empty hand. In the end, kime is kime, but your body feel and body mechanics are greatly improved if you practice kobudo. But I recommend to start training in karate-do first, so you develop an strong base for the weaponry aspect.

Has your karate changed over the years?

Of course. I have less physical power and this affects the way I move and perform my karate. I tend to use more natural and circular motions in my technique. When you are young you can go straight all the time, but after a certain age you need to develop ways so your body can move fast naturally. You need more than simple basics. You cannot do karate as if you were 20 years old. You must train in your basics but use different and new training methods that help you to accomplish what you're looking for. There are always physical limitations and I'm trying to find new ways of improving myself. Since karate-

do has become a way of life for me, I sometimes question myself about the role of karate in my life, and about my existence - but that's part of my evolution as a human being. My advice for the younger practitioners is to not get scared because you'll question yourself as to why you are doing it. It's OK, it's normal - everyone gets depressed with their own progression in training. What is important is to feel and spot these depressions and find a way to motivate yourself. Books, videos, and seminar with experts visiting your city or country are excellent methods of pushing through the bad patches.

What is your opinion of combat sports such as kickboxing?

I think these modern disciplines have their place for people who have to go through a certain personal development. Unfortunately, kickboxing can be very unhealthy and detrimental in the long run. Karate can be practiced for life but all these other combat sports cannot. They offer a certain amount of excitement until your body cannot take the punishment anymore. But to me they are sports -very effective and efficient sports - but sports nonetheless, and not budo.

Do you get tired of all the traveling you do?

Yes, I do get very tired but I also enjoy it. It is my responsibility to perpetuate the art my father Kenwa Mabuni developed. So I truly do it with joy. My actions speak for me. I judge myself and my own actions. I have to live with myself and as long as you're honest with yourself and the people around you, everything is alright. It's good to see the art of karate being practiced all around the world but the

real and true art of karate is very rare. It's important to be humble, to understand the simple things in life and training, to respect the senpai and your teachers. Even if they are old, they are still your teachers and respect should be paid to them. Tradition is not about technique, it is about ethics and morals. I don't believe in a soft approach to karate but in hard training, because for me karate-do is a martial art - it is budo and not a sport. I believe in good etiquette and discipline in and out the dojo.

How important is Zen training?

Zen is a big aspect of the Japanese culture and is deeply related to budo. Zen is something that you cannot teach in a karate class. You can show a little bit but it's something the student has to pursue by himself in order to find its real meaning. I consider it a very important part because it is mental training, and the mental training will carry you when your body can't perform anymore. Zen training can greatly help your karate and in the end, help you in life. Real spiritual training is present in every moment of our lives. But don't forget that Zen training is not only done with your head, but also "with your flesh and bones," as the master said.

How does one really understand karate?

Karate begins with the physical aspect, then is followed by the mental. But don't forget that to really understand you must to forge your spirit through the physical. There is no other way. Karate training give us something special that cannot be found in other sports such as football or basketball. It doesn't make us different, but more aware of our inner selves. Karate-do is a way of life, and we shouldn't forget the "do" in our training. Don't limit your training to develop your body but also develop your mind and heart as well. Karate-do must be part of a person's life, not separate from it. The path of karate-do is not an easy one, it is full of struggle and disappointments. As in life, not everything always goes right - in fact it seldom does - but if we have the strength to pass these obstacles then we'll reach a higher level, not only as a martial artist but also as a human being.

104

KENZO MABUNI

STAYING THE COURSE

HE WAS A CAPTIVATING AND COMPELLING MAN. BORN UNDER THE PRESSURE OF BEING THE SON OF ONE OF THE MOST IMPORTANT KARATE-DO TEACHERS OF ALL TIMES, HE HAD A RICH UNDERSTANDING OF THE MARTIAL ARTS. MASTER MABUNI TALKED IN ITALICS WITH EXCLAMATION POINTS TACKED ONTO THE END. HE WAS PASSIONATE ABOUT THE IMPORTANCE OF KARATE-DO, BUT YET AT THE SAME TIME PATIENT AND UNDERSTANDING TO THOSE WHO PRACTICE IT.

HEAD OF THE SHITO RYU NIPPON KARATE-DO KAI, THE ASSOCIATION FOUNDED BY HIS FATHER, KENWA MABUNI, KENZO MABUNI TAUGHT THE STYLE OF SHITO RYU ACCORDING TO THE ORIGINAL AND AUTHENTIC METHODS DEVELOPED BY THE FOUNDER. ALWAYS ON A VERY BUSY AND EXTREMELY TIGHT SCHEDULE, THIS REMARKABLE KARATE-DO TEACHER WAS CONSIDERED AMONG THE MOST INFLUENTIAL AND BEST-KNOWN KARATE MASTERS IN THE WORLD. IT IS WITH DEDICATION AND FORESIGHT THAT KENZO MABUNI - WITH A HIGH APPRECIATION FOR THE AESTHETIC, SPIRITUAL, AND PHYSICAL BEAUTY OF THE ART - EMBRACED THE TASK OF PERPETUATING THE ORIGINAL METHODS OF SHITO RYU KARATE-DO.

What were your beginnings in martial arts?

I started karate training when I was 13 years old and have continued until today. This makes more than 60 years of training. I also trained in kendo and judo when I was young and my training in kobudo involved the bo and sai methods of the Tawada tradition. I don't think it is necessary for a karate practitioner to train in other arts such as judo or kobudo, but it definitely helps you to get a better appreciation of other arts, and how your style or system can be used if you face an opponent who practices those other methods.

What do you consider to be the heritage of the shito ryu style?

My father devoted his life to the development of karate-do. This was unknown to the public and he received neither fame nor monetary rewards. The great inheritances of shito ryu for the future generations are the traditions my father learned from his two great masters - Yasutsune Itosu and Kanryo Higaonna. Of course he received instruction from other people but these two traditions are the basis of his legacy. He left a great gift for us and I have a mission to teach it correctly to the next generation. Therefore, I must be steadfast, study further, and endeavor to clarify.

What do you think are the most important qualities an instructor should possess?

An instructor has a big responsibility on his shoulders. It's important that the instructor study the way of karate-do together with his students. I think that an instructor should be godan (fifth degree black belt) and a certified shihan to fully instruct the students. He must posses a trustworthy character with strong will. I often fing many instructors who falsify their ranks and create their qualifications by themselves. That has caused the chaos of today and misled innocent students. It's important the teacher knows how to instruct with accuracy and correctness. The instructor should teach the art through current applicable ethics and the logic of their society. He has to accept the role of father to his students. In doing so he has a big responsibility to teach them the foundation of karate as well as the etiquette and morals. You must practice what you believe and believe what you practice.

Shito ryu has a very high number of kata; do you think is important to know all of them to master the style?

It's true that the shito ryu style has a high number of kata that represent both the Itosu and Higaonna traditions. My father knew over 90 different kata. He created some kata of his own but he didn't teach all of them in public. This fact shows how important kata is in the shito ryu tradition. It's not necessary to learn all the kata, but each kata teaches something unique - that's why they are a precious treasure. Kodansha should know about 30 to 40 kata, and that can take somewhere between 15 to 25 years of continuous training and dedication to master. I don't consider any kata to be more important than another - all of them are important if you really want to have an understanding of the authentic shito ryu legacy. Of course, each instructor and practitioner will have their own preferences and their favorite kata to perform - but it doesn't mean they won't learn, train and develop the rest.

From your point of view, what's the real problem with competition karate?

I believe the problem in modern competition has more to do with the judges than with the competition itself. The great hindrances to competitions are unqualified judges. Oftentimes, these are people who only possess their positions by passing paper examinations, even though their own karate-do knowledge and backgrounds are inadequate to qualify them to even test for the position. In many cases, I find that some person become a judge for certain political reasons or their own selfish motive to gain titles. Of course, if one is not even qualified to take a test, then he is clearly not qualified to judge.

What's you opinion of combat methods such as kickboxing and full contact karate?

I have seen kickboxing and similar disciplines but I consider them to be an sport, not a martial art which involves the aspects of budo.

Has your personal training changed over the years?

Of course! My birthday is May 30, 1927 and I'm not 20 years old anymore. My daily training consists of kihon movements for one hour. I practice bunkai for another 30or 40 minutes more, and kumite-bunkai for half-an-hour. Usually I train by myself for another 30 minutes. There are changes and alterations to training methods according to the ages of practitioners and the instructor's applications. It's important to understand your own body so you can adapt your private training to that. Every karate-do practitioner should practice diligently within the dojo and should neither copy other people nor other styles. It is important that one must personally practice techniques through their own physical exercise and gain experience through their own diligent efforts.

Do you consider makiwara training essential for a karate-do practitioner?

The training with the makiwara post is to make the fist stronger by clinching the fist harder. This makes the technique more effective and the practitioner will learn the proper body dynamics of expansion and contraction of the body as it relates to correct techniques and stances. Its use is not just to toughen the knuckles, but it teaches and prepares the whole body to absorb the shock of landing punches. In the past, just about everybody had a makiwara to train with, but the times have changed. Nowadays, even the karate world champions don't use it. I think that part of the reason for this is that they concentrate too much on the sport contest aspect of karate where hard contact is not required – makiwara training seems to have no place. I don't agree with this point of view and I still believe that the makiwara should be used because it is another important tool that forges a strong spirit.

Do you think that too much emphasis on kumite might prevent the student from reaching a full understanding of your father's teachings?

I think kumite practice is effective, but my father's teachings are steeped in tradition and it is up to us to retain those important aspects. If karate is to retain the elements of traditional martial arts, we cannot let it to be reduced to a pure sport. Shito ryu, from my experience in other martial arts and karate styles, is a very systematic training program developed by my father and style founder Kenwa Mabuni. The emphasis is on polishing the basics and this attitude is deeply related in the Japanese culture and the idea of paying attention and going very deep into every detail. It reflects the true Japanese view towards martial arts and life. This is the reason why kata practice has to be done with an emphasis on perfection and not just by going through the motions.

Have your goals changed over years?

My goals have definitely changed. My body is not the same as it used to be. It happens to every martial artist in the world. The way you think changes, as does your training. When you get older the art is not about winning tournaments or similar things, it is about health and integration with yourself.

Bringing your body and mind together becomes the main issue. What's the meaning of training? Why do I am doing this? What is my objective? As your body changes and your priorities change, the reason for your daily training changes. The objective changes as you do. We become more aware of what our body means to us and how to keep it in health and perfect condition. I think that karate is different for everybody and if your goal or objective is different, then your karate is different. The development of your mind and heart turns out to be the main goal. This is not only important as a martial artist but as a human being as well, and karate is a good vehicle and a powerful way to help you to understand yourself better. Karate is a very special experience.

Karate is perceived as a 'hard" method. What's your opinion about using the concept of relaxation?

Relaxation is very important in the art. Until you really understand how it works, and how beneficial it is for your body and technique, your training will be limited. The soft aspect is the other half of the equation. Power comes from a state of relaxation that allows you to bring the maximum kime in your technique. It allows you to use a little bit more stretch for explosive power in the physical movement. Of course, your body structure has a lot to do with that, but a deep understanding of how the soft aspect of the physical techniques work will bring your karate to a higher level. I think many karate practitioners lack of this soft aspect. Please don't misunderstand me, hardness and strong muscles are not a problem but we need to develop a higher control of our bodies and in order to achieve this, the understanding of the concept of "softness" is paramount. By being relaxed you can have overall awareness and a deeper sense of body control. The idea of "shizentai" (natural body) becomes more important as we get older. Our karate should be natural. This kind of control of tension and relaxation is very important for kata training since it is the integration of the body and the imagination. Kata is good for your mind - it is moving Zen.

What does kata mean to you?

For me, kata is an expression of daily human conduct and many of the principles are understood from studying many kata. For a authentic karate-do practitioner, kata must be the first priority. My personal feeling is that the karate professional must spend three years on a kata and three months in kumite as a proper ratio. Kata is not just a bunch of basic techniques organized in sequences. Kata, as I said before, is for the integration of the practitioner's mind and imagination. I don't have a preference for any specific kata in particular. My father studied and developed certain kata because he felt it was important for the shito ryu practitioner to learn the complete syllabus of the styles practiced in Okinawa. It is a well-known fact the other karate masters came to my father to learn kata. For instance, Master Funakoshi and my father were great friends, they practiced together and exchanged ideas. In 1945, Master Funakoshi took his students Masatoshi Nakayama and Isao Obata to Osaka to study under my father, and later he introduced the shotokan version of unshu (unsu), niseshi (nijushiho) and gojushiho. The shito ryu style contains beautiful kata, and yet I have found few instructors who teach the deeper meaning of the movements and the right appreciation of the more advanced aspects of training. It is important to understand that it is sometimes necessary to return to the most basic kata to correct one specific body motion used in an advanced kata, or to perfect a point in a particular technique. Unfortunately, in some styles, the study of the body mechanics has replaced the traditional approach of actually learning how to apply the technique and this is not good. We must strike a balance. As old saying goes, "The person is the kata, and the kata is the person."

Kenzo Mabuni

Is competition or sport karate bad for karate?

Competition is not bad, it's a modern aspect of the art. When you are young you want to test your skills, and competition is good for that. When you enter competition you face fear, insecurities, and other emotional aspects. What is really important is how you deal with these circumstances - how you control these psychological elements. Anger and fear are the two emotions that can make you get into a fight. In competition you deal with one of them. So I think that as long as you know the right place for the competition aspect in your karate training and you know how to use it in order to become a more mature person and karateka, competition is good. The problem appears when you only train for competition or you perceive the art of karate only as a sport. To me this is a mistake and a diversion from the true origins and goals of traditional karate. The old argument of kumite verses kata is only a problem in sport karate. In budo and traditional karate, kumite and kata go hand-in-hand. There is no argument, no contradictions whatsoever. Sport karate and competition training not only takes its toll on the kumite aspects but on kata as well.

It's very common these days to see competitors who are more concerned about the look of the kata rather than the meaning of what they are doing. Kata competition, because of the sportive aspect, has become more of a gymnastic test due to the practitioner's attachment to the aesthetic values. The demands of kata competition have caused kata to evolve in ways opposed to the traditional criteria. In these contests, kata is purely performed for the visual effect of the movements, regardless of their meaning for application in a real situation and things such as heavy breathing and unnecessary pauses have been introduced to impress the judges. Sometimes karate is not logical and

the same is true with kata. If you take kata literally, and try to explain it, you're going to have some difficulty making it work. You have to look at kata with a deeper approach than just as simple external movements. Karate is greater than the parts and in order to fully appreciate kata we have to learn to look at it from the correct angle. We have to study bunkai because in the end kata is kumite, and it is only through a deep study of bunkai that the practitioner can learn and develop a knowledge of the close-quarter or grappling methods hidden in karate. The grappling, throwing, and arm locking techniques in karate are part of the self-defense aspect and not useful for sport competition. If you don't research bunkai you lose the most important side of the art. The right bunkai is dangerous and not beautiful to watch. Sport karate evolves as the development of the competitive aspects of karate-do evolves. However, the budo essence of karate-do is the same as that represented by the godoshin - sho-shin, doryoku-shin, reisetsu-shin, jyo-shin, and wa-shin.

Why is it so difficult to reach a middle point between sport and budo?

Personally, I believe that we can find a middle point where sport competition helps karate and karate keeps the traditional values. For instance, let's take shobu ippon kumite - there is only one point and only one final action. The old samurai fought with swords and it was a matter of life or death. The loser died. In real fighting you could only make one mistake and if you did, you're dead. This is the same spirit we need in competition today. It requires not only physical and technical training but mental training as well. If the practitioner keeps in mind that he is "looking death straight in the face," that he is "at the edge of death," then his attitude will fit into the budo precepts. The spirit that is facing death needs to posses a certain philosophy. He has to keep his mental and physical balance and not lose composure. In dealing with a life or death situation the technique is a very relative thing, not something absolute. This is what budo is all about. But if the karateka thinks about the shobu ippon only as a game, then we lose all the important aspects of traditional training that goes far beyond the physical technique. To really understand budo you have to look at it from a variety of angles because it has many facets. Technique is not that important but its history and philosophy are, and these transcend the physical technique. But don't fool yourself, transcending the techniques implies that there is technique in first place. It is possible to win a competition even though you don't have good basic karate technique, and this is not good. You may have good timing and sharp speed to score but lack good karate basics.

Have you modified or changed any technique to suit modern times?

Execution will always improve. It doesn't mean we have to change the technique. These days, the instructors have a better understanding of physics and modern technologies so they use them to better perform and to explain the karate techniques. The technique doesn't change per se, but the way we move and understand the movement itself is at a higher level. We use modern technology to improve the art of karate - a more academic approach. A lot of the information we have at our fingertips today was inconceivable a few years ago. But as George Bernard Shaw wrote, "All progress depends on the unreasonable man."

Your mother played a very important role in your father's life, didn't she?

Yes, definitely. She understood my father's goal and his dedication to karate-do. My father shared his views and thoughts about the development of the art with her. She was there all the time next to my

father, supporting him and the family so my father could develop the art and pursue his training. She devoted her life to my father. She also had a very strong character and she used to help him with his training. For instance, my father used to hit the makiwara every day, rain or shine, early in the morning, pretty much the first thing after waking up. If it was rainy, my mother used to take an umbrella and hold it above the makiwara post so my father could punch it without getting soaked. A woman like that is very difficult to find and my father was fortunate. I truly think she deserves a lot of credit.

Why do you think that most of your father's top students split off and developed their own styles after his death?

This question should be asked to all those who claim to be a shito ryu stylist. Some people don't even have a real connection to the shito ryu family. This upset me very much. All I have to say is that the Shito Ryu Nippon Karate Do Kai was founded at #2-5-32, Ikue, Asahi-Ku, Osaka, Japan. This site exists to this day as my residence. After my father's death my mother suggested that I preserve the continuity of my father's dojo through his traditions, technical lists, personal notes, and shito ryu katas without any alterations. My mother appointed me the successor and the true heir of shito ryu. Then my older brother Kenei Mabuni, who ceased training about twelve years prior to our father's death, founded shito kai with many Osaka region and Toyo University college graduates. In 1955, Ryusho Sakagami of itosu kai, Masaru Watanabe of seiki kai, Kenjiro Tomoyori of kenyu ryu and Chojiro Tani of shuko kai separately claimed their independence by their own styles. As for as myself, I keep my father's traditions and teachings the way he taught them. It's my job to preserve his art and knowledge as purely as possible.

MINOBU MIKI

A MODERN TRADITIONALIST

ONE OF THE WORLD'S HIGHEST RANKING SHITO-RYU STYLISTS, SAN DIEGO-BASED MINOBU MIKI IS FROM A JAPANESE FAMILY STEEPED IN THE TRADITIONAL ASPECTS OF THE MARTIAL ARTS. KNOWN FOR HIS VERY TECHNICAL AND PRECISE KATA, MIKI HAS A DIRECT TRAINING LINEAGE TO SHITO-RYU FOUNDER KENWA MABUNI THROUGH KENWA'S SON KENZO. RECOGNIZING THE NEED TO MODERNIZE KARATE'S TRADITIONALLY HARSH TRAINING METHODS, MIKI HAS NEVERTHELESS REMAINED TRUE TO THE ART'S HIGH SPIRITUAL AND MORAL PRINCIPLES. WITH ONE FOOT PLANTED IN THE PAST AND THE OTHER ROOTED IN THE PRESENT, MINOBU MIKI IS A LIVING EXAMPLE OF HOW KARATE'S HONORABLE TRADITIONS CAN SURVIVE THE MODERN WORLD'S QUESTIONABLE VALUES.

How did you get started in martial arts?

The era was only a decade after WWII ended, when I was a child. I saw many injured war veterans who had lost legs and arms. I also witnessed many of shelters and saw many playgrounds that had holes from the bombings. So as a child, I developed a subtle insecurity and feeling of danger being around me. I was raised in a martial arts environment. My father was a judo black belt and my family was associated with iaido master Masayoshi Shinoda. Mr. Shinoda later received the Medal of Honor from the Japanese emperor, Hirohito. My aunt had a degree as a dance master and my whole family was involved with Japanese cultural arts. Both of my sisters trained extensively in Japanese dance. Additionally, the iaido master, Mr. Shinoda, and my family had a very close relationship which supported both arts.

I began my martial arts training in Japanese swordsmanship, or kendo, at the age of 8 while in elementary school. I also trained at a dojo located in a nearby police station. Then in junior high school I began training in judo both at school and a neighbor's judo dojo. I started karate-do at the age of 16. My friend and I commuted to a dojo a few towns away by train. There were only a few karate dojos then and there were no children involved like today. As a matter of fact, many high schools forbid their students from taking karate-do. They thought the training was too damaging to proper growth and too violent for students. My first teacher was Mr. Koshi Yamada. I hardly saw my master since we had many high-ranking instructors who came to teach us.

The entire dojo was made of wood, including floor and surrounding walls. But the school was not well-kept and many of the windows were without glass. When it rained, the students close to the windows would get wet. In the summertime, the instructor often had to halt our class to kill mosquitoes himself since if we moved even a little, he would shout at us or hit us with a shinai stick. In the wintertime, there was no heating. On snowy days, the instructor told us to run outside in only bare feet. In the

wintertime, the dojo floor had frost around the perimeter. So, everyone would try to arrive first in order to stay in the center part of dojo that had no frost. When I joined the dojo in late spring, my sensei told me, "If you can bear us for three days then you can make it." Of course this was after I paid the initiation fees and monthly dues. There was no dressing room, we simply had to change clothes in the corner of the dojo.

After a few years, the dojo moved to a location that I could no longer commute to. So I was forced to change schools to seido-ryu. The master there was Seido Mizuno whose style was one of the generic shito-ryu styles. This dojo had more people in the classes and was not as intense as the Koshi Kan Dojo where you were taught how to knock down the opponent. But at this dojo too, the workouts were very hard. At the first class, the beginners were taken outside where the makiwara posts were standing. We had to hit them until the skin on our knuckles came off. Then the instructor said, "Okay, it looks good. You must hit the makiwara post everyday to toughen up your fists. Do you understand?" While we were standing in front of the makiwara, a few other students were pulling carts full of roof tiles. The instructor picked one of the tiles up and suddenly broke it on his forehead. It shattered with a loud sound. We were all stunned by this demonstration. The instructor said, "These roof tile are good," as if he were tasting some fine food. After such an act, we did not want to argue with him.

In our modern society where empty-hand fighting is not an issue anymore, is the art of karate-do still beneficial?

Karate offers a way of self-defense, firstly by technique and then by mental attitude. Through the practice of the art, an awareness of the self develops along with an understanding of how to avoid conflict. We end up looking more for "human harmony." Karate-do is an education, a lifetime study, and if we study the origin of the art we'll learn correct values and many good lessons. That's why I believe that deeply studying the original methods will bring us a greater insight into the way of the empty hand. This is one of the reasons why I think 14 is a good age to start training karate. The mind is a very important tool in the development of yourself as karateka. Under this age, the mind is not sufficiently developed and the training is just play. Personally, karate has allowed me to develop mentally and physically in a manner I never would have been able to without it. The amount of control that regular karate training gives you is easily explained, but the overall feeling of being "in control" that one gets, is not so easily defined. In fact, I think it's impossible to explain to someone who doesn't train.

The ultimate goal of karate-do training is to make a better person, one who contributes to society as a whole. This is accomplished through disciplined physical and mental training. It creates a disciplined person who will develop self-esteem and confidence from this training. You should not look only at the physical aspect of karate-do and the development of effective techniques that can be harmful to others, you must develop the correct judgement that will allow you to abide by the law, humanity and common sense. How and when to use devastating techniques on others is important. It is like gun control, if a firearm is used to break the law, it is a crime. But, if it used in the correct way, it is a very powerful and effective tool to keep one's safety and peace. It is best if you never have to use it in your life. Karate-do practitioners should know the consequences of using their force.

How do you think sport affects the budo of karate do?

A simple sportive conception of the art is the responsible factor in losing many effective techniques found in the kata bunkai. They can't be used within the competition framework so practically nobody practices them anymore. Sporting kumite is good but this point should be kept in mind. Freestyle fighting is good for the sport but there is the danger of digressing from other important aspects of the martial arts. In Japan, our budo of the past was something extremely bloody and viscious as to what methods one could resort to. In looking forward to a peaceful future, the conversion to a competitive sport is the best way to spread the outstanding points and benefits of budo to the world - if it is done properly, that is. On other hand, the sportive science has evolved greatly and this allows practitioners to be more prepared and in better condition to absorb and perform the physical techniques.

Karate-do is a part of budo, and karate competition is a part of karate-do as a whole. It is true that karate-do has developed and spread rapidly due to competitions and sporting events. This has led to many practitioners believing that winning techniques and certain kata performances are the ultimate karate techniques. Sport karate is limited in the type of techniques allowed, for the safety of the competitors. On the other hand, budo is a way of killing an opponent. The sport aspects of karate encourages and develops athletes with goals that are different than the ultimate goal of budo.

What order of importance do you give to kihon, kata, and kumite?

Kata is the instrument or material used to teach students. This inheritance from the masters contains their ideology and methodology that is called the style or ryu-ha. Kumite is the physical application of movements from a particular style. Today, there are no obvious differences between the styles at sports competitions. It used to be that you could tell what style they practiced by their first kamae or stance. Also, techniques have become international and universal at world competitions. If one contestant is very successful at scoring or winning, immediately those movements and tactics are copied. Even in kata competition, if a certain kata wins in world competition, immediately that kata becomes popular and many other competitors begin performing it. This is another bad aspect of sports karate - only winners are praised in competition scenes. There are many inferior international judges who do not really know the kata's original methodology and content. Instead, they tend to look for and give higher scores to the kata that was performed using only strong physical movements. If sports competition continues to diverge from the budo aspects, then the realistic and original ideologies of karate-do techniques will be lost. Kihon is the basis for correct execution and the method to develop the physical and ideological characteristic of each style. The kihon of the style must used in both kumite and kata.

SHITO RYU MASTERS

If the students want to develop a good understanding of kata, they need the kihon and the kumite aspects to be properly balanced. One without the others is no good. The basic requirement for a good karate is kata. Kata cannot be just remembered in the mind only. Many physical repetitions are necessary to add it to the memory as well as perfecting each movement within the form.

What are the real differences between shito-kai, itosu-kai, tani-ha, shito-ryu, hayashi-ha, and shito-ryu?

After the founder of shito ryu, Kenwa Mabuni, passed away, shito-kai was created by mostly Toyo University graduates with Mr. Kenei Mabuni and late Mr. Manzo Iwata as their leaders. However, there was problem within the organization. Osaka area instructors had learned directly from Kenwa Mabuni whereas the Tokyo area instructors learned mainly at Toyo University. These two groups are technically different even in their kata. Only recently after many meetings have they been able to come to an agreement and produce some videotapes. Their curriculum was changed recently by a majority vote of their senior members. If karate-do is budo, it is not correct to decide the curriculum by the will of the majority. They created many new terminologis, movements and altered kata from the founder's shito-ryu versions. The eastern Japan (Tokyo) group had more voting rights than western Japan which was the home base of shito ryu. The name was changed to shito-kai in 1968. They collaborate with the national karate organization of Japan, the Japan Karate-Do Federation.

The late Ryusho Sakagami created itosu-kai after Kenwa Mabuni died in 1952. He claimed that was Kenwa Mabuni's last wish and that the itosu inheritance and traditions were to pass on to him. Obviously, Sakagami altered many of the kata to his version of shito-ryu, and therefore created his own itosu traditions. Since Sakagami was the senior student of Kenwa Mabuni, his methodology has influenced many generic shito-ryu practitioners - especially the eastern Japan karate-do practitioners including the eastern shito-kai group under the late Manzo Iwata. Even shotokan practitioners have been influenced by Sakagami's methodology, as evidenced by the fact that they have learned many shito-ryu kata and then altered them to their own style. Tani-ha shito-ryu was created by the late Chojiro Tani who also created the shuko-kai branch of shito-ryu. He was famous for his creative new methods and kata. When he performed some kata, he wore a mask and kimono while demonstrating. The style of shuko-kai is very unique and most shito-ryu stylists do not consider it a part of shito-ryu. Teruo Hayashi separated from seishin-kai to create his own version known as Hayashi-ha shito-ryu in 1970. Kosei Kuniba, who founded keishin-kai, was the landlord of that dojo. The dojo was originally one of Kenwa Mabuni's branch dojos in the southern part of Osaka City where the late Kenyu Tomoyori, who founded Kenyu-ryu, mainly taught. When Kuniba started an independent dojo listed as a shito-ryu dojo, senior shito-ryu instructors refused to recognize it. He then went to Okinawa and received a certificate of authenticity from the late Shoshin Nagamine of shorin-ryu, who called Kuniba's school motobu-ha shito-ryu. They also affiliated the Nippon Karate-Do Rengokai (organization) with Sakagami, and learned many kata from itosu kai traditions. Hayashi-ha shito ryu is from seishin-kai. However, according to the heir of shito-ryu, Kenzo Mabuni, it was not directly affiliated with shito-ryu or Kenwa Mabuni. Most of the high ranking shito-ryu practitioners say that Kenwa Mabuni wished to have Soke Kenzo Mabuni inherit his style. In fact, Kenzo Mabuni inherited his father's organization, Shito-Ryu Nippon Karate-Do Kai. More importantly, he inherited his father's entire curriculum, including personal notes and especially kata that were not published. Mr. Mabuni continued his father's guidelines and methodology. The most important aspect is that he never altered his father's kata or curricula.

Do you have any favorite kata in the shito-ryu system?

I do not have a favorite kata, but I have learned a few kata directly from the heir of shito-ryu, Soke Kenzo Mabuni, which were left unpublished by his father and founder, Kenwa Mabuni. These unpublicized kata including kenosha, quench, and others. By learning authentic shito ryu kata, I have learned much history and many of the reasons why kata has evolved to today's competition. I also have a lot of interest in other style's kata that stem from original shito-ryu kata. Kenwa Mabuni really influenced all of major styles' kata. Many unpublished kata that Kenwa Mabuni left behind are very interesting. I am proud to be one of the only people in the world who knows these kata.

Do you prefer kata or kumite?

Kata is the instructional material or textbook of each style and thus is essential to that style. Kumite on the other hand is the application of the techniques – kumite for fun, kata for learning. I do not have a preference. Kata is the instructional material and inheritance within the style or school. The unique strategy and tactics for that school or style are taught through kata. It is most important to understand kata through furyu monji. In the Zen sect, these words can be translated as, "One must learn through one's own physical experiences that which one cannot express by written form." Even many traditional instructors do not know the correct bunkai or oyo, much less the meaning and purpose of kakushi-waza or the hidden techniques.

What do you think about the unification of kata in the World Karate Federation?

This has been on the agenda many times at the WKF Technical Committee meetings. But the committee has never come to an agreement to have kata from all styles conform to only one certain form. There must be many different stages in the development of kata which reflect the major styles of the four founders: Kenwa Mabuni, Chojun Miyagi, Gichin Funakoshi and Hironori Otsuka. There are many controversial differences even within the same style. Each senior instructor will tell the student, "This is the way I learned." But there is no consistency. With strong influences from the International Olympic Committee, there is pressure to allow kata events to permit new free-form or open kata.

The agenda of making new free-forms was proposed by many European countries to our WKF Technical Committee meetings when I was a WKF World Technical Committee member. Their idea was that only a few kata have been winning in the last two decades and if the Olympic event is to see the

highest possible individual performance, then it must create a form to give a more objective scale to measure the performances, rather than depend on the judges' subjective and personal experiences. The kata judges often do not have enough knowledge of all the kata of all the styles. Most of them are only knowledgeable in one style; some of them do not even know all of their own styles kata well, and what they do know is often from only one instruction that they have received. Kata competition has many aspects of individual timing and personal movements. If the timing of kata changes, then the meaning of the movements changes; but the judges usually give higher scores to the demonstrator's looks rather than technical performance aspects and ignores certain styles' traditions and methodology. The judges tend to give higher scores to the performers who demonstrates power and focus even though the original kata requires no excess power or focus. The competition kata judges will give the scores to the competitors by the genetic ideas of competitions and the rules, not necessary to the tradition or methodology of the style.

What do you think about the kata competition compared to the traditional way of doing the forms?

Well, first we have to understand that there are limitations on what the judges can or cannot judge. These days, in sport kata competition, there are other factors more important that the meaning of the technique. A real kata doesn't have to be appealing or attractive, but a competition kata has to be. In sport, there is too much emphasis on beauty at the expense of power. And power is important to perform a kata well. There is a trend to over-emphasize the form, as there is no need for power. The general style is softer, the breathing rhythm sometimes has nothing to do with the meaning of the technique. The timing of the movement has been altered to allow the judges and the audience to better perceive the physical action. A kata must be neither too quick, nor too slow. Some parts must be fast and some slow, according to the demands of the movements and application. The judges must look for a fighter as well as an artist. The modern derivations of the old kata are more concerned with the external appearance rather than with the meaning behind it. The interpretation of the kata is a personal matter, but kata is good for the mind; it is moving Zen and can be learned and understood on many levels.

On other hand, I'm a strong believer that you should incorporate techniques from kata at a very early stage. I also understand some of the criticism of classical applications in kata since I have seen some impossible bunkai which any man in the street would undoubtedly question. But if you truly understand the art of karate, then kata is kumite. I believe that the person who looks seriously at the kata of karate, can be said to be studying the art.

How important is the students' ability to think during the bunkai phase?

It is very important. The mental aspect or attitude is paramount in this aspect of karate-do. However, the physical side is more important in the beginning. You must push the physical side first using your mental power, then both start to interrelate. The student must understand the way his body works, because this is crucial in order to execute the physical techniques properly. The practice of bunkai should be carried out slowly for a better understanding - at least at first. Once the bunkai is understood, then it must be practiced at full speed. Otherwise, there is no reason for doing bunkai - it's pointless. Kata without the element of realism is a waste of time. Unfortunately, these days we are not aware enough of these important elements in training, and even the simplest physical task becomes a chore. We depend too much on devices that do work for us!

It is correct to say that you're a mold and that many karateka are trying to copy you. Do you think students should try to copy their teacher?

It is normal for a student to try to emulate his sensei. There's nothing wrong with that. The problem lies when the students don't have the understanding of the basic principles within that particular technique and tries to copy directly from his sensei. Likewise it is wrong for a teacher to insist his students copy him. His work is to improve the student's technique as best suits their physique. Also, the student has to understand that "quality" is more important than "quantity." We must stick to the traditional way but if we stay "too traditional," then this might stop the development of karate. I always emphasize the traditional side of karate and when one is an instructor, one should always do your best. When I see students do some movement the wrong way, I sometimes think that the way I explained the technique wasn't all that good. The teacher has to learn how to communicate with students of different levels in order to assure they understand properly what is being transmitted. It is wise to have various approaches to teach the same movement or technique.

You are very close to your students, how have they affected your own progress?

Sometimes I have the opportunity to train with my peers. When I practice with them I must be better than them because they are equal and above me. Therefore when I train with my students, I must also practice my best and give them the proper role model, which involves the best technique, attitude and mental alertness. I think of my student as my teacher. Another interesting factor is that when you train with your peers, the techniques are direct and correct. There are many factors that make everything difficult, such as his mental alertness, the respect not to attack or counter without reason, et cetera. A lower grade student will present a series of untimed and uncoordinated random movements which are very hard to deal with. So as a teacher, I must learn to deal with the unexpected. If you try to do the same things, they won't work because the teacher has progressed above this level. Then he has to adapt.

How important is physical conditioning to you?

During the early days, the training methods were very primitive. We all carry wounded bodies because of that! Personally, I don't want my students to suffer the same injuries I had in my youth. This is my responsibility to them. The karate practitioner must treat his body with utmost respect. It is very important for the modern teacher to study anatomy and physiology in order to understand how the body works. Then he can eventually develop teaching and training methods that help the student to improve their technical skills without getting injured. Some of the old conditioning methods are not so good for you in the short or long term. These days, karate-do is not just for self-defense but also to live a longer, healthier, and happier life. I believe that training must be as natural as possible. Of course, you can use weights. I don't really think there is a need to increase muscle size but it's better to improve your speed with maximum kime. Lots of techniques can be practiced this way and I find this is an excellent way to get better in the art.

What do you think of makiwara training?

I use it. It's a very useful tool to develop focus. It also helps to forge a strong spirit, but pain is part of the process. If you don't know how to do it, it's easy to damage your hands irreparably. I think traditional training is the best. It builds stamina and technique. But it is very important to know the right way of doing it. Most people think that makiwara training only had meaning in the past because the hands and feet had to be deadly weapons, and with sport competitions taking over there is no need for that. Well, this is just one part of the whole equation. The makiwara is not only good for your conditioning but it also teaches you a lot about the proper kime and the right positioning when delivering the technique. Unfortunately, people think that the bigger your calluses are, the better you are at the art. Calluses are just a by-product of the training. As I said, it develops your wrists, elbows, hips, knees, et cetera. My advice is to find a true master that can teach you how to properly use this piece of equipment. The concept of kime has recently changed to a much lighter physical definition. It looks like fewer practitioners are using makiwara training than in previous generations. The idea of ichigeki hissatsu from Japanese budo, that was inherited from Japanese sword methodology, seems lost in modern competition techniques. The concept of maai should not be translated only as "distance" but should also include many other essences involved with controlled distance or effectiveness. On the bad side, competition creates conceited individuals who are contradictory to the idea of budo.

Do you think people's perception of what karate-do is all about has changed in the last decade?

Definitely. The level of awareness in the practitioners is higher than ten years ago. A great responsibility lies on the instructor's shoulders. The teacher must educate the students about the real art, the real karate-do, not simply about the sport. High technical standards must be kept in order to assure future generations the quality of the art. This is the only way to grow in a positive direction. We must sacrifice and train toward the goal of achieving high levels of technical and spiritual mastery and settle for no less. Keep high standards because this is the best way to preserve good karate. The body is like iron - the harder you beat it, the harder it becomes. By the same token, we have introduced important changes in the way the art is being taught these days; there are some exercises that are not used anymore. As you know, a lot of long-term karateka have hip, knee, or foot problems since the training was brought in line with a need to be "tough." I agree that it was a bit barbaric and now we are finding that there was no need, that we created more problems than we solved. Today, we have a better knowledge of physiology and biomechanics and there is a better understanding of the legal and insurance aspects. Teachers are more inclined to look after their student's welfare and this is very good for everyone.

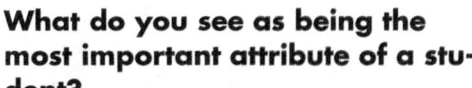

What do you see as being the most important attribute of a student?

Attitude. A good student is one who is willing to listen and learn. Attitude is the most important aspect. If the student is brought up the correct way they will understand that winning tournaments is not the most important thing, but that loyalty and having an open mind are far more desirable attributes. For me, always persevering and trying to do your best throughout your life are the most important things that karate training has taught me.

What about the non-technical aspects of the instructor. What kind of characteristics should they have?

They may soon need to have a four-year college degree just as public school teachers must have now. This is in addition to their skill in karate-do. Today, we see so many fake

degrees being touted just because that person likes to use the title of a Ph.D. This, even though they bought it through a mail-order correspondence course. Further, stricter health codes should be enforced. Since this is a physical sport, instructors and students come into regular contact with each another. Health safety should be one of the primary goals of instructors.

What are the most important points in your teaching?

I am like a translator in that I digest the knowledge of the East and hand it down to the West. I try to be the karate-do instructor that will teach students the correct, authentic traditional shito-ryu ideology and philosophy. I wish to have students who will inherit this virtue through my instructions.

AKIO MINAKAMI

A WARRIOR'S JOURNEY

Born and raised in Tokyo, Japan, Shihan Minakami began his formal martial arts training at 7. He belonged to the Jujitsu/Kodokan Judo School under Takagi Sensei. Takagi Sensei was a 9th-degree Kodokan black belt. Minakami moved to the United States in 1963. During his first years in America, Shihan Minakami made a name for himself as an outstanding karate man. By age 21, he was the first man ever to win both kata and kumite at the All-Hawaii Championships.

His most outstanding accomplishments include winning five gold medals at the Hayashi-Ha Shito-ryu Kai International Championships and five gold medals at the All-Japan Karate Championships. He was also the first man ever to win five gold medals at the AAU National Championships.

In 1983, Minakami received his Shihan certificate from both Hayashi-Ha Shito-ryu Kai and from the Federation of All-Japan Karate-do Organization (FAJKO). Shihan Minakami was the first to receive a unanimous passing grade, meaning all 11 masters (representing the four major styles) on the examining board gave him their approval. This is an amazing honor for which he will always be known. In 1985, Shihan Minakami founded the Minakami Karate Dojo. It was his goal to teach traditional Japanese karate and pass his knowledge onto dedicated students who would learn and enjoy the techniques, as well as attitudes, of the true martial artist. He is quick to make every opportunity a blessing for karate and is dedicated to improving the art and creating more interest in it. "Nowadays, karate is available to everyone who really wants to learn. I can't take it with me, and I want to leave something of value behind," he says with a smile on his face.

How long have you been practicing the martial arts?

My father is a martial artist and naturally I played and wrestled with him as a boy. Our house was only 50 feet away from the Judo Dojo in Koenji, Tokyo, and I grew up listening to good kiai every evening. On August 12, 1956, following an interview by Kiyokazu Takagi Sensei, I enrolled at this dojo. Takagi Sensei was a Kodokan 9th Dan. Before the war, he was Shihan at the Military Academy. After the war, he was Shihan at the Tokyo Metropolitan Police Department. He explained to me that the martial arts are not for fighting but to discipline one's self to become a good citizen. He said that our spirit must

SHITO RYU MASTERS

be strong enough not to be drawn into petty quarrels, even if it means running away. He used to say, "Kunshi ayaukini chikayorazu," which means that a wise man never courts danger and "Kichigai nihamono," which means that a crazy person with a weapon is dangerous. I was 7 years old and just wanted to learn how to fight. It's funny, but the older I get, the more I understand what he meant. Now I teach the same way.

In how many styles of karate or other methods have you trained?

I practiced karate at the JKA when the headquarters were in Suidobashi, Tokyo. I also practiced kyokushinkai and met Oyama Sensei. I had seen his book, What is Karate?, and I thought he was going to be big. I was surprised to find that he was short. He was a powerful man, friendly and humble. I learned tekenjutsukai from Mr. Bingo in Hawaii. I also practiced with my friend's uncle, Professor Chow, the founder of American kenpo. I remember him pounding a huge flagpole and making it ring loudly with each hit.

In 1965, I met shito-ryu instructor Chuzo Kotaka Sensei. I had never seen a front kick like his. I thought that no one could withstand his kick without being hurt. I wanted to learn this kick from him so I joined his dojo. In 1974, Kotaka Sensei introduced me to his teacher, Teruo Hayashi Soke. I have been with the Hayashi-Ha Shito-ryu Kai ever since.

When I was 28 and a fifth-degree black belt in karate, I wanted to broaden my martial arts practice — not only to become a stronger fighter — but also to become more skilled in natural movement and discover greater wisdom and spirituality. Luckily, I found Nobuto Omoto Sensei, 7th dan in kendo. He was a graduate of the Budosenmongakko in Kyoto, which was shut down right after General McArthur occupied Japan. People say that this was the last samurai school. Omoto Sensei explained that the kuden or verbal teaching between the student and the teacher at the Budosenmongakko was usually done in a relaxed, private situation. Omoto Sensei said that he learned a lot of the inner teachings of the martial arts when he was serving tea to his instructors in their office.

When I put away his bogu after each class, Omoto Sensei would talk to me about how to be a samurai. He did not talk just about fighting. He also talked about bushi no tashinami or the etiquette and knowledge of a martial artist, including taking care of equipment, sewing, cooking, singing and even partying.

Also, I am a good friend with Toshihiro Oshiro Shihan, and I have been lucky enough to meet his teacher, yamanni-ryu Master Chogi Kishaba Sensei. I have had the opportunity to talk to him many times about the martial arts.

I have a black belt in Kodokan judo from Kiyokazu Takagi Sensei, a 3rd Dan in kendo from Nobuto Omoto Sensei, a 5th Dan in yamanni-ryu bojutsu from Chogi Kishaba Sensei, an 8th Dan in hayashi-ha-shito-ryu kai from Teruo Hayashi Soke and a 7th Dan from the Japan Karate Federation.

With all the technical changes during the last 30 years, do you think there is still "pure" shotokan, shito-ryu, goju-ryu, etc? What is your opinion about mixing karate styles?

There were no styles before Funakoshi Sensei, Mabuni Sensei, Otsuka Sensei and Miyagi Sensei. The original ryu-kyu bujutsu — which includes what we now call sumo, bo, sai, nunchaku and empty-hand fighting — was originally called simply "te" or "ti" in Okinawan pronunciation.

We all study how to kill a person as quickly and efficiently as possible. If someone is doing this better, it seems foolish to say, "I won't do it; it's not in my style." We all have a body, two arms, two legs and so forth. And we have books, DVD, TV, seminars and are more informed than ever. So forget about style and be smart!

Karate should become better with time. If nothing changes, then you must wonder about the teacher's practice. Isn't it the same with electronics or cars? Don't they get better every year? Open your mind and look at things around you. If you see something that works, take it and make it yours. No style is better than the others, but the person practicing and the person teaching make a difference. Sadly, I have seen many people who think that their style is best … people with a limited outlook. We should always stay open-minded and be aware. Be a martial artist.

For instance, Sean Roberts Sensei leads my dojo in Hawaii. His background is in shotokan from Enoeda Sensei, but he incorporates my karate and teaching into his shotokan. Although I don't know the sequences of shotokan kata, I still can help Roberts Sensei with how to kick, punch and move more naturally. He endeavors to blend his karate experiences with my karate teaching.

How would you describe the life and dedication of your teacher, Soke Hayashi Teruo, to the arts of Budo?

There was a time when Hayashi Soke visited Okinawa so he could learn from a particular master. At first, he was not accepted as a student. He was monzen barai or kicked out at the gate. Thus, he slept under a bridge to hide from the weather. He tried again day after day. He didn't give up until finally he was accepted. Soke knows how to be at the bottom as well as at the top of his field. I don't think many teachers in mainland Japan have done things like this.

Back in the early 1970s, Soke put less emphasis on the aesthetics of the techniques. Nevertheless, his karate was extremely dangerous. Later, when he became chief referee at the Second World Championship in Los Angeles in 1974, he began to emphasize more "modern" or athletic karate that was safer and easier to learn. Tournament karate has since flourished around the world.

Soke disguised his natural movements to superficially look like "modern" karate. Just six months before he passed on, I was privileged to have private lessons with him. We worked out together strenuously for three hours a day, five days in a row. His karate was fast, strong and precise. It would have been impossible for him to move like this at his age without natural movement.

Soke always allowed us the freedom to try different ways to learn natural movement. As a result, our training methods changed and even our kata changed over time. When we went too far astray, Soke would make corrections. Many times we may not have understood his adjustments right away, but it was inappropriate to ask for further explanation without first trying. After a few years of effort, if we had to question, then we went through the chain of command. Tadashi Hashimoto Sensei headed the Hayashi-ha technical department, and he usually answered for Soke. He researched natural moves more than anybody else in the organization, and his karate is very dangerous.

Karate is nowadays often referred to as a sport. Would you agree with this definition or do you think it is only Budo?

Of course, karate can have a sporting element. Competition karate has many regulations and is safe. It is a sport enjoyed by many people, especially kids. As long as it is fun, then it is a good thing. However, if poor etiquette and rude conduct should emerge, then we should stop hosting tournaments.

I don't believe that most people appreciate Budo, which should be distinguished from bujutsu or fighting techniques. Budo is to empty one's self through the martial arts … to be fully present here and now with no extra thoughts in mind. Just deal with whatever you are doing now and that's all. This is challenging because we are thinking animals. It is like reading a book and not remembering what you've read. The mind is easily distracted.

Awareness and control of breathing are important if we are to be present in what we are doing. This is why the samurai practiced so much zazen or sitting meditation. It is an essential part of Budo. It is not for relaxation. It is to control the mind, and this is difficult!

How do you see the state of karate in the world at the present time?

Competition kumite has been similar in every style for a long time, as competitors adopt the movements of the champions. The same evolution is happening now even in kata tournaments. I went to the All-Osaka Championship. I was surprised to see the competitors all doing the same kata from the JKF. I couldn't tell the difference in styles like before.

My friend Oshiro Shihan is an excellent shorin-ryu and yamanni-ryu teacher. Each year he is invited to Europe to teach — and not only in shorin-ryu dojo. These days I think that many people appreciate that karate skill is beyond any particular style. Such open-mindedness is important and promotes development. For example, the late, great Enoeda Sensei gave me permission to teach at some of his European shotokan dojo. I really respected his open-mindedness.

Do you think that karate in the West is at the same level with Japanese karate?

There used to be a big difference because the Japanese were smaller in stature. But now, because of the change of diet, Japanese people are taller and larger than in the past. In terms of competition, everyone is the same. However, I think that the general skill level is much higher in Japan. In the U.S., maybe 30 people out of 100 look good. In Japan, 80 out 100 look good. It comes from the educational system and the culture. In Japan, the people tend to think more alike. Everybody is going in the same direction. In America, there are so many different cultures and so many different ways of thinking. Everybody is going in a different direction. If the American educational system were different, American karate could be different.

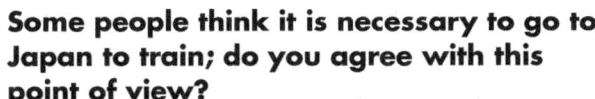

Some people think it is necessary to go to Japan to train; do you agree with this point of view?

No. Nearly all karate populations blindly follow their teacher and do not recognize good karate. This is equally true in Japan as it is in the rest of the world. So, while there are many good traditions that can best be experienced in Japan, it is not necessary to go to Japan to learn karate dogma. Take advantage of wisdom that is all around. Learn from other's kindness. Be hard on yourself and be kind to others, wherever you are. This brings discipline to your practice and harmony with fellow human beings. Eventually, with a good heart, you are able to make your own traditions and culture. With good culture and experience, you will develop wisdom and the ability to see good karate.

What are the most important points of your karate philosophy?

Be self-reliant. Karate training is for you and for no one else. Make yourself strong and be smart. Avoid violence whenever possible but fight without fear if you must. In an emergency, there is no one to rely on but you.

Kanto no seishin means to do your best with all your vitality. Have a fighting spirit and a good kiai.

Fukutsu no seishin means to never give up, even when the going gets tough. To quit is to die.

Hissho no seishin means to have a sure-win feeling no matter what. Even when faced with a superior opponent, you still have a chance. Keep in mind that he is not perfect and you will find a way to win. Without this confidence you will surely bring defeat upon yourself. Even if you were to lose, you did your best. Like the ancient warriors said, "That which burns to ashes has no regrets."

Be calm. Keep a cool head no matter what. We realize our potential with a calm mind.

Be strong. Keep a good spirit to withstand anything and persevere.

Be proud. Not better-than-you proud but afraid-of-nothing proud.

Be happy. Karate is a life-long endeavor that can bring us happiness. If it doesn't, then we should look for something else to make us content. Either way, keep smiling. If your practice is too serious, then it is no fun and you won't want to practice.

Make mistakes in training and in life. It is OK to make mistakes. It is necessary to make mistakes. Learn and try not to make the same mistake again.

Be sincere. Don't waste time doing things half-heartedly.

Be patient. If you want to prepare fast food, it may take you a couple of weeks to learn the ropes. However, if you want to be a good French chef, it will take many years and you never stop learning. Karate is the same. There is always more.

SHITO RYU MASTERS

Do you feel that you still have further to go in your studies of karate and Budo?

In college, you take classes, get a degree and then you're done. In Budo, or spiritual training through the martial arts, there is no graduation. There is no end to experience and wisdom. If you go deep into Budo, it is no different to the Chinese Dao and the Japanese Zen. It teaches us to do good and not evil — like religion.

Even physically, as we grow older and weaker, we still have the opportunity to discover and develop natural movement. There can be no such thing as a perfect kata. We can go deeper and deeper into one kata and continue to uncover hidden skill. This too is a never-ending process.

What is it that keeps you motivated after all these years?

I make every effort to empty myself through the ryu-kyu martial arts. It keeps me more aware of how vast nature is and how small I am. Hayashi Soke describes karate as being full of gokui (secrets) and students need to be wise enough to figure them out. Karate is a beautiful art. The deeper you go, the better it gets. There is so much to learn and each small moment of discovery is blissful and ecstatic. So I keep trying. I find it spiritually rewarding and definitely worth the effort.

Karate is a personal experience in nature that needs nothing and no one else. It is always freely available, here and now! I feel lucky to be alive and to be able to practice karate. I feel grateful to my parents for bringing me into this world.

One day we were at a park in front of a huge pine tree. My teacher, Hayashi Soke, told me not to become like this pine tree. It was straight and tall. He said it was tasteless. Become like the pine tree on a beach that is weather-beaten and has character. I relate to this because I have been living in the United States and so, for the most part, I am self-taught. I have made and continue to make many mistakes. But this is who I am. I developed my own character like Soke's pine tree.

It is not always easy. I remember having a bad financial problem and being depressed. Soke Hayashi came up to me and asked why I was so depressed. When I explained the reason, he started to laugh. He told me not to feel sorry for myself. There are people in this world who are without food and very ill. You are not sick and not starving. Just work hard and you will recover in no time. So practice with good spirit and kiai! Soke helped me to realize that depression is all in the mind. I thank Soke Hayashi for his inspiration.

How do you think a practitioner can increase his understanding of the spiritual aspect of karate?

We are born into this world with pure, uninhibited feelings. Whether a boy or a girl, we don't cry half-heartedly. We are completely free and confident. We don't care what people think of us. We just do our own thing. We cry with all of our might. Our first kiai is the loudest. As we grow up, we change slowly according to our experience. By observing our surroundings and through our intelligence, we learn how to act. Don't be an actor. Don't act cool. Don't act tough. Be true to your original self. Be true to your heart. Live like your baby-time kiai … with no hesitation and with all your might. Abandon small-minded images of who you want to be. Don't waste time pretending to be somebody that you're not. Just get on your life now! This is genuine confidence. This is your true self. Like a baby, you are free. Be patient. Re-discovering our original confidence is a life-long task.

Soke Hayashi was an expert in the weaponry art of kobudo. Do you think it helps empty-hand karate physically to train with weapons?

Our body is the same whether we are holding a weapon or not. The stances, steps, direction changes and upper body movements for kobudo are just the same as for empty-hand. It should be no surprise then that weapons give you clues to understanding natural movement and hidden fighting techniques. Both weapons and empty-hand should be practiced to fully appreciate ryu-kyu bujutsu. Even the founder of shotokan karate, Funakoshi Gichin Sensei, practiced weapons.

Also, if you practice weapons you don't need to lift weights or do most other types of supplemental training. Using weapons strengthens the body, legs, arms and grip, all of which are necessary in fighting.

What's your opinion of makiwara training?

Target training is important to make sure our joints are correctly aligned, stable and coordinated with our breathing at the moment of impact. This we can do with makiwara, punching bags or even portable targets. Each practitioner should use whatever works for him. I prefer to use punching bags that allow me to hit with all my might without risk of injury.

What advice would you give to students on the question of supplementary training?

Stretching must be done every day. I like running for fun. Weight training should be done only hodo hodo or moderately. Too much muscle will prevent you from being able to move smoothly and naturally. None of these are necessary if you practice weapons such as bojutsu or saijutsu.

To achieve good self-defense skills for a real situation, do you think it is necessary to engage in free fighting?

Free fighting and self-defense are completely different. Free fighting has rules. Self-defense has no such limits. In self-defense, just think, "What can I do?" at every moment. Do whatever it takes. For example, you could even throw a teapot to distract your opponent and then poke him in the eyes.

Do you think bunkai is important in the understanding of kata and karate in general?

Kata teaches us how to naturally move our bodies from point A to B. When done correctly, such natural movement is delightful. Nothing compares; it feels like bliss. This is the true wisdom left for us in kata by the ancient ryu-kyu warriors. It is up to us to discover, temper and polish this wisdom. Furthermore, natural movement will stimulate and unclog the meridians in our body and therefore bring us good health and great ki or universal energy. Movements that use just muscles and tension will strain the body and, sooner or later, cause injury, especially in older age. By comparison, bunkai is easy. Knowing the bunkai is not enough. If the movement is not expert, then the art will be at a low level.

SHITO RYU MASTERS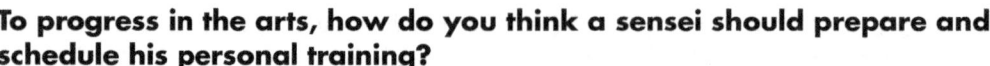

To progress in the arts, how do you think a sensei should prepare and schedule his personal training?

First, we should practice our conduct 24 hours each day. Physically, we must train in class with the students, not necessarily the whole class, but at least here and there we need to show the students what to do. When demonstrating, it is important to move well.

We should learn from books. We should study other martial arts. We should scrutinize old photographs of ryu-kyu teachers, but it is important to be selective because not all famous teachers are highly skilled. We must solve many puzzles. Why did they practice kata in preparation for combat? Is our kata suited for combat? Can we find similar movements in other Japanese martial arts? For example, kendo and kenjutsu can help us to understand how karate developed from te. Their kata are far more natural and suitable for combat than the karate kata that we see in tournament these days. Why? The master will keep researching, whereas a novice will be satisfied if he can take a step. There are endless secrets in how to take one step, so how can we master it in one lifetime? Never give up; research in one skill extensively. Keep scrutinizing and analyzing kihon and you will be an expert in the jutsu or art some day.

There is no limit to the secrets hidden in the kata. I am not talking about bunkai. I am talking about natural movement, such as how to take one step forward or make one turn. Often, this requires a very sophisticated level of kihon or basics. For this reason, kata is important. We should practice kata. Being a sensei will take a lifetime. Isn't it nice to have a lifetime's work?

What do you consider to be the most important qualities of a successful karateka?

For me, success as a karateka is measured not by how famous you are or how many students you have, but by the quality of your movement. How much did the person research natural movement? We must realize or become enlightened to a better way and find out the secrets. This is not easy. If a person is enlightened to the natural moves, the person is successful in karate.

What do you see as the most important attributes of a student?

A good student will do his or her homework. He does not practice only in the dojo. He takes responsibility for his own development and does not expect only to be taught. If he wants to learn, he has to make an effort. Nobody has to teach him anything.

Whom would you like to have trained with that you have not?

I would like to have studied Zen and sword under Tesshu Yamaoka. He was the Emperor's bodyguard after the Meiji restoration in Japan. He was a highly spirited person and the way he thought and trained would have given inspiration to my soul.

I would like to have studied Zen under Takuan Soho Osho, and he was also known as a Takuan priest. He had no training in swordsmanship, but he knew about the human mind. He was very wise, and he could lead you in the right direction. He taught Munenori Yagyu, the Shogun's martial arts teacher, how to free his mind.

I would like to have studied under Musashi Miyamoto. His famous book Gorin No Sho or the Book of Five Rings, is a good technical martial arts book and highly recommended.

These three people have already passed on, but I am still learning from them indirectly, through their words. I have read their books many times, especially when I'm down or confused in my life. Their books give me ki or energy and direction. I am here now, free and I can do anything I wish. All my suffering is delusion. It will pass and be forgotten in time.

What is your thought on the future of karate-do and what's your opinion about karate entering in the Olympic Games?

Olympics or not, karate can develop much further in the future. My hope for the 21st century is that karate becomes more widely understood for its philosophy and as a way of living. Karate should be recognized as representing the emptying or abandonment of extra thoughts and the awareness of what we are doing now. We develop this attitude in our training in te and carry it into all our learning and life. This way, moment to moment, we live life to the fullest. That which burns to ashes has no regrets!

Anything else you would to add for the readers?

While I was writing this article, my teacher, Soke Hayashi Teruo, passed on to the next world where we all have to go some day. I experienced impermanence in a very strong way.

During my last visit to see him, we practiced Monday through Friday for three hours each day. We worked with vigor and vitality — training with all our might. We performed kata together at full speed many times so that he could teach me the slow and fast parts of the kata at the same time. He left the tatami two to three times, for about five minutes at a time, and that is all the rest he took.

Two weeks later he was admitted into the hospital and never came out. He passed away six months later. During this time, only his family and two of his disciples knew where he was. His wish was not to show his ill self while lying down. This is the samurai teaching of not showing your sleeping face to your retainer. Now that he is gone, we remember him only as a strong warrior. He was truly a 21st century samurai.

SEINOSUKE MITSUYA

THE DISTANT DREAM

HE IS ONE OF THE MOST EXPERIENCED KARATE MASTERS IN THE WORLD, AND HIS KNOWLEDGE OF SHITO-RYU IS ABOVE AND BEYOND WHAT MOST OF THE CURRENT INSTRUCTORS OF THE ART KNOW. STUDENT OF THE LEGENDARY HAYASHI TERUO, MITSUYA SENSEI ADHERES TO THE TEACHING OF HIS INSTRUCTORS AS MUCH AS POSSIBLE AND INSISTS THAT TECHNIQUES HAVE NOT CHANGED MUCH. "KARATE TECHNIQUES HAVE NOT CHANGED FROM WHEN I STARTED. DEVELOPED? YES. BUT NOT CHANGED. SOMETIMES THEY ARE TAUGHT INCORRECTLY OR ADAPTED BECAUSE SOME INSTRUCTORS ARE UNABLE TO CORRECT TECHNIQUE, BUT THIS IS NOT BECAUSE THE TECHNIQUE IS LACKING."

IN DEFENSE OF YOUR LIFE, SENSEI MITSUYA BELIEVES THAT YOU MUST BE CAPABLE OF KILLING YOUR ENEMY WITH ONE BLOW. THAT IS WHY HIS TEACHING EMPHASIZES THE TRUE ELEMENTS AND PHILOSOPHY OF JAPANESE BUDO. LESSONS WITH HIM ARE MORE THAN A PHYSICAL WORKOUT. THEY ARE ALSO A KARATE HISTORY LESSON. "THE PHILOSOPHICAL ASPECTS OF KARATE-DO MUST BE LEARNED FROM THE KARATEKA'S VERY FIRST VISIT TO THE DOJO, SO THAT, FROM THE OUTSET, HE WILL PROGRESS BOTH PHYSICALLY AND MENTALLY. IN THIS WAY, AS THE COMPLEXITY AND POWER OF THE PHYSICAL TECHNIQUES INCREASES, THE KARATEKA'S DISCIPLINE AND CONTROL EVOLVES TO COMPLEMENT IT."

MITSUYA SENSEI HAS REACHED A LEVEL OF KARATE THAT — FOR THE MAJORITY — IS NOTHING BUT A DISTANT DREAM. HE REPRESENTS THE TOTAL KARATE EXPERIENCE.

How long have you been practicing the martial arts?

I have been practicing for more than 45 years and that includes both karate and kobudo simultaneously. I also practiced sumo between the ages of 6 and 12 and judo between 12 and 18. I started in karate (Hayashi-ha shito-ryu) at the age of 14. My first teachers were my elder brother, Jinichi, and Soke Teruo Hayashi.

Tell us some interesting stories of your early days in karate under the guidance of Grandmaster Soke Hayashi Teruo.

Soke Hayashi used to give very little explanation about the technique. He just gave his commands to perform the techniques and the kiai. That's all. It was up to us to watch carefully when he was moving and notice the details of the techniques. Our ability to do this was directly related to our level of knowledge and maturity in the art. But I also was very lucky. Somehow, when Soke wanted to study, analyze, and practice techniques and actions he would call me aside and make me attack him. He would tell me which atemi to perform, and I was unaware of what would happen next. I couldn't really see much, but I surely felt it. I was very lucky that he chose me. At that time, no one else but me was used for that purpose. I learned very much from those intense training sessions. Not only were they were very satisfying, but they stimulated me to continue karate with more passion and dedication than before. At night, the only thing I could do was rest so I would have the energy to train the next day. It was very intense training, and my body literally dropped after the last workout. Today, virtually nobody is willing to undergo such training, and that may be simply because this is a different time.

When you began teaching outside of Japan, how did you find that the Westerners responded to traditional Japanese training when they visited your dojo?

Western people are generally very interested in those aspects [traditional Japanese training that] they like, especially [things like] ethics and morality. They also wanted to learn about the traditional art and today's Japanese culture. The Japanese culture of yesterday, as well as the one of today, is very much interconnected with the spirit and technique of Budo.

Were you a natural at karate? Did the movements come easily to you?

Yes, for me it came quite easy. I felt it inside myself from the beginning. However, even if it is easy and natural [for anyone], it is important to always improve. There is no end to that. It is necessary to coordinate your thoughts and actions, and you need to continuously practice hard every day and never give up your personal training. Obviously, I always try to improve, and I continue learning, studying and practicing. I realize how the maturity of the physical techniques develops through time, especially when I trained with Soke Hayashi.

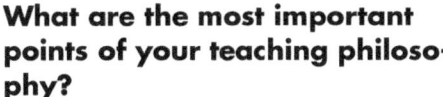

What are the most important points of your teaching philosophy?

Harmony among mind, spirit and body. Also, I make sure that I teach the right strategy (mental and spiritual) and tactic (action). There should be coordination in the body and in the mind, too. To get the maximum benefits from the art, it is very important to learn how to put together and coordinate all the mental and physical elements of karate.

With all the technical changes during the last decades, do you think there still are "pure" styles of karate?

Masters transfer the "purity" of the styles to the students who are strong spiritually and technically, because these students have the "strength" to continue the tradition. That's why they are "real" masters; they are the ones who have a serious school and a real grandmaster. Each style represents a different flavor in the big landscape of the art of karate.

A ryu (a style or system) is a method, and it is tradition, manners, philosophy, culture, science, technology, et cetera. Styles are different methods of training and represent different answers to the same problems. All of these aspects are like a sort of genetic identity or a DNA. The more talented old masters studied for many years ... even the smallest details. Some of the characteristics of Hayashi-ha shito-ryu include the trust and credibility that Soke Teruo Hayashi gained through [many] great sacrifices. Every style reflects the method, the correctness and the rectitude of the master who created it. Some great masters have practiced for many years under their teachers and then created their own style and unique method. After years of study, they implemented the most effective and functional techniques. Master Teruo Hayashi traveled often to search for the most traditional masters so he could study their techniques, their kata, and their methods both in karate-do and kobudo. Through these experiences, he founded the Hayashi-ha shito-ryu of karate-do and the kenshin-ryu of kobudo. Soke Hayashi was a man of great temper and charisma, as well as a great fighter. He gained respect from the most relevant masters in Budo — and became one of them — due to the great depth of his knowledge in martial arts. He demonstrated this knowledge on a number of occasions, and many considered him No. 1 among the current masters of karate and kobudo. He not only prepared technicians and fighters on a very high level, he successfully asserted his school all around the world.

How would you describe the life and dedication of Soke Hayashi to the arts of Budo?

Soke Hayashi practiced karate-do and kobudo with the spirit of the Japanese Budo [Yamato Damashii] for all of his life. For decades, he demonstrated the art in world championships and events in front of the most respected martial artists and politicians around the world, and the public always anticipated his presentations the most. And this is how people from all cultures and styles were able to recognize the art and the value of these arts. Because of his enormous knowledge, he was president of the referee council of the WKF (previously known as WUKO) for more than 10 years, and he greatly contributed to the revisions and improvements of the competitions and rules. A change in kumite is one example of that. In earlier times, there was the ippon shobu, which was the traditional Japanese form. To make the competitions more sport-oriented, Soke Hayashi created the system of sanbon-shobu. While this made it more accessible to the rest of the world, it kept the traditional elements. Certainly, he was the person who has contributed the most to the development of traditional karate-do and kobudo.

Do you think that karate in the West is at the same level with Japanese karate?

If we talk about sport competitions, then the West and Japan are at the same level. Philosophically and culturally, however, the differences are obvious and this affects the way karate is not only practiced in the dojo but also how the practitioner understands the art. Generally, karate is a serious matter for Japanese; it is not simply a sport. Unfortunately, due to the differences in culture with the Western world, I often notice a certain lack of seriousness from the Westerners who are involved in the arts of Budo.

Do you feel that there are any fundamental differences in approach or in the physical capabilities between Japanese karateka and European or American karateka?

There should not be any difference in the sport competitions. The referees, however, make a difference through their interpretation of the rules, their ability and knowledge.

Karate is nowadays often referred to as a sport. Would you agree with this definition or do you think it is only Budo?

Sport is governed by rules for athletic reasons. Karate-do is fundamentally a study for the body, mind and spirit. Therefore, it requires physical and mental discipline. Due to these reasons, karate-do can be considered as Budo and can be practiced for life. Karate as sport is only a small part of karate-do and can only be practiced as such for a few years. A true practitioner of Budo must study and practice his entire life. The study of the martial arts is similar to the research of modern technology; you never stop learning and studying. Soke Hayashi was a perfect example of an individual who studies, practices and lives the art of Budo.

At the present time, how do you see karate in general and Hayashi-ha shito-ryu in Europe and the rest of the world?

In these last decades, karate has transformed a lot. It is following a sportive path more and more, and it is losing the effectiveness of its actions. In sport competitions, nowadays, what really matters is the spectacle. This is probably due to the big influence of the movies, but what you see in the movies has nothing to do with real fighting or real self-defense. Many referees, often influenced by the public, don't know how to be objective and thus lose credibility in front of competitors and spectators. The Hayashi-ha system, in my opinion, not only has excellent technique, but it's very efficient and functional, and it is rich in beauty, elegance and refinements. And this is how karate should be.

Does it help empty-hand karate physically to train with weapons?

Yes. Every weapon has its peculiarities, and the body has to adapt and become stronger when using the weapon. All this preparation helps a student improve the mechanics behind the physical movements of karate.

What's your opinion of makiwara training?

Makiwara training is not indispensable, but it can be useful if it is practiced properly. Young people and teenagers — especially — should not practice this before they have reached a certain physical maturity, as there is risk of serious deformations in the hands. The makiwara is necessary to develop precision of technique and resistance at the moment of impact against an object. However, practicing with the makiwara properly is very difficult, so a teacher must not only have thorough knowledge of this training but also a lot of common sense. He must make sure that a student's hands do not become deformed or bleed because that can lead to serious problems, including HIV and infections.

To progress in the arts, how should a sensei prepare his personal training? Once he reaches a high technical level, what elements should be emphasized?

He must dedicate special attention to the weakest parts of his body, acknowledge them and strengthen them, and continue to develop his strengths. When a sensei arrives at a high technical level, he must emphasize the coordination between the mental and physical because this is an important aspect of the whole picture. It is also important to search for a great master or teacher who can help him go forward and improve, assisting him in reaching the higher levels of the art.

When teaching the art of karate, is self-defense, sport or tradition the most important?

Self-defense, tradition and sport. That is the order of importance, but each one is individually important because they all support each other to create a strong unit. Thus, you should not focus on only one or two of the elements. Instead, you should try to balance your practice. Of course, when you get older, the emphasis switches to tradition and self-defense because the sport aspect is gone.

In training, what's the proper ratio between kata and kumite?

It is difficult to answer because it depends on the age, physical capabilities and character of the person, and all of these elements [combined] generally make the "perfect" proportion for an individual. When a student is young, it is easier to practice kumite, but this should be done with discipline and proper manners. However, after a student reaches the age of 30, maybe he will naturally feel more [inclined] to do kata.

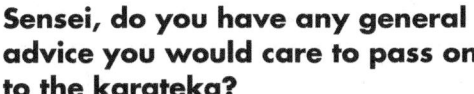

Sensei, do you have any general advice you would care to pass on to the karateka?

To the karateka of today, my advice is to always train with dedication and attention and, in addition to getting the proper education, you should incorporate the following values into your life: discipline, seriousness and respect. In other words, focus on technique, intelligence and spirit. For the art of karate-do, these are the most important values, and they are much more important than punching, kicking and muscle power.

Some people think it is necessary to train in Japan. Do you agree with this point of view?

Sometimes it may be useful if you don't have a good master, but it is not necessary because the best masters often travel outside of Japan [and thus are accessible] and many of them are already living outside of that country.

What would you say to someone who is interested in learning karate-do?

First, I'd say that it is a great idea! Learning this discipline brings much serenity to a practitioner's life and one should stick to the art and have a strong will to succeed. If the practitioner puts in the time and effort, everything is possible. For every age and everybody, there is a better way to practice karate. It is not necessary to use the same method or approach for every single student. Each practitioner must take care of the details. This is the essence of traditional Japanese karate-do. Personally, I try to follow this principle. Thanks to my passion and thanks to the teaching of Soke Hayashi, I have always been among the best ones [instructors], and I intend to continue being among the top instructors in the world. I have always wanted to do better than others.

What is your opinion about mixing karate styles? Does the practice of one nullify the effectiveness of the other or can it be beneficial to the student?

The mixing of styles often may cause mediocrity if [they are] studied superficially, because every style has its particular characteristics. The only way to attain time-lasting results is to carefully study the particulars of each style. Personally, I don't think that it is a good idea to study and mix styles, because it requires time and ability and a very high level of technical understanding that many people don't have. Thus, a serious karate-ka should dedicate more [time] to in-depth study of his style instead of jumping from one style to another without any logic behind [that decision].

Modern karate is moving away from the bunkai in kata practice. In general, how important is bunkai in the understanding of kata and karate-do?

Kata is essential to karate. Kata organizes the technical foundation of the style from the base (kihon) to very high levels of technical expertise. Due to this, the ratio between form and action is often hard to understand. Sometimes it is simply the student's lack of study or capability. That is also why the bunkai is sometimes very difficult to understand and tiring from a psychological point of view. I think that the best way to learn is to have a good and competent master who can truly teach you the essence of the form, its meaning and its applications, many of which are hidden, both for self-defense and for the health of the person.

What is the philosophical basis for your karate training?

Harmony among mind, spirit and body. This has always been the key factor for me. Also, I always wanted to study, learn and exercise to keep my body and mind in perfect shape.

After all these years of training and experience, could you explain the meaning of the practice of karate-do?

Self-control or seigyo, which is what we call it in Japanese. To apply this in your life, you have to completely understand it. It can be interpreted as seriousness and dignity, and as I said, it can be applied to every aspect of life. The practice of karate-do begins at black belt level — not at white belt. Prior to this phase [black belt], students are only going through a period of study and refection to try to understand their own tendencies. With correct training and the guidance of a good teacher, you can learn the right attitude, modesty, self-control and courage, and every black belt must maintain these principles. At that level, black belts must become examples for their kohai. The only way to understand every aspect of karate-do is through constant practice and dedication. As in any other activity, it is necessary to have professionalism and dignity.

Compared with those who were being taught in your early days, is there anything lacking in the way karate is taught today?

Generally, teachers today provide plenty of explanations, but they do it with more talking and less action [or demonstrations]. In the early times, there were few explanations, and it was necessary to pay strong attention. [In those days], there was more action and less talking.

Why is it, in your opinion, that a lot of students quit after two to three years of training?

The reasons vary from person to person, but the majority of students. After two or three years of practice, many believe that they are already good, and they don't think that they need to train anymore. They think that they are "there" because they have developed an evident skill [compared to when they started]. This is [the] wrong [approach], and the only way to prevent that is to teach the student he is still a beginner, regardless of how far how he thinks he has progressed … even if he has been training for two or three years. This is the reason why it is so important to teach the philosophy of Budo. It simply keeps the mind at the right place and prevents [the ego from] getting too big.

There is very little written about you in magazines. You obviously do not thrive on the publicity. Why?

I am not an exhibitionist. I have had chances to appear in magazines all over the world, but that is not my goal. I am well known in the karate world because I have always demonstrated my qualities and the authenticity of my teacher's art with actions and not just with words. The little publicity [I have received from] magazines may result from the fact that I never wanted to compromise [my goals] to anyone, and I have always kept my professional dignity untouched. I am Japanese deep to my core, and I have the spirit of the samurai. We all know what conditions of servility you need to undergo to be considered by the politicians of the sport, and I can't accept that. Now it should be easy to understand why I don't pursue publicity.

Is there anything else you would to add for the readers?

Seek and strive to be the best. Do not let yourself get dragged [down] by anyone's words or by what only appears to be good. This can be very deceiving.

KUNIO MIYAKE

THE POWER OF WILL

BORN IN 1946, MIYAKE SENSEI BEGAN TEACHING THE MARTIAL ARTS IN JAPAN. AT THE SAME TIME, HE WAS TEACHING MODERN JAPANESE LANGUAGE AND LITERATURE AT THE HIGH SCHOOL LEVEL. HE MOVED TO THE UNITED STATES IN 1985 AND — WITH PERMISSION FROM SHUKO-KAI TANI-HA SHITO-RYU AND SOKE CHOJIRO TANI — QUICKLY ESTABLISHED SHUKO-KAI U.S.A. IN SOUTHERN CALIFORNIA. FOUNDER OF SHUKO-KAI INTERNATIONAL, MIYAKE SENSEI CURRENTLY HOLDS AN OFFICIAL U.S.A. NATIONAL KARATE-DO FEDERATION 8TH DEGREE IN KARATE-DO AND A 6TH DEGREE IN SHORINJI AIKI JIU-JITSU. THE ALL-JAPAN KARATE-DO FEDERATION AND THE WORLD SHORINJI KEMPO FEDERATION ISSUED HIS INSTRUCTOR'S LICENSES. BOTH ASSOCIATIONS REQUIRE THE HIGHEST CALIBER OF KARATE AND JUJITSU KNOWLEDGE. IN 1982, HE WAS THE ALL-JAPAN CHAMPION IN SHITO-RYU SHUKO-KAI AND THE 1988 U.S.A. KARATE FEDERATION NATIONAL CHAMPION. HE WAS ALSO SELECTED AS THE REPRESENTATIVE AT THE ALL-JAPAN MARTIAL ARTS DEMONSTRATION (BUDOSAI) — A DISTINCTIVE HONOR BECAUSE REPRESENTATIVES ARE CHOSEN THROUGHOUT JAPAN BASED ON THEIR SUPERIOR SKILLS IN THEIR RESPECTIVE ARTS. WITH MANY YEARS OF EXPERIENCE IN THE ARTS OF BUDO, MIYAKE SENSEI IS CONSIDERED ONE OF THE MOST KNOWLEDGEABLE INSTRUCTORS IN THE ART OF KARATE. MIYAKE SENSEI HAS EARNED A HIGH LEVEL OF RESPECT BY SHARING KARATE-DO WITH LOVE, EMPATHY AND DEDICATION. HE STRIVES FOR A LIFE OF TRANQUILITY AND CONTENTMENT, REFRESHED BY THE SATISFACTION DERIVED FROM PURSUING THE WAY OF MARTIAL ARTS WITH DISCIPLINE AND COMMITMENT.

How long have you been practicing the martial arts and in how many styles have you trained?

I began practicing the martial arts when I was about eight. I started with kendo, and then I moved on to judo, shorinji-kempo, karate and iaido. Sensei Doshin So, the founder of shorinji kempo, was my first teacher. I had other sensei in kendo and judo, and they were extremely important in my training. Of course, in karate, it was Tani Sensei.

Tell us some interesting stories about your early days in karate training.

My early days in karate were based on simple and pure kihon training. Only a few people stayed because there wasn't anything very interesting [going on]; repeating the same techniques thousands of times is not amusing to most practitioners. In my shorinji kempo dojo, my senpai always came to me and told me that we [kohai] had to fight a yakuza for our black belt test. I didn't want to go to the test

for a long time because of this, and it never happened anyway. The main reason [I didn't go] was because I was still a kid, and I was afraid. From the physical point of view, I was a natural at karate. The kumite movements came more easily to me than kata movements. I believe that fighting is more natural for a human than learning a kata. In order to do a kata well, you have to "mold" your body so it "shows" the karate movement with precision and proper technique. Kumite seems to be a more natural approach, although it requires mastering other important elements that make fighting a different thing all together.

When you started teaching, how did the Westerners respond to traditional Japanese training?

In 1985, I started teaching in California, and most of my students were juniors. They never stayed quiet when I was explaining [techniques] in class. In Japan, the students are afraid of the sensei, so they don't move around ... let alone when the teacher is explaining a technique or a principle! In my dojo, it was impossible for me to give them traditional Japanese training because of the Western mentality. Traditional Japanese training means students have to do kihon drills everyday, and they have to be done with manners and patience. The sensei never explains anything, nor does he smile. Now, I teach traditional karate with manners but not like before when I was in Japan. I always explain why they need to do certain techniques, and they [seem to] enjoy traditional Japanese karate more. By providing explanations of why they have to behave in a certain way, it seems to help them truly appreciate the culture of Budo.

How has your personal karate developed over the years?

One way is my general approach to the art. In the very beginning, I always thought only about kumite. During my first years of training, I was not interested in kata at all. I only practiced kata for my rank testing because it was a requirement — not because I enjoyed it. As I grew up and gained maturity in the art, kata became more interesting to me, and I started to look at it from a very different perspective. Nowadays, when I conduct seminars, instructors and students ask me to do kata. They think that I specialize in kata instruction, which I don't, but it's very interesting to me because I enjoy instructing both kata and kumite. Life changes in very interesting ways!

With all the technical changes during the last 30 years, do you think there is still pure shotokan, shito-ryu, goju-ryu, et cetera?

When you compare current WKF rules with old tournament rules, you can tell the differences right away. In kumite, we were looking for one punch, one kill techniques, but now we stress speed to win. In kata, more variations are acceptable for tokuigata and competitors, to impress the judges, adopt fancier versions of the same kata. I noticed that Japanese kata champions are performing their kata differently in WKF championships than when they compete in Japan because the judges from the WKF have a different viewpoint on how the kata should be performed.

After karate became an international sport, every country brought its own flavor. As a matter of fact, the Europeans made the WKF rules. Anyway, to question whether things are pure is hard to say. First of all, we need to define what pure means because all the legendary masters learned from their teachers and then modified the teaching when they taught to the next generation of practitioners. We know, anyway, that karate has been changing rapidly for the last several decades, and it is very difficult to say that this or that style is pure.

Do you think different ryu are important?

Yes, because each ryu has its own characteristics. Depending on the style, kata has different sets of the principles that help you to develop the "flavor" in the art of karate. Unfortunately, modern kumite does not show the characteristics of each ryu anymore because everything is extremely unified in movement and approach. This is the result of sport competition. Back then, shotokan used zenkutsu-dachi and goju-ryu used nekoashi-dachi in kumite so you could tell the practitioner's style by just looking at the way he fought. Because karate now has a sport aspect, it has been losing a little bit of its own character. Nowadays, we have only two styles for kumite: Japanese and rest of the world. And even the Japanese are changing to better accommodate the sportive approach.

What is your opinion of full-contact karate and kickboxing?

I respect full-contact karate and kickboxing because those combat sports are extremely demanding and require a lot of dedication from the practitioners. For some, it isn't always easy to pursue good techniques. Sometimes fighters focus more on the efficiency of the technique and don't necessarily devote the proper attention to the development of the technical skill. Depending on what the individual person wants from karate or other martial arts, he should choose a style and try to do his best. I happened to choose traditional karate-do for myself because I wanted to practice the art my whole life. Combat sports are good when you are young and strong, but when you start to get older ... you simply can't perform them well.

In regards to karate, how would you describe the life and dedication of Tani Sensei?

Tani Sensei dedicated his life to karate more than any other karate-ka that I have ever known. Sensei used to think of karate all the time, and he had thought up new, unique ideas for the art, including the double-twist or kick-shock, which increases the power in the techniques.

Before Tani Sensei passed away, he insisted that the name tani-ha shito-ryu should be changed to tani-ha karate-do. Some senior students didn't like the idea of changing the name. I think he changed his karate's name because he was open-minded and wanted to make the style deeper by incorporating other styles. Eventually, it was not pure shito-ryu as he learned from Grandmaster Mabuni. After I studied goju-ryu kata, I understood naha-te more thoroughly than before. This is a good example of why Tani

SHITO RYU MASTERS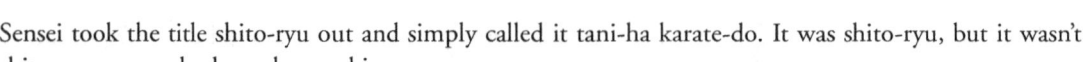

Sensei took the title shito-ryu out and simply called it tani-ha karate-do. It was shito-ryu, but it wasn't shito-ryu as everybody understood it.

In regards to approach or physical capabilities, are there are any fundamental differences between Japanese karateka and Western karateka?

When describing physical capabilities, there aren't many differences. Nowadays in the U.S., many children start practicing karate at an early age ... just as they do in Japan. Fundamentally, I feel that there are more differences, and I think that is because karate in Japan is taken more seriously than here. In the Western world, in some cases, karate is used as a way for parents to keep their children occupied or to teach them discipline. In Japan, from an early age, the discipline is already there and doesn't need to be taught. When the art of karate is taken seriously, karateka are able to learn much more easily.

If you compare karate in the United States today to 25 years ago, the art has improved tremendously. But still Japan generally performs at a higher level. Hopefully, the Western world will soon reach the level at which Japan performs.

Karate is often referred to as a sport. Would you agree with this or do you think it is only Budo?

As a younger man, I felt that I was seeing the sport aspect. Competition was exciting to me, and it was more of the driving force. Now, as an older person, Budo is more important as the driving force of my training. Karate and Budo are life experiences that never end. There is always another level of achievement to obtain, a higher plateau to be reached. The technical aspects are mastered earlier in life while the spiritual aspects become more apparent and are of more importance as you become older. I truly believe that age is an important factor in this matter.

In general, how do you presently see karate and shuko-kai around the world?

Because of the sport aspect of karate, the popularity has increased dramatically. The interest around the world is increasing; therefore, the exposure of Shuko-kai International has become increasingly more visible to practitioners. The increase in the availability of worldwide communication has brought my organization to the forefront of karate-do.

Do you think kobudo helps karateka to improve their empty-hand skills?

Weapons training is not an important aspect in my way of training. Karate and kobudo are separate and don't assist each other in the physical aspect. You can be a great karateka without training in kobudo, but it is very difficult to be an expert in kobudo without having previous knowledge of karate-do.

How should a sensei should prepare and schedule his personal training to progress in the arts?

As a younger sensei, I did daily repetition training similar to that of my students, and I truly thought it was important. However, I now feel that my personal training should revolve around the concept of quality. Of course, I spend time away from my students to prepare for my own training, but I also spend time exercising to stay in my best physical condition and to perfect my technique. The teacher should allocate time for personal training. According to his age, he needs to develop and maintain other physical elements such as agility, limberness, endurance and good health. These elements require specific training sessions separate from karate training.

When teaching the art of karate, what is the most important element: self-defense, sport or tradition?

My techniques are a balance of all three. As my students progress and obtain more knowledge, their techniques can be used for whatever avenue they want to follow. Many enjoy the sporting aspect; however, others report to me how many of their experiences in life are enriched by the physical training, focus, and spiritual teachings they have learned. For the sporting aspect, we focus on strength and physical abilities. For tradition, we focus our attention on knowledge and spirituality.

From the technical point of view and specificically for beginning students, we focus more on kumite to build coordination, speed and flexibility. As students progress, we introduce more complex techniques for kata to improve their form. Once they have obtained a higher level of achievement, I try to balance the training so their abilities increase for both aspects at the same rate.

Some people think that it's critical to go to Japan to train. Do you agree?

Not for everybody and not all the time. Right now many good karateka from Japan live overseas. Therefore, the level of karate all over the world is much higher than it was in the past. So, if you are going to go to Japan to learn karate, you should know what you want to learn, where you want to train and from whom you want to learn it. Otherwise, you will be disappointed. About 30 years ago, when karate was exported from Japan to other countries, any instructor in Japan could teach someone at the beginner's level better than a foreign or non-Japanese instructor. That's why if you want to go to Japan today to learn karate you must make a plan to determine where you are going to go, with whom you are going to train and determine, to the best of your ability, if you are going to learn what you set out to learn.

Whom would you like to have trained with that you have not?

The people I would have most wanted to train with would have been the founders of each style. It would be important to me to learn their philosophies, along with their techniques, to further enhance my own [techniques].

What keeps you motivated after all these years?

My motivation has always been to make myself stronger, both mentally and physically. As a young person, I was shy and the martial arts helped to build my confidence. As the years passed, the philosophies helped to motivate me in many directions and to achieve my goals.

When I began training, karate was known as an art form for people who wanted to learn aggressive techniques. At the time, there weren't that many people who wanted to learn, so there were not many dojo available. Now karate has evolved into a sport, and this has made it more attractive to everyone. As a result, the karate community has grown rapidly.

Do you think it is necessary to engage in free fighting to achieve good self-defense skills for a real situation?

I do not believe that it is necessary to free fight in order to defend yourself. If you prepare physically and mentally for tournament-style fighting, you should easily be able to adapt to the street … in most situations. But definitely, you need to understand that a sport competition is not real self-defense.

What is your opinion about mixing karate styles? Does the practice of one nullify the effectiveness of the other? Can it be beneficial to a student?

In kata, each style has its own character and flavor that shows the roots of the style. Therefore, mixing styles creates difficulty with mastering a true technique. However, in kumite, it is more acceptable because the object is to dominate your opponent, so having more techniques in your arsenal can enhance your ability to overcome the ever-changing situation.

How important is "bunkai" in the understanding of kata?

Contrary to what others may feel, my opinion is that bunkai is of great importance for the true understanding of kata. Different styles have different references, so if the bunkai of a style is not practiced properly, then there can be no true understanding of what the movements represent.

Do you have a particularly memorable karate experience that has remained as an inspiration for your training?

When I was in my twenties, I trained in shorinji-kempo and karate and did not have time to compete. But when I was in my early thirties, I began to compete. I enjoyed the competition, and it enhanced my experience and motivated me to train harder to be the best that I could. I concentrated on my kumite techniques and enjoyed the spirit of the competitions. It was an exciting time of my life, and it gave me the drive to better myself to this day.

How can practitioners increase their understanding of the spiritual aspect of karate?

Before you can increase your spiritual awareness, you must learn patience and realize that the karate experience takes many years of training. With this understanding, you realize — as in all spiritual journeys — that the more you know and realize, the deeper the spiritual experience. The first thing new students should learn is to enjoy all the basic aspects of karate-do. If they enjoy what they are doing, they will be more receptive to the disciplines that follow and be able to endure the rigorous training. Karate-do is a life-long experience that has many levels of achievement. As you experience the mental and physical aspects at different stages in your life, you seem to grasp the higher levels of knowledge and use these tools in all life experiences.

How much training should a senior karateka be doing to improve?

As a senior, you must learn to use your time and energy efficiently. A younger person can afford the luxury of longer and more repetitious training because the body can easily absorb the physical activity. When you are older, you do not have the same luxury. Thus, you have to train as intensely [as a younger student], but you cannot waste any energy that you need in the other aspects of your life.

Compared to the "early" days, is there anything lacking in the way karate is taught today?

These days karate has more of a sport aspect. Many people think the goal of training is to be a kata or a kumite champion. Some of these competitors think they are already the best because they have won championships. Many become champions by using only a few techniques or a few kata. However, these techniques or kata are only the tip of the iceberg. While some competitors focus [solely] on training to win competitions, they lose out on more important aspects of karate. Things like the right attitude, manners and respect. A karateka needs to remember to be humble, even after winning many championships. In my early days, the spiritual side of karate was emphasized. In the early days, there were competitions, but they were very different from now. If you were punched in the face, you did not show weakness. Instead, you would wait for an opportunity to hit your opponent back. After the tournament,

the fighters became friends because there was respect for each other. They would also compliment one another and humble themselves. This spiritual side of karate would also be shown in our dojo as well.

What advice on supplementary training can you give to students?

When I was competing, I used to jog about three miles four or five days a week, and I would lift weights three days a week to build speed and strength. You need to think about speed and power together — not separate. If you use too much strength, you will decrease the speed of your technique. For instance, the makiwara is an important aspect of training, and it should be used for achieving perfect form by practicing striking and relaxation techniques.

Why, after two or three years of training, do a lot of students quit training?

I think it's because there are a lot of very young students. Many of them seek other avenues of knowledge … may it be intellectual or sport. Our world has become a wealth of diversity, and it is difficult to concentrate on our subjects long enough to begin to understand the actual complexities and depth [of those subjects]. Children have a tendency to want to know about everything that goes on around them, and it is difficult for them to focus on one subject. Thus, we need parental guidance to help children focus on what is necessary … in lieu of what is available.

Character is one of the most important qualities of a successful karateka. If a student has good character, he will build a good relationship with the sensei. With a good relationship comes a good attitude and mutual respect. After this, the student's techniques will improve naturally because the technique is simply a result of the student's attitude. That's what Funakoshi Sensei meant when he said you should develop character through karate training. The more character the student has … the better and more mature the technique is.

There is very little written about you in magazines. You obviously do not thrive on the publicity like some martial artists. Why?

Fame is not what I seek. My quest is for the betterment of karate-do. I train and teach to be an example to my community. I must be in the best physical condition I can be and communicate my philosophy to my students. This is more important than being in the spotlight of the martial arts. My karate training has always been for the evaluation of my fears, and my philosophy is to always conquer myself. Fear is an emotion that is always tested in all aspects of life, and my training — both physical and mental — is focused on the release of fear.

What are your thoughts on the future of karate-do, and what's your opinion about karate entering in the Olympic games?

Although the Olympic Games may represent only one aspect of karate-do, I feel that it is important. The exposure to the world will increase the involvement of all nations and will help participants get funding through their national Olympic committee. This involvement will increase the amount of younger students who participate and encourage them to stay with the sport because they will want to achieve Olympic honor. In the process, they will obtain the deeper knowledge of karate-do with the additional years of training it will take to get to the Olympics.

Is there anything else you'd like to add?

When we are advanced [in age], we need to continue being strict on ourselves. When people get older, they often tend to become lazy. As a matter of fact, we often don't train enough as a karateka. Of course, it's natural to slow down and lose some physical strength when we get older. But if we become strict in our training, we can become mentally stronger and train with quality. Then, our advanced teaching will compensate for any loss of speed or physical strength. Karate-do is not only a method of fighting, but it's also a way of strengthening relationships between yourself and society. In the future, I hope that all practitioners and teachers continue to focus on the traditions of karate-do without allowing business or personal gain reasons to overtake them. Failing to concentrate on tradition and knowledge seems to be a new trend in the martial arts. People new to karate-do need to realize the difference when beginning their new experience. If a practitioner finds a teacher who has trained hard and has followed the traditional way, he will become a better martial artist — and person — in general.

SAM MOLEDZKI

NOT AN ORDINARY MAN

CHIEF INSTRUCTOR FOR SHITO KAI CANADA, HIS INTRODUCTION INTO THE MARTIAL ARTS BEGAN IN 1967 WHILE STUDYING BOXING AND COMPETING AS A MEMBER OF THE MIDLAND AVENUE COLLEGIATE GYMNASTIC TEAM. INITIALLY, MOLEDZKI SENSEI TRAINED IN THE CHITO-RYU KARATE SYSTEM FIRST INTRODUCED INTO CANADA IN 1958 BY THE MAN WHO IS REFERRED TO AS "THE FATHER OF CANADIAN KARATE," MASAMI TSURUOKA SENSEI. AFTER MANY MONTHS TRAINING SEVERAL TIMES A WEEK AT THE JAPAN CANADIAN CULTURE CENTRE, PLUS SPECIAL TRAINING SESSIONS AT TSURUOKA SENSEI'S OTHER DOJO LOCATIONS, MOLEDZKI SENSEI SUCCESSFULLY RECEIVED HIS SHODAN ON JANUARY 10, 1970.

SAM MOLEDZKI ALSO STUDIED OKINAWAN KOBUDO AS WELL AS KENDO, JODO AND IAIDO, AND HAS TRAVELED EXTENSIVELY TO JAPAN AND HAS TRAINED UNDER SOME OF THE WORLD'S GREATEST KARATE AND KOBUDO MASTERS, INCLUDING THE LEGENDARY RYUSHO SAKAGAMI SENSEI.

HE HAS BEEN A DIRECT STUDENT OF KUNIO MURAYAMA SENSEI SINCE 1991 AND NOW HE HEADS THE SHITO KAI CANADA, A MEMBER OF THE WORLD SHITO KAI KARATE-DO FEDERATION. FOR HIM, SPIRIT AND HEART ARE THE MOST IMPORTANT ATTRIBUTES IN MARTIAL ARTS TRAINING: "IN ORDER TO BE THE BEST," SENSEI MOLEDZKI SAYS, "YOU MUST HAVE THE WARRIOR'S SPIRIT – HEART." QUIET, RELAXED, AND SOFT-SPOKEN, THIS KARATE MASTER EXEMPLIFIES THE TRUE ATTRIBUTES OF A REAL MARTIAL ARTIST.

How long have you been practicing the martial arts?

It's been just over 40 years or so, since I first began practicing martial arts.

How many styles of karate or other methods have you trained in and who were your teachers?

Well, I first began training in the karate system called Chito-ryu from 1967 until 1969. This, by the way, was the most prevalent system of karate being taught all across Canada by Tsuruoka Sensei and his students. His chief instructor at the JCCC, when I joined, was Sensei Kei Tsumura at the Japanese Canadian Cultural Centre, from 1967 until 1981. Then, I personally chose to leave the Shito-ryu Itosu-Kai system to further my own knowledge of the martial arts independently. If you will indulge me for just a brief moment, I'd like to say that I remain to this day very grateful to Sensei Tsumura for teaching me the importance of developing good basics, in order to build a strong and firm foundation in karate. In my opinion, I still remember him being a very strict and demanding sensei who always had the best

interests of the students in mind, as karate-kas and, even more so, as human beings, whether we knew it or not.

I really learned a great deal about the value of how to persevere and apply hard work, honest effort, and patience in karate and in daily life from Tsumura Sensei, and I always will be thankful for that. As one of his top students at the time, I was afforded the fantastic opportunity to travel to the Honbu Dojo in Tsurumi, Japan. While in Japan, I had the great honor and privilege to meet and receive direct instruction from Grandmaster Ryusho Sakagami in the various martial arts, including, Karate-do, Ryukyu Kobudo, Iaido, Jodo, and Kendo. Sometimes, at the honbu dojo, Sakagami Sensei would simply supervise the karate classes and his son Sakagami Sadaaki Sensei would teach. Other times, he would let the sen-pai of the dojo Ichikawa Fumikaze-san, instruct the classes.

I have a great deal of respect for him, as he was a tough, no nonsense karate-ka and always a perfect gentleman and my senior who I called a friend. My actual direct relationship with Sakagami Ryusho Sensei really began in 1976, when I was sent to the Japan Itosu-kai Honbu for advanced training by Tsumura Sensei. At the time, I had specifically requested to learn more about the martial art of Iaido, and Tsumura Sensei arranged it so.

During 1975, in Toronto, I began training in a form of Iaido through a friend of Tsumura Sensei named Claude Vesque, an Aikido-ka and student of Mas Inokuchi Sensei.

When I arrived at the honbu dojo in Japan, Sakagami Sensei asked me to show him what I learned in the past year about Iaido. As I proceeded to show him what I knew, he immediately told me to stop and said that if I wanted to learn Iaido, then I would have to forget everything I had been practicing the previous year and start over in the Muso Jikiden Eishin Ryu system taught by him. Of course, I was dumbfounded, but not stupid enough to throw away the golden opportunity to be taught directly by him. From that moment on, I learned directly from Sakagami Sensei privately, every day, a minimum of eight hours a day, and sometimes ten hours a day, depending on what scheduled classes were being taught during the early evenings. I lived in an apartment owned by Sakagami Sensei, directly next door to the honbu dojo.

Depending on the schedule of evening classes throughout the week, I would attend classes in either Itosu-kai Karate-do, Shindo Muso Ryu Jodo, or privately with Sakagami Sensei in Ryukyu Kobudo, or sometimes part of Sakagami Sensei's Kendo class. Then, it usually would be back to Iaido training.

At the conclusion of my training in the Shito Ryu Itosu Kai Karate and Kobudo Association, Canada, in February 1981, I was at the level of 5th dan Shito-Ryu Karate; 3rd dan Ryukyu Kobudo, and 1st dan

Muso Jikiden Eishin Ryu Iaido. From 1981 to 1991, I remained steadfastly independent of any major national or international federation by personal choice, as mentioned previously, and took every opportunity whenever it presented itself to practice with as many senior Japanese instructors as possible.

As fate would have it, during our 1991 Canadian National Black Belt Championships in Vancouver, British Columbia, I had the great fortune to meet and practice with Sensei Murayama Kunio from Monterrey, Mexico, via Japan. And I haven't looked back ever since. Since 1991, I have been a representative of the Karate-Do Shito Kai Murayama family, and directly associated with the World Shito Ryu Karate Do Federation as the official representative for Canada, and in 2006, I was appointed a director of the WSKF.

In karate, what does kata really represent and how important is it?

I personally believe that throughout history, kata has been the method by which the founders of various martial arts recorded and passed on their secret fighting techniques. And by studying the kata deeply within a given system, one would be enlightened to the mysteries within the kata.

What are the most important points in your teaching methods?

We learn through various means and I prefer to teach using the Visual Method (demonstrating it), Audible (describing it by voice), and Physical (assisting the students by physically guiding them through it). I also feel humor is an important tool for teaching. In my opinion, humor cuts the tension in the learning process the best. I also believe the student needs to have an open mind, be patient, and never give up, but persevere.

Do you think different 'styles' are truly important in the art of karate?

I believe that styles or personal interpretations of the original founders' training methods are important because they help us understand something of what the actual founder of that particular system felt was important to preserve at the time he created the system.

Do you feel that you still have further to go in your studies?

Most definitely! I firmly believe that I'm at the stage where I have a lot better understanding of karate than I did even ten years ago but, I am still a long way from ever mastering it. I'm still very excited about learning more and more, as it is a never-ending study to reach perfection. And, as we know, no man is perfect, so the journey is what it's all about for me anyway.

I'll tell you quite honestly, when I joined the Shito-kai Murayama family in 1991, my karate knowledge exploded. I was introduced to a system of Shito-ryu karate that contained a whole new world of knowledge handed down from Mabuni Kenwa Sensei through Iwata Manzo Sensei to Murayama Kunio Sensei. Exploring the major influences from Mabuni Kenwa Sensei relating to in-depth understanding of Nage-waza and Gyaku-waza are part of this terrific system. Not to forget about the major influences of Fujita Seiko Sensei, (14th generation headmaster of Koga Ryu, Wada-ha Ninjitsu) that was passed down to Iwata Manzo Sensei and on to Murayama Sensei, and is one of the more significant developments. They include Fujita Sensei's mastery of Daienryu Jojutsu. In 1943, Iwata Sensei received his Shihan license in the short stick art, Shingetsu Ryu Shuriken Jutsu. In 1944, Iwata Sensei received his shihan license in the throwing-projectile art and Nanban Satto Ryu Kenpo Jutsu. In 1948, Iwata Sensei received the honor of becoming the 4th generation Soke of Nanban Satto Ryu, the art of jujutsu-like grappling combat techniques. Today, Genzo Iwata Sensei (Chief Instructor WSKF) is the 5th Soke of Nanban Satto Ryu Kenpo Jutsu.

Do you think it helps the karate student physically to train with weapons?

Kobudo weapons help a great deal, physically and mentally, to train and develop my traditional karate techniques. I believe the advantages are as many as there are particular weapons.

For example, the Bo could help you understand more about the need to develop a clearer understanding of the use of longer distance while the Sai may help you to apply the correct angle and direction of a technique at a closer range. The Tonfa, for instance, possibly may help in understanding better about how to generate hip torque, from the tanden or lower stomach, and transferring energy through back, chest, shoulder, arm, and wrist action. The Nunchaku also can help you to gain maximum power and speed by the use of proper hip rotation and the understanding of how to possibly overcome distance to an advantage over your opponent, while the Kama, I believe, is able to help you develop a more controlled and secure hooking and scooping action in your striking and blocking techniques.

Practicing with Kobudo weapons assists in your shifting into control of various offensive and defensive distances, to become a better martial artist.

Forms and sparring, what's the proper ratio in training?

I believe that in the world competition arena today, one should specialize in either forms or fighting. But as a traditional martial artist, kata principles should be trained more and not just the pattern or form of the kata or just the fancy techniques of some kata.

What do you consider to be the major changes in the art since you began training?

I've witnessed and experienced many changes, especially in the aspect of competition rules and regulations as a former international class athlete and later as an international referee.

These changes start with the kumite matches in the 1960s without the use of equipment (bare fists, no mouth guards or groin protection) to using a single point match method or two half-points, through the mirror judging system using the three-point system with six half-points and on to the present system of multiple points and superior techniques getting a higher value. In Canada, during the 3rd Canadian National Black Belt Championships in 1976, kata was first included. I had the honor of finishing in third place, behind Kim Wong in second place and Tak Samashima in first place.

A few years later, female Kumite was included and finally Junior Kumite, including the evolution of the kata performance from the mostly hard and all-powerful performances to the more aesthetic, artistic performances, with the present-day inclusion of demonstrating various theatrical self-defense aspects of the form.

And there's the fashion change in the basic karate uniform, including the use of designated competition belts and eliminating the black belt of grade. There's also the added use of specific types of uniforms for the forms competition and another for sparring competition. I also see the sporting aspect of karate evolving along the recognition lines of Tae Kwon Do if it actually becomes an Olympic event, with all the usual benefits of an officially recognized Olympic sport.

What is it that keeps you motivated after all these years?

I guess I'd have to say it is the thirst for knowledge in a very different art form, as well as trying to understand an ancient culture that I find fascinating. Also, to continually improve my understanding of the martial arts through constant mental and physical dedication to it.

Do you have a particularly memorable karate experience that has remained as an inspiration for your training?

In 1971, during my first visit to Japan, I competed in the Kanto District Karate Championships and became the first non-Asian ever to win the Black Belt Kumite title in Japan. In my mind, it proved that if I believed in myself, and my karate ability, even I could win in Japan. In 1991, at the Canadian National Black Belt Championships in Vancouver, British Columbia, I had the great experience of having one of my students become the first Canadian junior male athlete to win gold in both his kumite and kata division for his age group. And then, later in 1993, at the 1st World Shito-ryu Karate-do Championships in Tokyo, Japan, one of my female students won a bronze medal in Black Belt sparring.

And finally Sensei, what benefits did you get from the art of Karate-do?

That's a very difficult question to answer. Let's just say that, in my case, the study of karate-do has been a personal life saving experience. I grew up in a small town in Ontario until my early teenage years. My late father was a very physically abusive parent who used to beat me and my brother almost daily until I was thirteen. My mother was finally forced to leave my father for fear of her life. She left the family with a broken arm and broken nose, when I was just six years old.

My brother and I grew up pretty much unsupervised and on our own, and, eventually fell in with the wrong types, which led to us getting into trouble on a regular basis. Seven years later, in 1962, when my mother finally was able to return to rescue us, we moved to Toronto. Unfortunately, in Toronto, we fell in with the same element and continued to get into trouble.

When my best friend, Pinky, suggested we investigate the JCCC, I already was a seasoned, streetwise, street-fighting teenager, with no real direction in life. My introduction to the art of karate-do was the thing that personally saved my life. By beginning to learn about the power of mental discipline through a safe, organized class structure, with dedicated instructors and regular structured physical training, I was able to turn my life completely around. Karate-do has given me that, and a great way of life that I will take to my grave.

KUNIO MURAYAMA

A SOULFUL JOURNEY

Murayama Sensei was born on June 30, 1944, in Miyagi, Japan. A direct student of Manzo Iwata Sensei, the young Murayama made great progress in his karate while studying for an economics degree. His hard work and dedication to the art of karate was recognized by Master Iwata, who eventually invited him to become his uchi-deshi (live-in disciple). This great honor allowed Murayama Sensei to experience his master's great wealth of knowledge, as taught him directly by Kenwa Mabuni, founder of the Shito Ryu style. Murayama continued his training at Tokyo University even after his graduation in 1966. He captained his university karate team for two years more before leaving Japan in 1970.

Having earned his Menkyo (teaching license), Murayama Sensei sought a teaching career in the noble art he had grown to love and began his work to promote the Shito-Kai organization, quickly developing a large following through his work and growing reputation as a world-class coach, WKF official, karateka and teacher. Now in his fifth decade of study, Shihan Murayama Kunio is a respected master of Karate-do and a leader for the art of Shito Ryu around the world.

How was the training in your beginnings in the art?

The training during my early days was far from easy. Our sempai used to push us very hard. They knew that only by breaking our bodies would our true spirit come up so we could show how strong we were. This is part of the old traditional approach to Budo and Japanese martial arts. Karate and other

Japanese arts really started to develop after World War II. The Japanese spirit was that one from the war and every activity you did was related to the development of your spirit. All Karate training then and now should be structured on the basis of the fighting spirit a warrior should have. Then karate becomes a kind of model laboratory that teaches us how to survive in the outside-budo world. And even Karate must follow the path of the laws of Universe, the same laws that dictate the movements of the body or the four seasons.

What can you tell us about your teacher Master Manzo Iwata?

Shihan Manzo Iwata was well known for his in-depth and comprehensive understanding of Mabuni Kenwa's Shito-Ryu system. Later, following an introduction by Kenwa Mabuni to his friend Fujita Seiko, Iwata also learned Daien Ryu Jojustu and Nanban Satto Ryu Kempo, among other disciplines for which Fujita Seiko was renowned. He was a very special man and a dedicated karateka. His ethic as a human being was outstanding and that probably is the reason why Grandmaster Kenwa Mabuni chose him as one of his top disciples. Iwata Sensei dedicated all his life to the study and development of Shito Ryu karate. He is directly responsible for the perpetuation around the world of the style developed by Kenwa Mabuni. Sensei Iwata's non-political approach to karate made people willing to exchange knowledge and techniques with him. His son Genzo Iwata Sensei is one of the technical directors of the World Shito Kai Federation.

What is the first lesson that all practitioners should learn?

Do not make a "decision" of what karate is or is not. You must walk the walk before you can decide what it is. Some people have preconceived ideas and notions of what the art is and this attitude limits their progress. Don't think that everybody has the same reason to train. Some want physical conditioning, others health, others sport, etc. … Everyone has a different purpose. Karate offers many faces that we can use to improve ourselves as individuals.

What do you think are the major misconceptions about the art of karate, in general terms?

There are some but I would mention a few. Many practitioners think that in the past, the old masters had the single techniques isolated in a kihon format first, and later they were put into kata format. Actually, it is the opposite. The techniques were extracted from the kata to develop the kihon. Then, when the level of the isolated techniques (kihon) improved, the overall kata performance got better.

Another general misconception is that the karate techniques we train in kihon have to be used exactly the same in a free-style or self-defense situation. This idea is not correct. The practitioner uses the "mold" of kihon to bring a certain level of body mechanics and technical skill, but once these already are part of the karateka, the technique flows and is expressed in a natural way. One example of this is the hikite. In actual combat, we don't do "hikite." The hikite training is for other things and has its place, but not in a free-style sparring or a real self-defense situation.

How much protection (pads, gloves, etc.) do you think should be used in karate competition?

The safety of the practitioners is always a priority, or at least it should be. I don't think competitors should look like "robocop," though. But coming from a traditional training, I think sometimes is important to spar with no gloves, pads, or protections of any kind. This bring us to the feeling of "empty hand" karate. We must be able to hit hard without hurting our hands or feet, and also think that if we are hit by a punch or a kick, no pads will prevent us from being hurt.

Do you teach the same art that you practice?

I do. The techniques that I teach are the same techniques that I personally practice. Karate is a very complex art but its difficulty lies in the perfection of the simple techniques.

Are there any aspects where Japanese are physically different than Causasians?

Well, the bodies are little different but I think maybe the difference was more in the old days because of the traditions. Japanese always sat on seiza a lot during the day, so hips tend to be stronger; also, ankles used to be more flexible in Japanese people because of the sandals/slippers, but these are very small differences and the mastery in karate has absolutely nothing to do with that.

Do you think kata is a useful tool in order to perform well in kumite or self-defense?

Due to the fact that sport competition is getting more popular, the amount of techniques used in actual sparring is being reduced to those that actually can score a point in competition. Kumite is not competition sparring. Kumite allows more techniques that won't ever be permitted in a sport contest. So we should clearly differentiate between sport shiai-kumite division and karate jyu-kumite. Kata, when studied correctly, truly is a library for kumite or sparring. Kata has many fighting principles and concepts that can be used both in jyu-kumite and self-defense situations. The problem lies in the fact that many people who perform kata well and are great in kata competition never researched and analyzed the combat principles intrinsic to the kata. They never applied them in a sparring situation. Many, strategies, rhythms, and tactics in kumite come from kata principles. But not everybody recognizes them as part of kata ... they just learned them as "sparring."

What should be the main physical goal of karate training?

The main physical goal should be to produce the maximum power with the best possible body mechanics. Try to produce the maximum output from your body. That is the key. The only way to achieve that is to dedicate yourself to constant drilling and training of the basics, to correct and intense training of the fundamental techniques of the art. Once this point is a constant in your karate fundamental techniques, then everything falls into place. Kata becomes strong and powerful and kumite seems easy and natural. Always stress the basic and simple training and don't think too much about intellectualizing things. Do it instead of spending time trying to label things and understanding the physics of your body. This will come naturally if you do enough training.

What is your personal training schedule?

I do a lot of teaching so I do repeat basic movements many times. I do have time for my personal training that I follow according to my physical conditions. I do emphasize more stretching and above all the natural approach to karate that Shito Ryu is based on. I would like to emphasize that what is really important is not the technique you do in your training but the thought behind it. That, and the time you invest in it, makes you better. So right thought or state-of-mind and quality training time is the key, no matter what your age may be. There is no other magic formula or secret.

How has modern society and education changed the way karate is taught today?

To begin with, people today have a different kind of life compared to what we had many years ago. The young generation has more commodities that we had. Their families in general are better off than previous generations, so they have to work less. The idea of "constant sacrifice" for things is simply not there as it used to be. This affects the way young people approach their karate training today. You tell them to do a gyaku-tsuki 1,000 times and they will look at you funny. These changes in the society and culture are the main reasons for the differences between our old generation and the younger ones.

What do you think about Karate getting into the Olympics?

The development of Karate as a sport may be seen as taking the art away from its roots. Competition is only one part of karate and only a few of the people who practice karate actually are involved in sport competition.

The great benefit would be a contact point with a bigger audience around the world. Only then, and through the idea of sport, can people eventually learn more about what underlies the sport technically and spiritually. Also, parents would see karate as a possibility for their children to become worldwide recognized athletes. This would bring more people to the dojos around the world and it would be a great opportunity to teach people about the true values of karate as an art and a way of life.

One of the stronger criticisms of sport karate is that if we focus only on the competition aspect, only those techniques used in sport activities will be emphasized in training. All attitudes and strategies will be suited for competition and that will bring a serious deficiency in the overall balance of karate as an art. Competition is good and is healthy, but we always need to remember that karate is for one's life and not only for a few years. Do karate for yourself; always look after yourself. Don't think only in terms of the activity but in terms of "you" as an individual. The tradition of karate will be lost totally in the future if there are not instructors and students left to keep to the traditional ways.

Some people think traditional martial arts and/or karate have very little value for street situations because the practice is not reality-based.

Whoever is saying that shows how little knowledge they have of the martial arts. That is a very narrow-minded attitude to have. But in the end, it all boils down to the individual – the way you train martial arts, and your instructor may have an important influence in that. But it is still down to "you" as an individual whether or not you can make it work in a real situation.

What kind of mental preparation would you recommend?

The best mental preparation is to have confidence in what you do; and that confidence only comes from knowing that your art and training methods work.

Do you think kata competition may push the student to focus only in the "external mold" for the form?

Kata competition is a great challenge for any karateka, but there are things we can't forget about. You can get someone to copy the perfect technique. This technique might look great to the untrained eye, even to some trained eyes ... but it's purely cosmetic. It is important to understand and maintain the essential principles of the form without losing track of its concepts. You can be a world kata champion and have a deep understanding of

the essence of the kata you practice. There is no reason why not. I don't see any conflict; one is sport, the other is art and a challenging personal journey.

Shito Ryu incorporates the naha-te and the shuri-te aspects of Okinawa, and also tomari-te. How does that translate into the physical technique?

The hard and soft aspects of karate are intrinsic to the style developed by Kenwa Mabuni. When we think of strength, we have to remember that there are many forms of "strength" and that not all are the same. This is the case with the "soft" aspect of the art. From stances and blocks to punches and kicks, the art of Shito Ryu has many different ways of expressing the principles of hard and soft.

I don't think that any style of karate is "soft" or "hard" by nature. When we are young, we have to train hard, no matter what the style is. When we get older, we tend to use the strength and physical force in different ways, so our karate may look "softer" when actually it is not. The different breathing patterns also play a very important part of how these forces are applied in actual practice.

Do you think some people try to rely too much on who there is teacher to gain personal credibility in the world of Martial Arts?

Definitely! Karate is what karate is, and it doesn't matter who your teacher is because it won't do any good to you if you can't pull it off individually. I see many like to "drop" their teacher's name in order to get respect, but that doesn't mean anything in front of a real martial artist. I like to say that karate was here before me and will be here after me, so all that I can do if train hard and use it as a tool to improve

myself. My teacher can't do that for me. We simply are not our teachers' men or women. At the end, it is all up to us as individuals.

Is there any message you would like to send to the karate practitioners or martial artist in general?

Essentially, all martial arts are the same. The challenge and the personal journey is the same no matter what style you practice. In martial arts training, there is no ending, no completion. It is a constant and endless challenge and you always have to be questioning yourself as a karateka and martial artist and never be satisfied with your technical level and understanding of the art. Proper training is essential for progress but having the right mind is even more important.

HIDETOSHI NAKAHASHI

BUDO SIMPLICITY

When you meet Nakahashi Sensei you feel nothing less than the energy of someone seriously devoted to the study of the art of Shito Ryu karate-do. He started his training at a very early age in Kobe and became an extremely understanding, approachable and respectful teacher. His long years of experience have allowed him to internalize the important moral aspects of Budo and use them in his daily life. He is Internationally recognized as a Shito Ryu authority.

Nakahashi Sensei has spent a lifetime acquiring knowledge and experience of the art that he found as his way of life. What sets him apart is that he is ready and willing to not only train hardcore martial artists, but also individuals interested in personal development as well. He is a knowledgeable and fascinating man, full of interesting stories, and brimming with a positive attitude towards teaching. For him, spirit and heart are the most important attributes in karate training. "In order to be the best", Nakahashi Sensei says, "you must have the warrior's spirit and the warrior's heart.

Sensei, when did you start your karate training and when you arrived in France?

I was around eleven years old, when I got into Kenshukai Shito Ryu in Kobe, Japan but it wasn't until the year 1976 that I arrived to France.

Who was the instructor there?

Sensei Ogasahara Eiji, direct student of Kenwa Mabuni. He passed away on March 11, 2011.

Sensei, how do you see the art of karate today?

Obviously, after many years of development in different societies around the world, the art of karate

has shaped itself in different ways. We have the traditional approach and we have the sportive element to it. Sport has become a very integral part of what karate is today and is this aspect what really attracts youth to it. The young people of today are different than the young of 30 or 40 years ago. They have different goals, different upbringing, different culture, and all that affects how karate can be taught and is perceived by young individuals. Today, you simply can't have a teenager to punch 1,000 punches in a one-hour class; you can't have them do 500 punches on the makiwara and have their knuckles bleeding through the session, etc. These are different times. Youth is attracted to the sportive elements more but we should understand how to teach them the true principles and values of Budo. Discipline, dedication, respect, ethics, good manners, etc. are things that are part of Budo and there is no reason why we can't teach those today.

People always talk about karate-do as a "way of life" but how can we transfer karate training into our lives?

Karate does not end with kihon, kata and kumite training. Karate training is also outside the dojo but in order to get there the training at the dojo needs to be correct and above all, the mental training at the dojo has to be the appropriate. When you train, you do focus only in the training, your mind does not wonder about your life outside, your family, your job, etc. Concentrate on your practice only.

When you say the "dojo kun" at the beginning of a class and perform "mokuso", you must remember that this is the tool we use to "leave behind" our life outside. From that moment on, it is only karate training. Once training is done, we have developed something; the mind is clearer; the problems we had before seem different. Karate mental training takes us back to the samurai concept of going back to the simplest way of approaching our life and our problems.

What are the most important training aspects we should take outside of the dojo as far as self-defense?

After training we have to go back to the outside world. That world is not very nice and there is a lot of violence in it. We need to be aware of what is outside and who are those around us. We should never start trouble just because we know how to handle a physical confrontation. Never put yourself into a dead-end kind of situation where it is not possible to face your opponent. Nevertheless, we must be prepared to face an enemy at all times, in case we are attacked. A real martial artist never fights with people of a lower mental level. The best karateka is never in a street fight in his whole life.

Do you think it is important to study other arts?

This is a very interesting but tricky question. Definitely, I think any student must dedicate all his/her training to one art. Jumping from one style to another will refrain from reaching the higher levels in the chosen art. Sensei or teachers may research or study other elements that can be complementary to the art they are teaching but for personal investigation and development. You must to find a "common thread" that actually gives sense to your study or research. Trying to mix or put together different arts is another story. Unfortunately, this is a common practice these days.

What are the main differences between Bujutsu and Budo?

In Bujutsu we learn how to defeat an opponent. Budo basic teaching is to learn how to "one's cutting of oneself". This means that we have to realize that the opponent is oneself. This is the highest level.

How would you describe Soke Mabuni Kenei's way of Shito Ryu?

The way Mabuni Kenei Soke was expressing the art of Shito Ryu was different to other teachers and instructors that I had the opportunity to meet. He had a personal way of explaining the fundamental concepts and principles of the style and put them in a very "natural" way in order to express the physical technique. I was very honored and fortunate of spending a lot of time with him. I will always be grateful for his teachings not only about the physical techniques of karate but also about the "do" aspect of the art.

And, what about his approach to real self-defense?

He did a lot of research and found ways of doing many techniques in a more natural way. His studies about the wrist locks, armlocks, etc. were very interesting. He used techniques that if we judge based only on photo or video, would be impossible to understand, but once you felt his action in person you started wondering how he could do those techniques in that simple but effective way.

He developed a clear connection between the kata training and the self-defense application. Traditionally, we look at kata and kumite as separate aspects of karate, and to a certain extent they truly are but, the self-defense aspect is not kumite "per se". Self-defense is a whole different aspect of karate-do. It has nothing to do with the sportive version of kumite that we can see in tournaments but neither has any resemblance with the other versions of kumite that we practice in the dojo. There are some kumite elements that can be transferred to the karate self-defense approach but you need to know what are those and how to transfer them correctly. Mabuni Kenei Soke was extremely good at this.

What aspects did he like to emphasize?

The natural movement of the body. The use of simplicity, economy of motion and effectiveness in every action. He always applied the principle of "Tenshin Happo" or eight directions of movement and the five principles of the defense. Sometimes we tend to block and the counter the action. Mabuni Soke emphasized to hit directly [if possible] instead of spending time in blocking and parrying. Please note that not always this is possible, but still "simplicity" should be the main goal in our technical actions. One element that he stressed constantly was "directness". If a movement usually takes three steps in order to be completed but you can "simplify" the action and cut it to two or even only one, that is the secret for efficiency in self-defense.

SHITO RYU MASTERS

How do you feel about his passing?

Obviously, I was very sad when I found out. Then I remembered all our conversations... he knew his days were coming to an end. He lived his life like a "budoka". He was aware his final was close and embraced it with no regrets. This is the "way of the samurai". No regrets. He knew that the Shito Ryu legacy was assured and the style developed by his father was going to exist forever. It is important that all those who were touched by him will keep his legacy and teachings not only in our hearts but also in our dojo and amongst our students. Now the responsibility is on us. It is our duty to fulfill it as true "budoka".

How do you look at the old karate masters? What can we learn from them?

It is important for us to be humble and be mentally mature to understand their legacy. We need a critical eye to see this precisely. This critical eye is based on true honesty as karateka, as budoka, and allow us to see ourselves accurately.

What advise would you give us in the development of the technique?

In the development of the technical skills there are three stages that all practitioners should remember: First we must emphasize what we can call "big feeling" of the technique. Second, the power and third, pure speed. The idea is that first the mind leads, then the feeling follows the mind and finally the mind follows the feeling. What we understand as power, speed and proper form it comes from the "feeling". We should not start simply with the technical "form" but with the "feeling" of it. That "feeling" pulls the body into the proper form, and that proper form brings power and eventually natural speed. Many teachers forget to start the skill development of the technique with the "feeling" aspect and they jump straight into the many details of the actual form of the movement. This prevents the students to understand the importance of a big feeling in training and practice.

What about the actual form of the technique?

Every technique has many different aspects that must be developed in order to make the body parts to work together to generate power. Nevertheless, the most important element at this stage is to understand the use of our hips as the center and the connecting "piece" between the lower and the upper body. We have to use that big feeling I mentioned before to make the hips move every time. Your mind, your feeling and your hips must work and move together in every action. Then we add the rest of the technical details. That is how the technique can be developed to its maximum potential.

And how we develop the speed?

The speed should be related to the feeling and relation with the opponent. Pure speed is not always efficient. Whatever is that we do, we must refrain from eliminating parts of the technique in order to make the move faster. This will make the movement weaker. A fast move is based on the elimination of all the unnecessary parts of the technique, both mental and physical. You must always adhere strictly to the precise form. This is the true high level karate.

How the art of Zen and the Bushido is related to the art of karate?

Samurai had a very strong influence from Zen that was the "tool" they used to prepare for battle and facing death. Zen is not a religion. For a samurai, the sword represents justice, therefore it had to be a right reasons for him to draw the blade and kill. Otherwise, he was cutting his own ignorance and stupidity.

Zen teaches that there is no only a world or universe outside but also inside of us. This feeling is the foundation of Zen and all martial arts. As budoka we must to remove that distinction between us and the universe. The universe lies in our minds and our mind is in the universe. All the answers are inside of us, we simply need to learn the tools to discover the truth.

How do you see karate helping to the practitioners in our modern society?

The modern man has many complex and confusing philosophical questions. The answer to all those must be resolved using the perspective of a primitive and simple man. This is one of the main teachings of Budo: when troubled by abstract problems of today, think as you were living in a primate stage. Only this way we will find a simple and direct answer to our problems. This is related to karate training…if we have technical problems…we should go back to the basics.

How we should approach our karate training?

Karate training is a life long journey, like a marathon, not a 100 meters dash. He who maintains the proper technique, the best physical shape, the samurai spirit and vital health over the span of his life "wins". Nothing pains me more than to see a bright young talented spark in karate burn out after a few brief years, the victim of his own ambitions. Knowing your strengths and weaknesses and balancing your goal with your personal limitations are the key to be the best you can be.

Finally, what advise would you like to give to teachers and students?

It is important for all to understand that as a group we have a big value and represent a huge contribution to the society we are living in. If we look only to our personal benefit, then there is nothing positive to leave for others to benefit from. We must ask ourselves: "Why are we practicing for?" We need to know the "why"; the reason of our training. Like a good samurai, we must try to make our lives simpler, our associations and groups too: especially administrators and dojo teachers. Simplicity is the key factor. Don't forget that training is the most important factor… everything else is secondary..

172

YOSHINAO NANBU

WALKING HIS OWN PATH

ONE OF THE MOST GIFTED AND TALENTED KARATE PRACTITIONERS OF HIS TIME, SENSEI NANBU DECIDED TO BREAK FROM THOSE WHO CAME BEFORE HIM. WALKING HIS OWN PATH, HE DEVELOPED ORIGINAL KARATE METHODS AND STYLES THAT ARE A TRUE REFLECTION OF HIS PERSONAL BUDO JOURNEY.

HE IS A TRUE WORLDWIDE ICON OF JAPANESE KARATE. A PIONEER BY ANY MEASURE, THIS OUTSTANDING KARATE-KA WAS BORN 1943 IN KOBE, JAPAN. HE MOVED TO FRANCE AS A YOUNG MAN TO BREAK INTERNATIONAL BARRIERS AND SHOW THE EUROPEANS THE TRUE ART OF KARATE. RECOGNIZED BY THE LATE TANI SENSEI AS "ONE OF THE MOST GIFTED AND TALENTED PRACTITIONERS OF HIS TIME," SENSEI NANBU DECIDED TO BREAK AWAY FROM THE RESTRICTIONS OF THE PAST AND DEVELOP HIS OWN KARATE METHOD. HIS OPEN MIND AND FLEXIBLE SENTIMENTS ABOUT OTHER ARTS ALLOWED HIM TO INCORPORATE PRINCIPLES AND CONCEPTS NEVER USED IN KARATE-DO BEFORE. THIS ADAPTABLE ATTITUDE REVOLUTIONIZED THE APPROACH TO THE TEACHING OF KARATE. TODAY HE IS RECOGNIZED AROUND THE WORLD AS ONE OF THE FOREMOST AUTHORITIES IN THE ART OF JAPANESE KARATE. A TRUE WARRIOR OF BUDO, SENSEI NANBU HAS CONQUERED EVERY CHALLENGE HE HAS EVER FACED.

How did you get involved in the budo arts?

My family has always been involved in budo. My great grandfather was a great yokozuna, the most prestigious title in sumo circles. My uncle, Mr. Togashi, was a 9th degree black belt in judo and my other uncle, Mr. Yano, a master in the Japanese fencing art of kendo. My father was a 5th black belt degree in judo and an expert in the weaponry art of naginata. I was already a shodan at 19 when I entered in the University of Osaka. It was there where I met Tani Sensei, at that time a 9th dan in shito-ryu and one of the stylistic leaders in the world. Master Tani developed the method called shukokai, which is a personal approach to the shito-ryu style he learned under Kenwa Mabuni.

SHITO RYU MASTERS

How was the training at that time?

Extremely tough. Very hard and physically demanding. Every day we had to do 1,000 front kicks with kiai, and punch the makiwara thousands of times, not even stopping when our knuckles were bleeding. There was no way out. No excuses to quit. I was rapidly promoted to captain of the team. In 1963 I became All-Japan University champion. This was a very difficult title to achieve then. At that moment there was a total of 1,250 competitors. I remember my opponent in the final match had his gi torn apart from my front kicks! Due to this victory I was awarded the very special Medallion of "Grand Merite," a coveted national recognition presented by the president of the greatest student association in Japan, Mr. Ohama.

When did you decide to travel to Europe?

Mr. Henry Plee invited me to go to France and teach the art in Europe. I was very excited! I was on my way on the journey of my life. I left the university and went to France in 1964. I began teaching for Monsieur Henry Plee at his school in Montagne Saint-Genevieve. It was there I saw many new things for the first time in my life that opened my point of view as individual.

You competed in the championships held in France and Europe at that time. A Japanese instructor living in Europe and competing against the Westerners was very unusual. How did it feel?

It was an exceptional thing but I really wanted to test myself and I promised Sensei Plee that I was going to compete. I didn't have any problem with that. I know that it is very unusual to see a Japanese sensei enter a competition and fight against those who supposedly know less karate. But I never considered myself better than any other human being so I did not have a problem being a Japanese karate instructor in Europe and competing against Europeans. I didn't want people to respect me simply because I was Japanese and supposedly knew more than Westerners about karate. I wanted to earn respect and so I put myself to test. Only good things came out of that, The European karate community respected me highly and supported me greatly in anything I did.

I kept my Japanese and traditional approach to competition, though. My spirit said, "I have no right to lose a match." I was carrying a sword with me to all competitions to remind me that I should die if I lost a match. I won almost all the major titles at that time and gained a lot of respect from all French and European karate-ka. I remember that in the final match of the International Cup (forerunner of the European Championships) I faced and defeated the great Domique Valera, who was occasionally a student of mine! It was a great match and I have a lot of respect for him. I kicked him very hard in the stomach with a mae-geri and Dominque didn't even blink! Then he kicked me back really hard to my stomach. I kept a poker face. No sign of pain. Later on, in the locker room, I opened my gi and my stomach was black and blue. I looked at him and said, "Really good kick." Valera opened his gi and his stomach was also all bruised and he says: "Not bad, not bad at all." Domique Valera was an exceptional karate-ka – very talented. All I have is great respect for him.

When you quit competition?

It was in 1966. A little bit later I went back to Japan and Tani Sensei proposed me to be the official representative of shukokai for Europe and Africa. I accepted the offer and put myself into the shukokai shito-ryu style of karate in these two continents. Around the same time and during my visits to Japan I had the opportunity to train with several other people who opened my eyes to different conceptual approaches to martial art techniques and philosophies. It was very rewarding experience for me, not only as a martial artist but as a human being as well.

What happened after?

I have always been an individual in constant progression. In 1972, and after years of researching, fighting and training, I realized that I had many ideas about what I was doing. My martial arts journey has always been in constant evolution. The same year I decided to create the sankukai style. Of course, Tani Sensei wasn't happy about it and declined to see me again. I never meant to offend or hurt anyone but I had to be true to myself and follow my own path in life, regardless of what other's people interest may be. Sankukai was a very natural evolution of the shito-ryu method I was practicing already. That step in my life was not a way of saying, "I want to break free and do my own thing." It was a natural progression in my budo journey and something I couldn't deny. If I did denied that evolution I would have been denying my own existence. Unfortunately, some people didn't see it that way.

Sankukai was a great and almost immediate success, probably because of my established reputation in Europe. People loved it and karate-ka from all over the world realized how suitable that style was for competition. In 1973 I did 11 tours to teach the art. The lateral footwork (tai-sabaki) was the main principle in the fighting techniques. Using the opponent's force and momentum to counter his action is a wiser approach than using force against force as other karate-do styles use. In 1976, and due to the great acceptance of the style, I established the official World Sankukai Association to regulate the style in 43 countries. The same year we held the World Cup in Nice, France, and the World Championships in Monte Carlo, Monaco.

When did you first publicly demonstrate what you describe as "nanbudo?"

It was in 1978, when we were holding the 2nd Sankukai World Championships, that I decided to demonstrate something that I had worked on for many years without mentioning to anyone. I showed nanbudo to the world – The Way of Nanbu. Once again, it was a natural thing in my progression as a martial artist.

You retired for over a year in the south of France, in Cap d'Ail, Monaco. How this retirement affect your perception of the art and the direction of your research?

I was extremely happy with the success of sankukai around the world. If money was my reason to do things, I could have stuck to sankukai because it was working perfectly, but once again, my goal is different. Being isolated for over a year, Mother Nature became my teacher. I observed how nature works and tried to adapt those principles to the art of nabudo. The beginnings of nanbudo were very difficult because most all my sankukai students and affiliates around the world didn't follow me into the new expression of the art. In 1978, when I decided to drop sankukai, I was shocked and couldn't understand why they weren't following me.

I was not sure of the future due to the fact that the majority of my students weren't at my same level of development – both physical and spiritual. This is understandable. I accepted that, but I was not going to allow personal interest to prevent me from growing as a human being. Today, after starting the same process again, the art of nanbudo is recognized worldwide and practiced in more than 50 countries.

What is nanbudo?

Nanbudo is not a synthesis of different martial art styles and it is not an eclectic approach to budo either. It is a complete art. At first sight, due to the physical techniques and elements involved, people may think it comprises karate, aikido, tai chi, Zen, and some other elements. But the art of nabudo goes beyond that simplistic definition. Similar to a professional sport car designer who calculates the wind and speed to come up with a more aerodynamic shape for a new car, I have developed a mechanical way to use the human body in a wiser and safer way. The wind is still strong so the design is still evolving, like nature itself.

What is your opinion of the competition aspects of karate-do?

It depends on the individual. The bottom line is that if you know how to use it properly, the art of karate-do is a school for the formation of human character. Competition is simply a game that emulates the element of surviving in life. It keeps it real and in proper perspective.

How does the nanbu-taisho exercises affect the student's health?

While learning and practicing these exercises, there are considerable benefits to health, largely due to the strengthening on the internal musculature and increased blood circulation. It is particularly beneficial to the functioning of the heart, but there have also been improvements in some of my students in cases of asthma, and other illness. For this reason, many people of all ages take up nanbu-taisho just for their health, and some instructors teach it for health only. There is more to nanbudo than just a fighting.

The martial applications themselves are swift, subtle and very lethal. They are fully effective but cannot be learned or used effectively until a considerable groundwork of exercises and form have been laid down. In nanbudo, as in any other martial art, the fighter is only as good as they make themselves. Success will depend on the amount of effort personally expended. Some people make good fighters and some people do not. My method is similar to other martial arts — it contains the knowledge, the methods and the skills, some unusual, for fighting — but the rest depends on the student and on the student's patience, endurance and personality in confronting and dealing with violence. Possibly the only aspect in which nanbudo differs from most other martial arts is that everyone can reach their own level of strength and self-defense ability without getting hurt.

In martial arts systems like nanbudo or nanbu-taisho, the difference between one whose mind wanders and the student who is attentive is much more apparent than in any other style. Not only will the inattentive one get low marks, but what is more important, they will most likely be a candidate to have bones broken when a free-style fighting situation occurs. A person must always confront fear head-on, otherwise it will overwhelm them.

What is your opinion about individuals developing their own martial art style?

I know people who were white belts ten years ago and now they have their own styles and they are tenth degree black belts or whatever rank they've given themselves. It takes more than that to develop a new approach to the ancient arts. There is a price that has to be paid and some dues, too. The eclectic approach is very convenient for those who don't want to pay their dues. Definitely, this is not what I did when I created nanbudo. Everybody knows where I came from, what I did, what I accomplished as a young karate-ka, and the years I deeply studied the arts before expressing my own perception of the principles of budo.

Can you imagine life without karate?

That's not possible. Karate and budo are not just aspects of my life but very major parts of it. Learning karate has to become a way of life. I have shaped my life toward learning karate and budo. From this, one learns to marshal one's time in other areas — greater benefits come without the individual realizing what is happening inside. Budo is a vehicle for a deep transformation inside the human spirit. Don't get me wrong, nothing is free and an individual has to work hard towards that goal.

How do you think the modern approach to martial arts schools has affected the teaching methods used by the instructors?

I truly believe that those instructors who give into the demands for modernization are in reality cut-

ting off their noses to spite their faces, and are destroying their greatest students by ignoring spiritual assets without which the martial arts become no more than murderous forms of personal combat. If a student really wanted just that, and nothing else, the man would buy a knife, or a gun and would have a greater instant killing power than the average shodan – and the shodan's rank takes years of hard work, bruises and personal sacrifice to earn. Yet even with all his achievements, the first dan is still no match for the gun. The black belt-holder hasn't been born, no matter what their rank, who can block a bullet, or even jump away from one. That's why the martial art teacher has to be an impeccable example of integrity. Is that not what Western man wishes more than anything else – the ability to trust his fellow man? How can anyone have faith in a person who, to paraphrase the Western scriptures, "Sold his birthright for a mess of pottage?" Our culture, our discipline, our moral values and traditions make us what we are. If for the sake of our student's fees, we were to throw all this away, then we would be proven false because we had shown by our actions that we do not believe in our own birthright.

Do you see differences between Westerners and Japanese when it comes to the art of nanbudo?

To me, all individuals are the same. It is true, though, that I have found that Westerners are much better trainees in my system than are the Japanese – they seem to better understand what each movement means. They are more naturally curious and are continually asking questions. Why, I don't know. I guess it is part of the exuberance of the Western character! After all these years living and teaching in the

Western world, I have learned to look and feel in a very different way. I find myself in a balanced spot, where I don't see good or bad in the Western or Eastern society or culture. Both have good and bad things and the citizens are a reflection of these attitudes. We are no more than the product of our societies, but I truly believe that a thinking individual can go beyond barriers and cultural boundaries to really find the truth and the essence of their existence.

Are you a traditionalist?

That is a good question considering all the barriers I broken in my past and how much I have evolved since I began training karate! If by traditionalist you mean someone who is teaching the same techniques he learned 35 years ago then I am not a traditionalist, because everybody knows that the physical techniques I teach today are extremely different than those I used to teach when I was doing shito-ryu or sankukai. As far as the moral and ethical values of budo, I definitely want to preserve those, so to that extent you may say that I am a traditionalist. To be honest, I don't know why people think that being a traditionalist is something wrong. Morality and ethics are something very important in order to have good citizen and a strong society. Creativity is not an excuse for blind rebelliousness. Disagreement for disagreement's sake is not being creative. Unfortunately, a lot of karate-ka with that attitude nowadays. The great Taisen Deshimaru wrote: "Life's problems are different for each of us, and each of us needs a different way of solving them. Therefore, each of us has to create his own method. If you imitate, you'll be wrong. You have to create yourself." Martial art is not different from life.

Where does the budo spirit lie?

Karate-do, nanbudo, and all martial arts in general is something that can only spring from within. Because of that, you should inspect yourself as you would a weapon and notice your strong points and weaknesses. This internal journey will make you a better human being. There is something I like to call your "sphere of influence." As human being, it is within this sphere of influence that you can be more efficient as an individual. You simply don't want to go beyond the boundaries of this sphere because all your true power and energy will be inefficient.

180

YUISHI NEGISHI

A MODERN SAMURAI

Born in Togichi, Japan, on December 7, 1940, Sensei Negishi started his karate training at age 15 under the great Shito-Ryu teacher Manzo Iwata, a direct disciple of founder Kenwa Mabuni. He was educated in a family where the code of samurai governed the house and strict disciple was enforced. Graduating in economics from Toyo University, he became the captain of the university karate team in 1964 and the head coach the year after. Negishi also studied Myata-ryu batto-jutsu directly from his grandfather, Kazuzyo Hasegawa. He was the President of Nippon Budo Sosei-Kai Shito-Ryu and the leader of the traditional school of Japanese tai-jitsu, Nippon Shinkyoku-Ryu Tai Jitsu, where he was the founder's 10th generation direct descendant. Although he taught both arts as separate entities, his dynamic approach created an effective mixture of hard karate power and soft tai-jitsu techniques.

How has karate evolved since you began training?

The art has evolved significantly, especially in the last 20 years or so. This evolution has affected the technical aspects of karate. For instance, when I began my training the conception of fighting distance was quite different. We used to train short techniques such as kizami tsuki or mae ashi geri because they were better for real fighting. Nowadays, since the emphases on karate's sportive aspects is bigger, the fighting distance is wider and most techniques are delivered by the rear hand and leg. This is a subtle change, but it affects the way the art is taught in many schools around the world. Karate should be taught as a complete martial art which allows individuals who feel so inclined, to compete, practice and train techniques that are suitable for sport competition.

Are these changes good or bad?

As I said before, it depends on goal of the student. If you're thinking only about a physical activity and not about self defense, then it's fine. But if your mind is focused on real self-defense, the sportive aspect of the karate won't help you much. In fact, it can be negative for your mental approach to real self-defense. Evolution is inevitable, but the direction this evolution takes depends on the final goal of each practitioner. As long as you know where you are going, it's fine. Just don't get upset when you find you're a karate champion who can't defend themselves in a real fight.

Why are there so many different karate styles today?

All these variations depend on the instructor's perception of how to perform a certain movement and how to apply it in combat. It's very often taken as fact that when an instructor is young he teaches very differently than when he is old. This simple factor has caused misunderstanding not only in karate, but in martial arts in general. A teacher's perspective changes with time and their overall perception of the art varies according to that. In most cases, however, the essence and principles are the same but the physical way of applying the concepts changes. The understanding about the functionality of the physical movement changes, therefore, the way of teaching it changes also. A karate-ka doesn't practice the art the same at age 25 years as he does at age 55. If he is an instructor, then you can be sure that his age will affect the way he teaches a technique he learned 30 years ago. It's called "maturity."

Are some styles better than others?

All karate is good. The best advice I can give is to focus on the art that you can best use. There are some karate styles that are more suitable for certain kinds of physical configuration and in the long term this can make a difference in the external appearance of your technique. For instance, goju-ryu is a style of karate-do that suits a short body. You can be 6'3" and be a great goju-ryu exponent, but from the external point of view, goju-ryu is a style that looks better on short people. But if you are tall and big and you really enjoy goju-ryu, you shouldn't avoid this art simply because it doesn't fit your body type? The bottom line is to train in the style you feel most comfortable doing. Enjoy your training and keep practicing even if many things don't make sense in the beginning. Time brings understanding in the art of karate - you need time in order to mature and see things that are not visible in the first years of training. You need patience to progress and to understand the deeper principles of the art. By sweating in your gi every day, you'll be closer to the union of the body and spirit. That's when you will see what the art is really about.

How much personal influence should an instructor incorporate into their teaching?

Everything! The teacher is a vehicle to preserve the art. The way the teacher sees the art, the way the teacher feels the art, and the way the teacher express the art is the only reference that the student has. Every single karate-do instructor in the world influences and changes the art in some way according to his personality and point of view. That's a logical thing. There is nothing wrong with that. The art is

nothing but the expression of the artist, and in this case the art of karate is a vehicle used by the karate-ka to express themselves. Duplicating what you have been taught without thinking and analyzing what you're doing, is just to follow blindly - that not the right attitude of budo. You are supposed to use the art to elevate and grow, but not to follow without thinking for yourself. In the true expression of any art form a copy has no worth, only originals have value.

Are you against the growing movement of sport karate?

Not really. Sport is a small part of karate. It can be used wisely to develop positive qualities in young practitioners - but if the teacher focuses too much on sport, students will be missing the whole picture. Training has to be balanced. Real fighting is very different from point fighting or sport competition, not only in physical techniques but also how both situations are approached mentally. Sport karate can only be practiced for a short time, but the martial art of karate can be practiced for your whole life.

What is your opinion on supplemental training like running and weight lifting?

Anything you can do to improve your health and strengthen your body for karate is good. Having a good training to improve your wind, using weights to develop muscles, and practicing yoga to improve flexibility is something I recommend to all practitioners. The problem comes when a student gets caught up in physical training at the expense of the time he trains in karate. Don't fool yourself, running a marathon, lifting weights, or practicing yoga one hour a day won't improve your karate - it won't make

SHITO RYU MASTERS

your gyaku-tsuki faster or your kata more precise. Karate is should come first, then if you have extra time to dedicate to these other training aspects the better for you. Don't substitute your technical karate training for running or lifting weights because you will be making a mistake. You must first develop a strong technical foundation before you consider spending time in other physical conditioning aspects. When you reach the rank of shodan or nidan, then perhaps you can go and develop purely physical areas such as strength - but not at the expense of substituting your karate classes for weight training sessions. A strong karate technique has nothing to do with the way your body looks. Physical appearance has nothing to do with real karate.

Why did the old masters change the original karate techniques so much?

It's hard to answer that question. Master Funakoshi used to practice karate forms with a high center of gravity and short hand movements, much like shito-ryu. Then Master Nakayama came along next and changed the positions and developed a different form of karate. He pushed the art of karate as a form of physical education, and I guess he decided to modify certain technical aspects to better serve his new goal.

Do you think kobudo training helps the karate practitioner?

I think so. The old bushi arts involved weapons training, not only empty-hand techniques. They were different elements of warrior training and education. Later on, all these different aspects were separated; but in the beginning a warrior was a "complete package." Training with traditional weapons helps students to develop important physical attributes that will improve their empty-hand techniques. In the process of learning how to use a weapon, the student uses the body in a very different way compared to the simpler empty-hand movements. The body works differently when you are using a bo than when you are performing gyaku-tsuki. The body rotation maybe be essentially the same, but the timing of the hip-turning has to match the speed of the weapon in order to get kime in the right moment. If hitting with the bo takes longer time than hitting with your fist, the synchronization of your body torque will have to be adjusted to that particular speed. Once you drop the weapon and go back to empty-hand, you'll find that the body moves more in sync with the technique. It's something very difficult to explain in words without being too technical. But those who train in both arts – kobudo and karate – will definitely understand what I'm trying to say.

The legendary goju-ryu karate master, Gogen Yamaguchi, said that for a total understanding of his style students should embrace yoga and shinto. Are there any special spiritual elements that need to be studied in shito-ryu karate?

Zen training is paramount for karate-do development. The spiritual aspect is very important when you are practicing Japanese karate. You need both to have the complete art. If you only focus on the physical techniques there will be many aspects you'll overlook in your personal journey toward mastery. Not paying attention to spiritual and mental development will limit your progress and evolution as a karate-ka. This is not only true for karate-do but for all styles of martial arts as well. You need to find a balance between your body and mind. The body is trained through demanding karate sessions of kihon, kata and kumite, but the mind should be trained equally to counterbalance the physical side - this is only achieved through serious and dedicated Zen training.

Do you think the media is responsible for the public perception of martial arts?

Karate and martial arts are the result of many years of training, research and evolution. They contain cultivation and refinement, but unfortunately, instead of trying to preserve the heritage that our ancestors preserved for us – magazines and promoters have looked for the easiest and fastest ways to make money and have moved away from the basic principles of budo. Movies also share the blame in this. Young practitioners think that martial arts are all about Bruce Lee screaming and yelling with nunchakus flying all over the place. This is not real budo and I don't believe this kind of attitude is good for future generations.

In a few years, the kids that were educated under this modern philosophy will open their own schools and become teachers. What do you think they are going to teach? If you don't educate youth in the way of budo, don't expect real martial arts to survive - maybe the new approaches of full contact fighting but not true budo. If there is a lack of proper education, martial arts will suffer in the future.

Is it necessary to travel to Japan to learn karate?

Karate is a great art and its sportive aspects will help many young people to achieve what they want in life. Japanese aren't necessarily better than Caucasians, but they definitely understand more about the traditions of budo. If you want to go to Japan to experience the culture and learn the traditions of budo, then do it because you won't get that anywhere else. But if you are only interested in the physical side of the art, just find a good teacher and follow his guidance. These days, it is common knowledge that the majority of the great Japanese teachers are living outside of Japan.

Can a practitioner's physique make a difference in their kata or kumite?

It's true that a medium-sized person will make a kata "look better," but this has nothing to do with the true kata performance of a budo practitioner. The physical appearance may affect a kata competition by influencing the judges, but it doesn't mean anything to a karate-do kata practitioner. In kumite, a practitioner with long limbs will have a certain advantage against someone who is shorter. But the shorter karate-ka may be more dangerous in a real fight. For karate competition your physique may be a determining factor, but for karate-do as part of budo, definitely not.

How important is bunkai in the study of kata?

Kata in an integral part of the art of karate. In fact, karate can't be totally understood without a thorough study of kata. The analysis of the different karate techniques found in kata is very important. You need to understand that bunkai is structured in different levels of application, with varying difficulty. The first step is when you apply the physical movement from kata directly, without changing the movements. This very basic application opens the student's mind to how karate uses the technical mechanics for physical movements. The next step is to incorporate the principles found in that particular technique and apply a more creative approch without totally breaking away from the kata movement. This phase allows the student's creativity to come out. Finally, and only after you totally understand the intrinsic principles of that particular movement, you can enter into what we can call a "non-classical" phase. In this phase you use the principles of the technique but in a totally free format. You have already learned the principle, and now your application of the original movement doesn't look like that kata movement anymore. The principle is there - the main concept of the movement found in the kata is still there - but

your external application is different. That is when you can say you have truly transcended kata. Reaching this level of skill and understanding requires many years of dedicated training and study.

What is your advice to future karate generations?

I'm not planning on leaving anytime soon! Kidding aside, it is very important that all the top karate teachers in the world understand that the future of the art is in their hands. Whatever they put in their students' hearts is what will drive the art of karate in the future. Students should always remember that karate-do is not simply a sport; there is a sportive aspect but karate is not just a sport. Karate-do is budo and as such it has to be internalized. Budo is for the rest of your life and it transcends trophies and medals. Budo is about life. If students remember this simple fact everything else will fall into place because budo teaches your how to practice and lead your own life. Once you understand budo, the rest is easy. The tricky part is for teachers to make sure the students really understand budo, so the important values are preserved for future generations. Preserving physical techniques is not a big deal, but preserving the right attitude takes a dedicated effort. This is our responsibility as leaders of the martial art of karate.

188

TED RABINO

IN THE SPIRIT OF SHITO KAI

SENSEI TED RABINO BEGAN HIS JUDO TRAINING IN 1966 UNDER WATANABE SENSEI AND HIS KARATE TRAINING UNDER BOTH HIS BROTHERS SAM (SHORINJI KEMPO) AND PETE RABINO (SHURI-RYU). PETE RABINO WAS ONE OF ROBERT TRIAS'S FIRST CHIEF INSTRUCTORS IN THE USKA. TED RABINO RECEIVED HIS 1ST DAN IN KARATE IN 1972. ON THE RECOMMENDATION OF MR. TRIAS, SENSEI RABINO STARTED HIS TRAINING IN THE SHITO RYU STYLE OF KARATE. FROM THAT POINT ON, HE TRAINED IN MOTOBU-HA SHITO-RYU WITH SHIHAN BAYANI ADLAWAN, AND MATEO MANGOSING. MR. RABINO RECEIVED HIS 1ST AND 2ND DANS IN SHITO-RYU AND CONTINUED TRAINING WITH ADLAWAN SENSEI UNTIL HIS UNTIMELY DEATH. THEN, HE CONTINUED TRAINING IN MOTOBU-HA SHITO-RYU UNDER THE PERSONAL GUIDANCE OF SOKE SHOGO KUNIBA, FROM WHOM HE RECEIVED HIS 3RD AND 4TH DANS. AFTER THAT, SENSEI RABINO BEGAN HIS TRAINING IN THE SHITO KAI METHOD OF THE STYLE FOUNDED BY THE LATE KENWA MABUNI. PRESENTLY SENSEI RABINO IS THE U.S.A. SHIBUCHO UNDER THE DIRECTION OF SHIHAN KUNIO MURAYAMA AND THE WORLD SHITO KAI FEDERATION OF JAPAN.

How long have you been practicing the martial arts?

In the early years of my life, the early 1960s, while residing in farm labor camps throughout California and Arizona, I had observed various martial arts. The different origins of these arts were Chinese, Filipino, Japanese, and possibly Malaysian. The young fighters always would train by sparring and teaching each other on Sunday afternoons at the labor camps. Since a lot of the migrant workers did not have much money to spend, they would entertain each other by training, playing musical instruments, and holding chicken fighting events on Sundays. Each summer, while working in the grapes, we would spend time on the weekends mingling and trying to get information from these practitioners. Some would share, but quite a few would not. It was different than the regular street fighting that you would normally learn in the barrios (neighborhoods) of the rougher inner city South Phoenix, where we resided.

I have been training in various Japanese/Okinawan and Filipino martial arts since 1966, initially in Judo under Watenabe, K. Sensei here in Arizona. Watanabe, K. Sensei would teach us ukemi (falling), over and over. The art was taught in the backyard in both Peoria and South Phoenix and my father would take me to these training sessions. I always was curious but never asked questions. The Watenabe family had vegetable and flower harvest fields and my father, who was a seasonal migrant Filipino farm laborer, worked for them during the season. But we would spend off-season at home in South Phoenix.

SHITO RYU MASTERS

Mr. Watenabe was my best man in our wedding; it was a pleasure to know he was instrumental in my martial art career. And giving me life advice to help me stay happily married to my wife Sara Rabino, who I have been married to since 1976. She was instrumental in my contining my training. Without good support of your spouse, many a marriage has taken its toll on a martial arts career.

I also trained under my older brothers Samuel and Pedro (Pete) in my early years. My brother Sam was stationed in Misawa, Japan, while in the U.S. Air Force. During the late 60s, he continued his martial arts training, learning traditional Japanese arts such Iado, Judo, and Karate in Japan. My brother Pete began training under both Sam Rabino and Robert Trias (U.S.K.A. founder), since Sam was Pete's first instructor as well as mine. Sam had his orders to depart to Japan, leaving Pete to continue his training under someone who could further his martial arts training. Sam took Pete to fight in almost every dojo in Phoenix, attempting to find him a dojo where he could continue his martial training. Mr. Trias's dojo was where Pete stayed. With Pete's newly-found instructor, he furthered my knowledge in martial arts training by instructing me in this art that he was learning under Mr. Trias. It was Mr. Trias who advised me to seek a Japanese-based karate style; he suggested one of the four major styles: Goju-ryu, Shito-ryu, Shotokan, or Wado-ryu. I picked Shito-ryu karate and have not changed styles since. The variety of kata, kumite, and bunkai techniques always encourages me to look further into the arts. Murayama Sensei has been a living treasure with a source of information on this subject, and very loyal to the Iwata family.

But my true mentor to the martial arts was my father. My father (Cayetano Rabino), an immigrant from Santa Catalina, Ilocos Sur – Philippines. Dad introduced my brothers and me to boxing and basic stick arts (Eskrima/Knife). Later, Lonnie and Leto Acosta taught me a more regimented art of eskrima while working as a farm laborer in my early years. Felix Carbahal (Guji) taught Kajukenbo to us and to most of the Filipino community. Guji's dojo was located a block down from the Filipino Center and the Luzon Pool Hall, which was a part of the Phoenix's historical downtown Chinatown. This is where the Filipino men and women (Manongs and Manangs) could go to and meet their friends and acquaintances. Today, I am under the guidance of Shihan Kunio Murayama, a kind but stern man from Miyagi, Japan. He is my present mentor and master instructor, and a classical warrior in today's society and Shihan Genzo Iwata. These men are guiding me through a Budo experience of true karate and jujitsu that it like no other. I am blessed to have such instructors to teach a non-political martial art, whereas today Budo is being set back due to political organizations.

How many styles of karate or other methods have you trained in?

During my lifetime, I have trained in various Shorin-ryu factions (Kobayashi-ryu, Matsubayashi-ryu), Shito-ryu (Motobu-Ha Shito-ryu, Tani-Ha Shito-ryu, and Shito-ryu of Kenei Mabuni and Manzo Iwata), Goju-ryu, Wado-ryu, and Kodokan Judo Shuri-ryu. I also have trained in different views and methods of Filipino Martial Arts. Because of previous training of different arts, I always believed in having an open mind. But if you teach Shito-ryu, or whatever art that you instruct, that is what you should teach, not a blend.

Who are your teachers?

I presently am under the direction of Shihan Kunio Murayama (Shito-ryu) and plan to be under him until I learn everything there is to learn, which means a lifetime. He is a great and very technical master instructor.

Mr. Murayama was the Uchi Deshi to Sensei Manzo Iwata. Mr. Iwata taught him both Nanban Sato-ryu Kenpo (grappling art) and Shito-ryu Karate-do. Murayama Sensei is a kind but a no-nonsense instructor with classical methods of teaching. He has introduced me to bunkai as I have never seen or felt. At one training seminar in Phoenix, which our U.S.A. club sponsored, he literally knocked me out with a takedown utilizing technique from one of the intermediate katas. Practitioners take kata for granted; that is because they were not taught the techniques hidden in each kata. Sensei always makes me a believer in the classical arts of Jujutsu (Nanban Sato-ryu Kenpo) and Shito-ryu Karate. I always wonder what people are missing when they are not taught the movements of kata and their style's specific techniques. Murayama Sensei introduced me to Sensei Genzo Iwata (Shito-ryu) during a training seminar at the Copa Murayama, an annual karate tournament held in Monterrey, Mexico. Sensei Iwata is very precise in his training methods; his kata and kumite teachings are accurate and authentic Shito-ryu methods as taught by his father, master instructor Sensei Manzo Iwata. Mr. Genzo's instruction this year was Tomari Bassai kata; it always is amazing to train under such master instructors. It was a memorable event to be with this great company and to learn these inside secrets in the presence of Mr. Kanazawa and Sam Moledzki. Other instructors in the past that I have trained under were Soke Shogo Kuniba (Motobu-Ha Shito-ryu), Sensei Shogen Oyakawa (Kobayashi-ryu), Sensei Toshihiro Oshiro (Matsubayashi-ryu), Sensei Bayani Adlawan (Motobu-Ha Shito-ryu), and Watenabe, K. Sensei (Kodokan Judo)

Would you tell us some interesting stories of your early days in karate?

There are a few, but most memorable were with Oyakawa Sensei. He was a karate instructor by night; by day, he was a shiatsu therapist at a chiropractor business in Los Angeles. He was visiting for an annual Karate/Kobudo clinic that he taught four to six times a year, and afterward, we always would have a picnic, and he always was the umpire. The kids loved him, but one of my students, Sempai Doug Gill, who still trains and teaches for me, asked Sensei: "Can you teach the striking bunkai to the White Crane (Hakutsuru) kata" that he taught earlier. Sensei was about 5-foot-6 and Doug, who was a muscular 5-foot-9, threw a punch at sensei's request. Doug responsively held onto his chest after being struck by sensei. Visually, it looked as if Doug was having a heart attack, but sensei mentioned these are the secrets that are in the applications of the empty hand. These are the secrets that are not taught and are dying out with the old masters. Yes, they hurt when the answer is revealed, but the Eastern way is not to ask these questions. You, as students, need to ask these questions; if not you will not have the answers. This

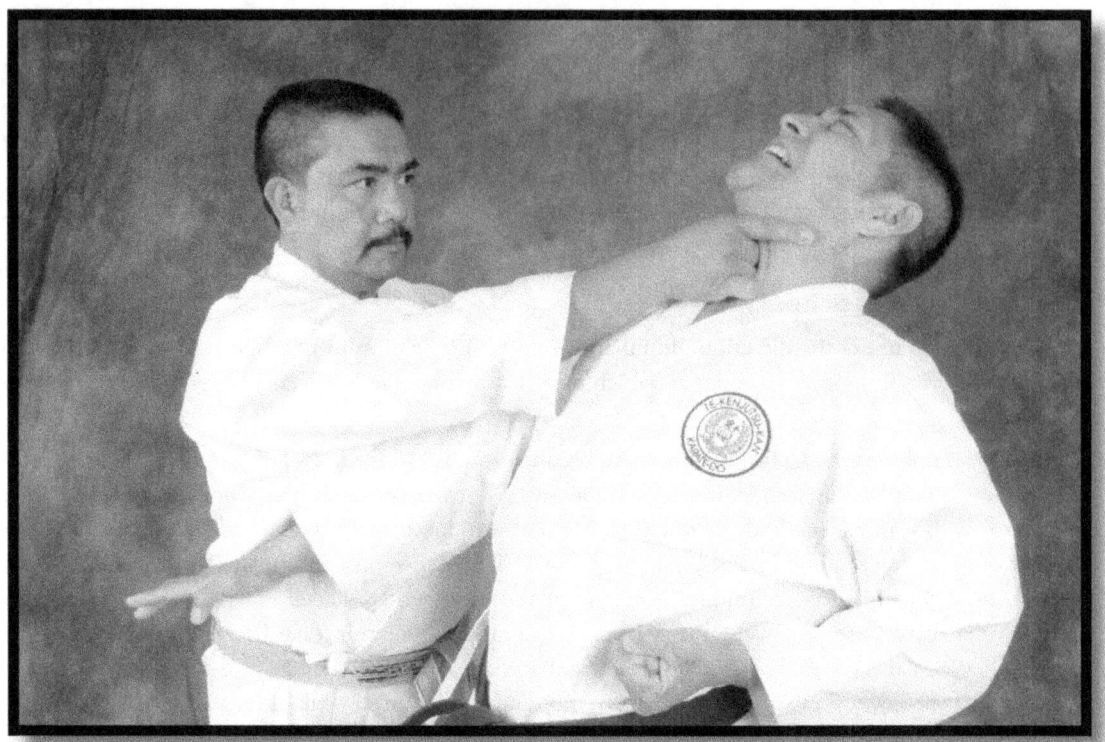

changed my martial arts frame of thought, thanks to Doug's hurtful encounter.

Which kata best represents you, and how important is it?

Kata Seipai is my favorite, due to its fluid technique and rhythmic tempo. The kata is internally energy driven, but that doesn't mean that all katas are not like this, just that Seipai is very powerful and very fluid-influenced. I really appreciate the bunkai; it is very physical and quick. It actually lets your mind wander while your body is in lethal cruise control.

Were you a 'natural' at karate; did the movements come easily to you?

I felt that I was, but this was due to my early experiences with Judo and Gung-fu. This helped with my relaxation and my ability to learn at an easier pace. Karate is an art that helps one to understand oneself. If the beginner karate-ka could refrain from battling his left side if he is right side dominant, that is half of the fight from training in a natural state. Sensei would call that the "wild horse"; he would say a wild horse would always do the opposite of the direction of the rider. If the reins are pulled to the right, the wild horse would go to the left. Understand your wild horse before your natural side can come out.

How has your personal expression of karate developed over the years?

Just as fads of martial arts change, so should your defenses and offenses. In my earlier years, I found myself moving more telegraphically, with a slight tension in my movement. In the dojo, our kata and bunkai stay the same, as traditional karate should. If one changes the movement, it is not considered traditional, but that doesn't mean that your classes should not include streetwise techniques. Yes, karate has every set of defenses available. But as famous military figures have said repeatedly, "to know your opponent is to know how they fight." Teach the traditions but open your mind; know your art very well before you start thinking about adding an adaptation to your rendition of your art. Sensei Murayama's teachings of Jujitsu have open doors to a more clear and complete art of Shito-ryu Karate-do.

What are the most important points in your teaching methods? And what are the most important qualities for a student to become proficient in the karate style?

I never can overstate the teaching of the basics. I think that in some of today's dojos, they go around the teachings of the kihon because the youth get bored easily and do not like repetitious movement. This is a part of our teachings – basics, basics, and more basics. What we also express is where to hit, not just throwing a punch or kick and wherever it lands is good. More important is what will stop your opponent and what the effects of a precise technique are.

With all the technical changes during the last years, do you think there still is 'pure' Shito Ryu karate?

Yes, because of the line of teachers—starting with Kenwa Mabuni (founder of Shito-ryu), and Mabuni's protégé Sensei Manzo Iwata, and Mr. Iwata's protégé Sensei Kunio Murayama. Karate-do Shito-kai Murayama U.S.A. teaches the Shito-ryu of Kenwa Mabuni. But how pure was Shito-ryu when Mr. Iwata was being taught? Most Karate styles have changed, depending on when the recipient learned from the master. At an older age, there were body movement limitations that altered the kata and techniques.

Do you think different 'styles' are truly important in the art of karate?

Yes, if there were not other styles, the argument of my style is better than yours would not exist (jokingly). Each style has its own flavor. Without different styles, there would not have been the various challenges in the development of these arts. It's like having only one football team; where would the competition be? This competition promotes improvements within; in turn, other styles will improve.

What is your opinion of fighting events such as the UFC and Mixed Martial Arts events?

I always have believed any martial art is good, but when events like these become more spectator sports, they become cloned in the streets. This makes today's martial arts evolve, which means instruc-

SHITO RYU MASTERS

tors should not become complacent in their dojo. Quite a few karate dojo do not include ground fighting; this is an Achilles heel to their art. If they do not teach it now, they should start to prepare their students better for that rough battleground—the streets.

Karate nowadays often is referred to as a sport. Would you agree with this definition or is it a martial art?

No, I do not consider Karate a sport. But the sport aspect has kept karate alive, in many ways. Sport karate (kumite and kata) has done well by giving youth a better out than street activity. Just like baseball, basketball, and of course soccer, karate has done a lot of good for today's youth. But martial arts still has to be taught along with sports, so they can understand the difference, such as where to strike and to truly understand timing.

Do you feel that you still have further to go in your studies?

Yes, we have 50 plus kata in our style of Shito-ryu. This is a very long path of trying to learn the kata, including their bunkai (applications). It is fascinating to learn the history, kata, and their bunkai; this is a true life endeavor as written in most Karate rank certificates—especially learning these studies from Sensei Kunio Murayama. He is very knowledgeable in the art of Shito-ryu; he is a wealth of knowledge.

How do you see Shito-ryu karate in North America at the present time?

This art has sprouted, thanks to Sensei Fumio Demura and his kindness as a true karate-do master. We also can thank Masters Shogo Kuniba (Motobu-Ha Shito-ryu), Teruo Hayashi (Hayashi-ha Shito-ryu), and Chuzo Kotaka for their contributions to the growth of Shito-ryu in the USA. We also have Sensei Kunio Murayama, who visited our dojo conducting seminars in Phoenix, Arizona, and Texas. We are looking to have sensei also conduct a clinic in Illinois. And we have talked to Sensei Genzo Iwata about conducting seminars in the USA. He is the technical director for the World Shito-ryu Karate-do Federation (WSKF).

Do you think it helps the karate student physically to train with weapons (Kobudo)?

Yes, I have believed that ever since the first time I picked up as pair of sai. The coordination that comes with weapons training is very rewarding for each student, especially two-man drills (Yakusoku kumite). Short/long weapons provide either weight or wind restrictions, making the resistance with weapons training very strenuous. It also makes the martial artist a very versatile karate practitioner.

How does the Shito-ryu karate style differ from other methods and styles of karate?

Shito-ryu karate is a unique style, due to the founder Kenwa Mabuni combining the kata and theories of the Tode (Chinese hand) styles of all three Okinawan villages (Naha, Tomari, and Shuri) where Okinawan Empty hand arts originated. Most styles are combinations; for example, Goju-ryu has Naha, Okinawa origins, plus the Gung-fu influence of Pa Qua Chuan of Fukien, China. Shotokan has Shuri, Okinawan influence from Itosu and Azato. By Mr. Mabuni (Shito-ryu founder) incorporating these origins to its style, we differ by including these Okinawan methods.

When teaching the art of karate, what is the most important element: self-defense or sport?

Of course, self-defense is the most important aspect of karate. But with a ratio of 60 percent more of today's youth training and filling our dojo, we have to teach sport karate, without the martial art included.

Forms and sparring, what's the proper ratio in training?

The ratio we go by is 60 percent kata and 40 percent kumite. Kata (form) teaches movement and versatility, but jyu-kumite (free sparring) improves timing and builds reflexive reactions. Kata teaches you good attacks and defenses, and kumite tweaks your confidence, spirit, and of course timing/speed.

Do you have any general advice you would care to pass on to practitioners in general?

As most practitioners would say, keep training your basics. But I'd like to add something different, and that is to not just train in the basics but also try to understand your movements. Listen well, and respect your instructor and senior classmates. Conduct yourself in a professional manner, especially in front of the younger classmates. You may be tomorrow's mentors, and how you act will be mimicked by your peers.

What do you consider to be the major changes in the art of Shito-ryu since you began training?

Some Shito-ryu practitioners have modified the kata to look more flowery for competition purposes. Shito-ryu forms are beautiful just as they are, without any modifications. I also have noticed that there are more 7th and 8th Dan now then there were in the 80s or 90s, and quite a few red/white belt bearers.

Who would you like to have trained with that you have not?

I would like to have trained with Kenwa Mabuni; the stories of his training methods are historic. I also would like to have trained with Manzo Iwata. I always have been fascinated at how Shito-ryu karate might have looked in the early years. I always ask Sensei Murayama this question: "Can you teach me the way that Mr. Iwata taught you?" He always says, "These are my present methods of teaching. Nothing has changed but my age and my hair. I have less."

SHITO RYU MASTERS

What would you say to someone who is interested in starting to learn karate?

Why do you want to train in martial arts? Is this something that you want to do; will you be able to make a commitment to your training? Make sure you do your research on schools in your area before you commit. Write questions down and take them with you to the school that you have an interest in; spend time to ask the instructor what you might expect. Do your research and let yourself know you are going to get hit.

What is it that keeps you motivated after all these years?

I always have been motivated since I have trained with some very good mentor instructors. I never have had one karate or kobudo instructor swear or curse in class or around students; I have kept the same tradition. Since they have been great mentors, I am trying to keep the tradition of these great master instructors. This goal keeps me learning and teaching year to year. The most important factor is seeing the face of some of the young students testing for their first belt ranking; their smiles are so pure and truthful. This is my highlight and motivation, that I have changed someone's life for the better—hopefully by setting a good example by teaching the culture/customs and respect of these martial arts.

What is the philosophical basis for your karate training?

To continuously train and teach the tradition of an art that was taught to me, so the next generation can benefit from yesterday's martial arts discoveries. I find this to be a lifelong commitment, which motivates me to continue to learn more and hopefully to fulfill my goal as an instructor. Part of the base is to abide by the meaningful principles of Shito-ryu fighting philosophy. For instance, Rakka, in which the principle is to powerfully parry the attack; Ryu Sui (Water Flow), in which the principle is to evade the opponent's attacks without parrying them; Kusshin (Body Bending), in which the principle is to parry the adversary's attacks by bending your body; Ten-i (Position Change), in which the principle is to parry the purpose of the adversary's attack by displacement; Hantsuki (Reflection of the Attack), in which the principle is to reflect the attack by matching the adversary's move. These examples of Shito-ryu's martial philosophies are only a few of the highlights in our art.

Do you have a particularly memorable karate experience that has remained as an inspiration for your training?

I was invited to a training seminar for instructors taught by Sensei Kunio Murayama (Shito-Kai), and the class was on basics. But it wasn't the subject that fascinated me; it was the method of how he taught, and the overall classical Eastern way of doing things. Sensei was not rude, but he was stern, and he taught the courtesy and the martial ways of the Japanese. He kept going over how to teach strikes, kicks, and blocks—the fundamentals. I looked around the room and not one participant looked bored; it was the basics and everyone enjoyed it. Sensei sat everyone down with the command of "Seiza." He began to teach us the rules of the dojo and how to treat students. This was very memorable, because how many instructors teach their students how to teach students? True master instructors are instructors who truly teach instructors. How many really do that—not just advanced kata or kumite, but what martial arts really are about? This is what Sensei Murayama and Sensei Genzo Iwata have done for my true martial experience, and have kept the light burning in my martial career.

After all these years of training and experience, could you explain the meaning of the practice of karate?

To practice in karate is to follow all Japanese and Okinawan Dojo Kun (The Place of the Way Rules) and follow the true traditions of respect. Leave all of your thoughts and emotions outside, and let your body demonstrate mental expressions by executing kata with kime (spirit).

How do you think a practitioner can increase his understanding of the spiritual aspect of the art?

Martial art teaches the practitioner how to look deeper into his/her inner self by learning about the body's limitations. By preparing for their periodical evaluations / testing period, the students ready themselves mentally and physically. By this preparation, they learn to minimize errors, to push and strive for a better character, not to earn another level belt but to gain an accomplishment that improves inner spiritual confidence.

Is anything lacking in the way martial arts are taught today compared to how they were in your beginnings?

I think manners and respect are lacking in today's dojo. I alwaysthought martial arts were all about respect, but instructors are lacking in teaching these methods and conveying these rules to their students. If these rules are not conveyed, the idea of respect will be lost. Otherwise, the domino effect occurs—if they never were taught, how can they teach the next generation of black belts? This is one concern; the other is the teaching of yesterday's methods of martial arts.

I find that when I travel to Monterrey, Mexico, and Japan for training, the teachings are the same as yesterday's. One fear here is that in the USA, today's teachers are refraining from past methods due to possible lawsuits. You hear in the past of shinai being used to correct improper moves; also shime (body testing) methods for proper body tension. Some of the Naha-te schools still use these practices of yesterday.

Could I ask what you consider to be the most important qualities of a successful karate practitioner?

I believe they have to know what their goals are or should be, such as life. If their success is just acquiring a black belt, they only are on a partial path to their martial progression. Learn your Budo (warrior way) history/customs, where/how to strike, and find your true self.

SHITO RYU MASTERS

What advice would you give to students on the question of supplementary training (running, weights, etc.)?

Today's athletes have improved their performance by far. This did not happen because they were the plain Joe/Jane. They have learned "how," "when," and "what" nutrients to consume and how to push their limits in isometric and weight training. Jyu-kumite (free sparring) training drills are, in many ways, better than most machines or free weights; they can offer as much as gym equipment. But the karate-ka may need to get a physical checkup to know one's limits. Knowing these facts may prevent possible injuries.

What do you see as the most important attributes of a student?

The will to learn, and to have patience. I know that when learning a technique or kata, one always wants to learn what is next, just like a movie. Learn and practice what you have at home. Patience and practice are two attributes that students need to have a little more of. They may have one or the other, but not both attributes.

Why is it, in your opinion, that a lot of students start falling away after two-three years of training?

I think that in three years they may have attained their black belt and, after acquiring this, they believe mentally that they have reached their goal. We know this is where one really starts to learn, but to the majority, this is a completion. Another reason is that if they did not acquire their black belt, they wonder why not? So they may go to another dojo that might give them an easy way out, by accepting a black belt from another teacher. The last is they may have been burned out on the same old routine. Again, this relates to my comment on patience. In today's world, where everything is fast paced, they may believe why not martial arts?

Have been times when you felt fear in your training?

Actually, yes, during a training session in which Sensei K. Murayama was teaching the finer points of both Nanban Satoh-ryu Kenpo (Jujitsu) and Shito-ryu kata. This was the first year we brought Sensei to visit this first USA and Hombu dojo. Thanks to my Sempai Sam Moledzki, my sponsor in the Japan Karate-do Shito-kai, Sensei asked me if I knew ukemi (how to fall/roll). I replied, "Hai Sensei (yes)." Mind you, I had just picked him up at the airport from an international flight, with no practice and not knowing what he was going to do. At the seminar, he asked me to grab his lapel. He commenced to

throw me around like I have never been thrown. But in Nanban Satoh-ryu Kenpo, the positioning is to place your opponent in a bind where they cannot preventively roll out of the attack. Let me tell you, I wasn't as fearful as I was astonished at what he did. I remained on the ground with my students viewing this technique that Sensei just did to me. I was down for maybe 20 seconds, but it felt more like 20 minutes. After the session, my students were impressed to see what Sensei did to me—but not as impressed as I was.

Do you think the Olympics will be positive for the art of karate-do?

Yes, the exposure of karate in the event will be great. I know a lot of traditionalists are against this move and there are karate organizations that are working hard to see this happen. And, do you know what? They are doing a fantastic job. But the question that always is asked is: what are the rules this year? Do we have to get certified again, how much will this cost? Cost is a big question, because when money is involved, a lot of funny things happen. We hope for the sake of the competitors that they are not the ones paying for political gains.

What are your thoughts on the future of karate?

Karate is moving forward and growing as an art and as a sport. But a few of the qualities of yesterday's traditions are drifting slightly. I have observed that respect and loyalty, which are great humane qualities, need to be reinforced in today's dojo. Quite a few young black belts are leaving their Sensei and opening their own dojo, for one reason or other. Some of the finer points of karate are taught when acceptance of black belt rank merit has been achieved. Leaving their dojo is a growing issue. We talk as senior instructors and wonder what will become of tomorrow karate-ka generation. We only can pray for the best, and just train and sweat and practice our kata and kumite as our styles' originators would have wished it to be.

RYUSHO SAKAGAMI

THE GENTLE MASTER

Ryusho Sakagami exemplified all the qualities a master of Budo should. Born on 1915 in Kawanishi City, which is in the Hyugo Prefecture, Sakagami Sensei began his martial art training at age 10. The Nihon Budo Kyogi-Kai gave him the highest Budo award — the Budo Koro-Sho medal. His extensive training in the art of karate-do under grandmasters of the caliber of Choki Motobu and Kenwa Mabuni, among others, made him one of the top and more knowledgeable masters of his generation. With an extensive training in judo, iaido, kendo and kobudo, Sakagami Sensei used the Budo principles and his education to lead an honorable life. He stayed active at his dojo in Tsurumi Ward, between Yokohama and Kawasaki, until his very last days of life. His teacher, Shito-Ryu founder Kenwa Mabuni, asked Ryusho Sakagami to succeed him in the heritage of Itosu Anko's orthodox method of karate, appointing him the third generation leader of the Itosu-ha seito.

In 1980, the Federation of All-Japan Karate-Do Organizations awarded Master Sakagami his 8th dan in karate-do, and in 1987 he received his 8th dan in Muso Jikiden Eishin Ryu iaido.

The most important karate federations in the world acknowledged Grandmaster Sakagami to be a living treasure and a repository of the history and knowledge of Budo. Ryusho Sakagami — a true legend of the art of karate, an honorable human being and a gentle master — died from heart failure on December 28, 1993.

Master Sakagami, please tell us about your beginnings in the art.

My grandfather was a kendo master. I trained in iaido under Nakayama Hiromichi Sensei, who was a meijin, and in aikido under Hirai Minoru Sensei, who was a direct student of O'Sensei Ueshiba. I traveled often to Okinawa – though my parents didn't know it – to train in karate, because I was informed that there was an excellent master in Osaka. His name was Kenwa Mabuni, and I began my training under him around 1935. Training at that time was very different than today. I also trained under Choki Motobu. I have also trained in judo, jodo, kobudo and other classical arts of Budo.

Did you meet Funakoshi Gichin Sensei?

Yes I did. He visited Mabuni Sensei, and he had some of his students learn kata from Mabuni Sensei. Later on, they modified things to better fit the style Funakoshi Sensei was developing. Mabuni Sensei had a good relationship with Funakoshi Sensei.

Why did you take over the Itosu-kai heritage after becoming one of the oldest students of Kenwa Mabuni Sensei?

Mabuni Sensei was the founder of Shito-ryu, which is a combination of naha-te, shuri-te and tomari-te. In Japan, the son is always the heir to his father's throne. Mabuni Kenei, although a junior to me, had to be the leader of his father's heritage. Kenwa Mabuni Sensei, knowing that I was a senior, suggested that I carry on with the tradition of the Itosu-ha, which I honored and accepted. Mabuni Sensei learned from Master Itosu Ankho. Master Itosu was the teacher of other great masters like Chosin Chibana, Funakoshi Gichin, Choki Motobu, et cetera. For me, it was a privilege and an honor.

Master Sakagami, how much influence of Zen is there in Bushido as a code of the samurai and Budo?

The spirit underlying the arts practiced by the samurai was part Shinto and part Zen. This discipline was adapted from the Zen monastery and imposed on the martial arts elements and training. The most mundane act was to be performed with the utmost perfection. That ritual and tedious repetition in training provided not only technical expertise for the warriors but also a spiritual connection to the ancestors.

How do you feel after so many years of training?

I feel great about myself, but I'd probably be better if I had had more knowledge of the human body and proper nutrition. Knowing what I know today, I would have suffered fewer injuries and could have trained harder. To make their training and life more productive, new generations should study all of the information they have today. With that, they should be able to go farther than we old teachers did. In doing a martial art, the mind, spirit and technique should all be fully expressed. If your technique is correct and your mind and spirit fully expressed and arrived, you will progress very fast. In this case, you will get a different feeling everyday. Students should carefully realize this. If your technique, your mind and your spirit do not arrive, you are wasting your time and will never succeed.

What should be the main principles on which training is based?

All forms of martial arts start with courtesy and respect. The main idea of Budo is to remove all arrogance and pomposity and replace them with humbleness and the right spirit, and it's important to display those qualities that were established and sustained by generations of dedicated and devoted martial artists. The true Budo spirit is not something that you can put on and take off at will. It is something you become. It is in everything you do and permeates through all your acts. It puts us in accord with the flow of the universe. It is true that the value of a martial art depends on its application, but the goal is not always self-defense or self-protection. There are some other higher goals in Budo training. In a true martial artist, all of the actions are geared [or designed] so that there is no dishonor or loss of face. The most important thing to keep in mind is that all forms of Budo are not courses of study, but rather, a way of life.

Sensei, what do you think is the most important thing a teacher should make sure the students learn, and what is the most relevant principle the student should keep in mind?

It is important that a martial art instructor foster a sense of self-responsibility in his students. For the students, the best way to learn is to practice, persevere and think about the intent behind the technique. It is too easy to look for magic while the real secret is sweat. There is no magic in the martial arts, just a good teacher and a lot of hard work. The key is to practice, and I have always been an advocate for teaching the students everything I know. Holding back just weakens the art. The old principle of saving a little, which implies not teaching the whole art, has caused the deterioration of the martial arts.

Do you think a certain amount of knowledge is lost when the art is taught from generation to generation?

Yes. The reason that techniques are lost is not because the teacher withholds the knowledge. Instead, it's because today's students don't work to understand what lies behind the physical movements. Sometimes you have a situation in which there are two students, and you spend a lot of time and effort on them. One turns out to be very good and the other turns out poor. The martial arts are not something you can copy. You must learn what lies behind the technique. The martial arts are taught today only like a good physical exercise. Unfortunately, they are lacking the true Budo spirit. The training is not geared to a real life-or-death situation, and this single fact changes the whole approach.

A student should be humble and honest with himself, because he should know his limitations and true possibilities. The martial arts are great as a physical exercise, as well as an excellent vehicle for mental health. Anyone should be able to become strong and more confident if he trains with the proper direction and goals in mind. Don't expect miracles though, because the martial arts won't bring any kind of mystical powers! It is important that a martial art instructor foster a sense of self-responsibility on the part of his students.

Is it correct to change elements of the art and modify things that our teachers taught us?

I don't advocate change for change's sake, and this is what has happened recently in the world of martial arts. People with a limited amount of knowledge put together a little of this, a little of that, give it a new name and [suddenly] we have a new, complete martial art system that will liberate all the practitioners in the world from the useless, traditional methods. I feel sorry for those students [who train with them] for not knowing any better. They follow these "instructors" and give them their money and their time. The traditional styles were put together with a sense of balance. Everything in a particular style was designed and glued together with meaning and reason. The techniques, the strategies and the principles found in the forms, et cetera, [all] work perfectly together like the pieces of a puzzle. If you have all the pieces and keep the final puzzle as it meant to be, you'll have a nice picture once you are finished. On the contrary, if you try to mix pieces from several different puzzles, you'll have a mess with no foundation and no reason to exist. People who do this often show big contradictions; they spend too much time repeating the words of other martial artist because they have nothing to offer and no central philosophy in what they are trying to teach. The old masters weren't so naive when they designed the different styles. Give them the credit they deserve because there is more in the traditional styles than what meets the eye. These martial artists who create new styles operate under the misconception that they are creating a perfect fighting method. To me, this concept is simply an illusion. The perfect style doesn't exit. Perfection is something that sounds very good, but it is unattainable. By simply eliminating classical techniques and replacing them with boxing does not make a new method better or superior. It makes it different. That's all. By changing the old styles and thinking that we have developed a superior method, we are creating a foundation for failure because that's another illusion. There is no perfect person, and there is no perfect style but the one that fits you and brings understanding and a peaceful spirit to your existence as a human being.

Many people criticize the martial arts because they are loaded with rituals and protocols that are not necessary in the West. What is your opinion?

The martial arts are more than fighting. In Japan, they are part of Budo. In China, they represent a way of life and a way of thinking that involves the principles of Taoism, and the same happens in every place where the arts were developed. Protocol and rituals have very little to do with the actual fighting, but they are vehicles to preserve education, politeness, etiquette, et cetera. All these are very important values for a student. The people who criticize this simply don't have the knowledge of what these aspects represent. The courtesy and proper protocol found in the traditional schools are the essence of the education. They are the true bones of what's happening and keep everything within a serious environment for education. When you take away the protocol, the rituals like bowing and paying respect to your opponent, you are taking away from the history, from the legacy, from the bones and the essence of what a true martial art is all about. People should learn to differentiate between the rituals and the essence represented in these rituals. Maybe then they will realize why they are so important for the future generations.

How important are the basics?

The technical foundations, which were dwelled upon for years, are unfortunately and often glossed over in a matter of a few months of part-time work. It is very important to train hard in the basics of the art. Never ignore these. Forms are composed of single movements or parts that make up the whole form. To become an expert, you should strive to learn how to use these parts. The basics, which are known as kihon, apply to the art of karate-do, as well as to the foundations of Budo. It is very misleading [and wrong] if you move on and never give the basics another thought once you have learned them. To keep the foundation strong, you always have to go back to it, regardless of how many years of practice you have accumulated.

Sensei, what kind of additional training is helpful for karate?

Traditionally, we had a series of supplementary training aids. They are classical implements that helped karateka to strengthen their bodies and prepare them for combat. The makiwara is one of them. Kobudo training also helps the wrists and hands.

Is makiwara training beneficial for a practitioner?

If the student is guided by a knowledgeable teacher, it is definitely positive. You don't want to hit the makiwara without having a previous understanding and knowledge of what your goals are. You need to know the purpose of [training with the] makiwara, and the purpose is not to develop calloused hands. That's simply a consequence of the training. Your body, through correct training in the makiwara, will learn how to absorb the energy sent back to it after your fist hits an object. Thus, you will learn how to develop the right positioning when hitting an object with full force. It is a different [phenomena] to practice your punches and kicks in the air than it is to hit a solid object. The positioning of your legs, hip, back, shoulder, elbow, forearm and wrist must be properly aligned to exert all the possible power from your body and to absorb the shock of the impact. Basically, makiwara teaches you the right technique. If you do makiwara training simply to develop big knuckles and calluses, you won't get any benefit from it because that's not the purpose.

Does the sportive approach change the teacher/student relationship?

Well, unfortunately, many people today think that karate is a sport, so they train for specific tournaments and competition, pretty much the same way that a basketball or football player trains for a game. Because the goal for every training session relates to sport competition, the person training them, correcting their movements and guiding them is a trainer or coach. Never a sensei. The word sensei has very different connotations and meanings that extend way beyond winning a tournament. There are no coaches or trainers in Budo.

The person who teaches you to discover yourself and your place in the world is not a coach. He is called teacher, master or sensei. He teaches you loyalty, courtesy, etiquette and all the important values that make a person a better human being. The person who trains a boxer is a trainer; the individual who trains and teach a karate-ka is a sensei. If the training is focused to win tournaments in a sport environment, other important qualities intrinsic in the true Budo training, such as courtesy, loyalty, et cetera, are simply lost and forgotten. There can be an appreciation and respect for your coach but not in a Budo way. Etiquette and proper attitude disappear. That's why we see coaches and competitors complaining constantly in a tournament if a referee's decision doesn't go their way. Proper etiquette is lost. Style is not as important as the spirit of the art.

Is there anything you would like to add?

Yes, dedicate yourself to reach the higher levels of Budo and put your heart and soul into it. The key to understanding the art of karate-do and most other Budo arts is the underlying philosophy that runs so inseparably through all the forms of Japanese life. The principles of karate are based on the principles of life and the universe. It is the realization of an existing phenomenon – such as a punch or a kick – that gives meaning to that phenomenon, and it is the understanding of that meaning that allows one to master the phenomenon. It is for this purpose – understanding – that a person learns the art of karate-do.

SADAAKI SAKAGAMI

IN THE NAME OF ITOSU

THE SAKAGAMI FAMILY TREE TRACES ITS ROOTS TO THE GREAT ANKHO ITOSU WHO WAS REGARDED AS ONE OF THE BEST KARATE MASTERS EVER PRODUCED IN OKINAWA. SADAAKI SAKAGAMI HAS FOLLOWED IN HIS FATHER'S FOOTSTEPS AND IS NOW KNOWN AS ONE OF THE MOST KNOWLEDGEABLE MEN OF KARATE AND THE SOKE OF THE "ITOSU RYU" STYLE. DESCRIBED AS AN UNSELFISH AND DEDICATED INSTRUCTOR, SOKE SAKAGAMI TRAVELS AROUND THE WORLD SHARING HIS KNOWLEDGE AND EXPERTISE. IT IS SOKE SAKAGAMI'S DESIRE TO PRESERVE AND SPREAD THE ORIGINAL ART DEVELOPED AND PASSED ONTO HIS FATHER BY THE GREAT KENWA MABUNI.

FOR SOKE SAKAGAMI, SPIRIT AND HEART ARE THE MOST IMPORTANT ATTRIBUTES IN KARATE TRANING. "IN ORDER TO BE THE BEST," HE SAYS FIRMLY, "YOU MUST HAVE THE WARRIOR'S HEART AND SPIRIT".

HE IS A KNOWLEDGEABLE AND FASCINATING MAN, FULL OF INTERESTING STORIES, AND BRIMMING WITH A POSITIVE ATTITUDE TOWARDS TEACHING AND LIFE. IN THE MODERN WORLD OF DISILLUSIONMENT, HE IS TRULY A UNIQUE INDIVIDUAL AND A TRUE KARATE MASTER.

How did your father, Ryusho Sakagami, become the successor of the Itosu Ryu style?

According to what I heard from my father Ryusho Sakagami, he was invited to his teacher Mater Kenwa Mabuni's house a few months before he passed away. At that time, Master Mabuni offered my father to be the successor of the Shito Ryu style.

But my father respectfully refused his offer because he had his own business and also he had never thought he would be able to live on karate at that time. So, my father told him: "I am not worthy to be the successor. Also, you have a son. So, please give him Shito Ryu Soke's title."

But Master Mabuni said, "If you don't be the successor, I will feel very bad and sorry for you. So, if you don't, please be the successor of my teacher, Itosu Sensei's orthodox lineage, using the name of "Itosu" instead of "Shito" to describe the style you will be teaching after my death".

SHITO RYU MASTERS

How did your father start training Shito Ryu with Master Mabuni?

The reason my father started practicing Shito Ryu is that my father went to Kokushikan University in Tokyo to practice Kendo, and he met a classmate who was from Okinawa and was also a karate practitioner. My father started practicing karate when he was 12 or 13 years old in his hometown, Hyogo. He learned the art from a man from Okinawa.

Anyway, one day he was practicing karate's kata by himself at the University, and his friend from Okinawa surprisingly looked at it and he asked if it was karate or not. And my father replied to him by saying "Yes, it is Karate."

His friend also asked "Who did you learn it from?" My father replied to him that he learned the art from an Okinawan man in his hometown. The father of his friend was actually a karate teacher and he even owned a karate club in Okinawa. So, he asked my father to go to Okinawa to practice karate together. And while he was a University student, he often went to Okinawa to train.

After he graduated from the University, he wanted to keep training karate near his hometown in the Osaka area. So, he asked some Okinawan teachers if they could introduce him to a local karate teacher. They said that Master Kenwa Mabuni lived in Osaka [at that time] and he was a very good and reputable teacher. After the proper introduction, my father started training with Master Kenwa Mabuni.

Would you please define and explain the main characteristics of the Itosu Ryu style?

Master Kenwa Mabuni was the founder of the Shito Ryu style. So, what my father learned from him was actually the complete Shito Ryu method but before Master Mabuni passed away, he appointed my father to be the successor of Master Itosu's orthodox lineage, but what he was doing was actually Shito Ryu. Master Kenwa Mabuni knew he had to pass the Shito Ryu style to one of his sons and that is the reason why he named my father the leader and successor of the Itosu lineage. However, one day my father thought he had to distinguish the Itosu orthodox style from the Shito Ryu style, so he officially named it "Itosu Ryu".

Shito Ryu is based on Itosu Sensei's lineage and Higashionna Sensei's lineage. It was named after those two great masters' first kanji character, "shi" and "ito". So, we consider the Itosu Ryu style to be one of the roots of Shito Ryu and we keep cherishing the style although it is true we have the 'naha' elements and kata from the Higashionna lineage as well.

When did you start training in Kobudo?

The reason I started training Kobudo is because Master Shinken Taira started living at my father's house in 1957 or 1958 and was teaching Kobudo at my father's dojo. I directly learned Kobudo from Master Taira.

Karate was getting popular at that time, but Kobudo was not. I was wondering why we had to practice Kobudo at all. So my focus was relatively more on karate than Kobudo. However, since Master Taira and my father were living in the same place, I couldn't run away from Kobudo training. So, I trained and practiced Kobudo everyday. The sessions with Sensei Taira were very demanding and hard. With time I found practicing Sai strengthening the power of the wrist even for regular

punching; training Bo is good for making sure distance is correct when facing an opponent. These discoveries made me practice Kobudo harder and harder so I could improve my karate at the same time.

Those practices in my young days became a part of my body, and they are a treasure for my martial arts' life today.

How did you actually feel when you became the successor of the Itosu style?

It was personally very shocking to me when my father passed away for obvious reasons. Then, a lot of my father's students, who were actually my 'sempai', senior students to me, told me that I should be the successor of the Itosu Ryu style. After thinking about it and getting the support from my 'sempai', I agreed and succeeded to be the successor of the style.

I received the huge responsibility to preserve the art which had been passed down for three generations: from Master Itosu, Master Mabuni, finally to my father Ryusho Sakagami, At the same time, I had strong feelings that it was my mission to promote the Itosu Ryu style to the world.

Please tell us about the evolution and development of your personal training in the arts of Karate and Kobudo.

I directly learned karate from my father, so obviously I have huge influence from him.

However, there are a lot of styles in karate, for instance Shotokan, Goju Ryu and Wado Ryu, and I thought each style must have had wonderful techniques. So, I actually asked a lot of questions to many of the styles' instructors, regarding their techniques, and I especially asked about applications.

SHITO RYU MASTERS

For instance, I went and asked other top instructors questions like; "In our style we have this kind of application, but how do you interpret this technique in your style?" This is how I studied the difference between the Itosu Ryu style and other styles.

I thought, "If I don't ask, I cannot develop Itosu Ryu itself. Learning other styles is also very important for having a full understanding of what my style, Itosu Ryu really is." This is how I accumulated my karate knowledge besides training under the guidance of my father.

How do you see the Itosu Ryu style around the world?

These days it is actually very difficult for any instructor to promote karate worldwide. Our karate organization is based on our karate techniques. However, not only the techniques but also humanity and communication skills are very important for international promotion. Also, there are cultural and economical differences in the world. Filling up the gap is a very difficult task these days. So, I always think spreading Itosu Ryu to the world is a very hard job because there are many other elements that affect the task.

What do you think about Budo and the sport aspect in Karate-do?

It is a very difficult issue. It is just like a diamond. If we look at a diamond, we can see a lot of glitters according to the angles. Karate is also same. According to the angle, there are a lot of aspects and facets. Some people consider it as Budo - the way of martial arts, but other people think it is sport. Budo is Japanese traditional martial arts which pursues the mental and physical ability through hard training. It is self-discipline. The idea of Budo is deeply related to Zen Buddhism. We have to have very hard training for that, and the final goal is developing ourselves.

But if you consider Karate-do as Budo, then the mental and spiritual aspects are very important, and it is a very difficult idea for regular people. I don't mean sports do not have a mental aspect, but the goal of sports is winning at a sportive competition, and that is the main purpose. Of course, any sports need hard training, but winning or losing is not so important in Budo training. Developing ourselves and especially our spirit is the focus of Budo training. That's the biggest difference between Budo and sports.

So, nowadays many people tend to forget about Budo's aspects, and they just focus on only winning tournaments. But I think Budo's aspects are very important in karate, and that's what I want to teach and pass onto my students and the followers of the Itosu method of karate.

We actually cannot say "This is the definition of the borderline for Budo or sport." Also, we cannot say, "Budo is better than sports" or "sport is better than Budo."

Furthermore, we have to teach both Budo and sport aspects to our students. So, now we - all karate instructors are in a difficult position. Actually I think not only Karate instructors, but also other martial arts instructors, such as Kendo and Judo, must have the same issue.

Real martial arts training has nothing to do with trophies and black belts. In fact we should learn the other way: think of losing your black belt or your trophy. Like the Zen master Sawaki Kodo said, "To gain is suffering; loss in enlightenment."

Can you elaborate on that Soke?

The main difference between the old time practitioners and today's is that old martial artists understood and looked at their training as a "loss." They gave up everything for their art and their practice. Today's practitioners only think of gain: "I want this, I want that." We want to practice martial arts but we want nice cars, a house, a lot of money, fame, etc…

It is important to not forget the spirit and determination of the great masters of the past.

Please tell us about the traditional principle of "Shu-Ha-Ri."

The term "Shu-ha-Ri" came from Kendo. Actually, many Kendo words were introduced to the art of karate-do.

"Shu" means "Preserve." It means we firmly preserve what we learned from our teachers. We have to follow what our teacher taught us, and we have to practice it very hard.

"Ha" means "to add our own idea on what we learned from a teacher" and it is an idea for further personal study. "Ri" means "Being away from the idea of "Shu" and "Ha," and create our own style."

But there are a lot of people who do not understand the idea of "Shu" and try to do "Ha" and "Ri" right away instead of dedicating many years of practice to the concept of "Shu."

Many karate styles have this problem. There are a lot of groups and branches in any style now. I mean, many people make their own style by themselves simply to break away and be 'leaders'.

If anyone decides to make his own style, nobody can stop it. It is true that there is no such rule that we can't make our own style. That's why more and more styles and groups are created now without really bringing anything new. I let people judge that for themselves.

"Shu-Ha-Ri" is a concept of Budo, and it is actually for self-development. So, I believe the most important thing in Budo is that we have to preserve what we learned from our teacher…and later in life…follow and develop our own path.

What kind of message you would like to give to all karate practitioners?

I always ask this question to my students, "There are a lot of arts in Budo such as Judo, Kendo, and Karate-do, but why did you chose karate?" Some people simply say, "Because I like it," but I always ask them "Why do you like karate?"

They might reply; "Because it looks so cool!" and "Why do you think it is cool?"

They say; "fighting looks so cool!" But I finally tell them "I don't think it is the right answer," and I explain "Budo is for self- discipline, and we acquire it through hard training. If you just want to pursue the sport aspect, you will eventually quit karate-do."

Nowadays, most of the students are actually children. It is very difficult for them to understand what Budo means. It is very complex for them.

So, what I always do at first is "try to amuse children through karate training," and I let them understand "what is Budo" and little by little, taking time to do it.

How do you want everybody to remember the legacy of Itosu Ryu karate-do?

I think the most important element of a style is "Kata." The character of our Itosu Ryu style is preserving the art as much as possible, which has been passed down for three generations: from Master Itosu, Master Mabuni to Ryusho Sakagami. This is my mission, and I want everybody in the world to know what the Itosu Ryu style truly is.

Would you give us some final advice?

In Budo you learn "to do the most natural thing in the most natural way." But to find the most natural way and execute it in the more natural manner, it is not easy and that may be one of the biggest obstacles not only in our training but in our lives too.

Sometimes we seem to be unlucky in life and we start thinking negatively about training and about ourselves. Feeling sorry for yourself is self-defeat. We need to keep training and pushing forward because then the barriers will reveal themselves as teachings and a better understanding of things will come out of it. Just because the world is not going the way we want it is not a reason to surrender or to become negative about our lives.

Budo training is not about playing out our fantasies. It has to do with your own life and death.

SHOKO SATO

MOVING FORWARD

IT'S QUITE AN ACCOMPLISHMENT TO DELVE DEEP INTO THE MYSTERIES OF THE ART OF KARATE BUT VERY FEW PRACTITIONERS HAVE THE PATIENCE, LET ALONE THE SELF-DISCIPLINE, TO MASTER THE ART'S INTRICATE SKILLS. IT'S A DISTINCT HONOR TO HAVE TRAINED WITH THE LATE MANZO IWATA, WHO IS LAUDED WORLDWIDE AS ONE OF THE SHITO RYU'S MOST CELEBRATED INSTRUCTORS. SENSEI SHOKO SATO IS AMONG THE HANDFUL OF ELITE MARTIAL ARTISTS WHO TRAINED DIRECTLY UNDER THE LEGENDARY KARATE MASTER. BORN IN 1945 IN MIYAGI, JAPAN, MASTER SATO ENROLLED IN THE PRESTIGIOUS TOYO UNIVERSITY IN TOKYO, ALSO KNOWN AS A KARATE POWERHOUSE. WHILE THERE, HIS SKILLS WERE HIGHLY REGARDED AND AS A RESULT, HE WAS APPOINTED AS THE CAPTAIN OF THE UNIVERSITY TEAM THAT LED THEM TO BECOME ALL JAPAN KARATE CHAMPIONSHIP DURING THE LATE SIXTIES. HIS WORK AS A KARATE INSTRUCTOR HAS BEEN RECOGNIZED ALL OVER THE WORLD, AND HIS REPUTATION WITHIN THE SHITO KAI COMMUNITY IS SECOND TO NONE.

SENSEI SATO POSSESSES PANORAMIC INSIGHTS INTO THE TECHNIQUES AND PHILOSOPHIES OF THE ART OF SHITO RYU. IN THIS INTERVIEW, HE SHARES A TREASURE CHEST OF INTIMATE EXPERIENCES HE HAD WITH HIS LEGENDARY MENTOR AND REVEALS MANY LITTLE-KNOWN FACTS ABOUT HIS BELOVED ART. HIS DEDICATION, DEEP KNOWLEDGE, AND EXCELLENT ABILITY TO COMMUNICATE MAKE HIM ONE OF THE GREATEST MASTERS OF HIS GENERATION. MASTER SATO CONTINUES TO TRAVEL THROUGHOUT THE WORLD TEACHING KARATE.

How long have you been practicing karate-do?

After the WWII, training in a martial art became mandatory. That is how I did enter in judo as a kid. I started training karate at age 15 with a group of friends but it wasn't until I entered in the University that the training became "real".

When I did enter in the University, many clubs from several sports came to select student and athletes for their disciplines; not only for karate but for other sports like gymnastics, track and field, judo, etc. I always felt attracted to karate so I decided that it was the right choice. I did and I have spend the rest of my life dedicated to the art of the "empty hand".

With the exception of judo as a kid, I didn't practice any other martial art. Karate was my first and the only one I dedicated my life to. I understand some people may feel the need to study other arts but since I was training under Manzo Iwata Sensei and felt very fortunate, I didn't see or felt the need for immerse myself in any other style or method of martial arts.

SHITO RYU MASTERS

Was your early karate training difficult?

In the beginning I really felt that the training was extremely hard. Iwata Sensei forced us to reach our physical limits and we needed a lot of personal discipline just to keep going. The sessions were long and very demanding. It was not only about developing good karate skills but also about building the true 'warrior spirit'. We train skill and spirit. The techniques were not easy to absorb by my body and took time to "mold" my body to the art of karate. I remember that there were other students that progressed at a faster pace than me. But I was determined to reach my goals and kept training and enduring the hard sessions. It is true that I thought about giving up a couple of times but I realized that "giving up" was not an option for a true karate practitioner.

What are the most important points in the Shito Ryu method?

Shito Ryu is a very complex style of karate. It absorbs elements from the three main "branches" (shuri, tomari and naha) plus other additional influences. Nevertheless, I can mention three aspects that are essential to the style: a) Natural Movements: all movements have to be natural for the body. This principle opens the training for kids and elders; b) Short and economical movements: simple and direct technical actions improve and shorten the reaction to attacks; and c) Five Principles of Defense: Rakka, Ryusui, Kusshin, Ten-I and Hangeki. All defensive actions are found in these five principles of the Shito Ryu style.

Karate is nowadays often referred to as a sport... would you agree with this definition or is a martial art?

Karate is more than a simple sport. It can be used as a sportive activity in our society but it is an art and the Budo spirit should be present in everything related to it. Even in sport events, the Budo spirit must be there. Budo karate is for all and can be practiced forever. As an athlete, you will reach one day when you can't compete anymore and that is the end. But as a karateka, you keep training and practicing for all your life.

I know that many people are attracted to karate for the sportive aspect of it but the main reason to start and train in karate should not be winning medals and trophies. Karate-do is not about tournaments and medals but about developing yourself as a human being and perfecting your character as a budoka.

How important is competition in the evolution of a karate practitioner?

Sport competition is an interesting element of the karateka's evolution and development. It is a good way to test the skills and see where the practitioner is. It develops confidence and tests the karateka's ability to deal with pressure. If you join sport competition for these reasons, then is positive because is part of the evolution; but if you compete just for the medals and trophies, then you are not doing "real" karate.

Do you think Kobudo training is beneficial for a Karate practitioner?

I truly recommend training in Kobudo since teaches you other important elements in the use of weapons and how to apply the body mechanics when holding a weapon. The Bo is a very good weapon to learn and train and I think it is beneficial to all karateka regardless for the style.

How do you like to train yourself? Has this changed over the years?

My personal training has substantially changed throughout the years because my body has changed. I had to adapt my personal training to those changes. My perception of karate has not changed at all but the physical approach to my personal training did. One thing that has given me a very different point of view of things is traveling all over the world and understanding that every country has a different culture and that culture "shapes" the way people of each country perceive and feel about the art. As a teacher you need to understand these nuances and try to present the art in the best possible way for each culture. It is definitely harder than it sounds.

Kihon, Kata and Kumite, what's the proper ratio in training?

I think that kihon training should be at least half of the training and then, kata and kumite equally distributed; like a 50/25/25 ratio. Without a solid kihon there is no good kata and not good kumite. Many groups in Japan, when preparing for a competition, focus on kihon and not excessively in kata and kumite. Kihon training brings the necessary technical elements that are paramount for a good kata and a good kumite.

SHITO RYU MASTERS

What really means "Ikken-Hissatsu" and how it applies when used in Karate?

"Ikken-Hissatsu" means to finish the opponent with a single blow. This is not always possible but it teaches us the idea that every blow we deliver must have the intention of being a "finishing" strike in action and spirit. There is an important element here about the "intention" of the attack… it is not about throwing combinations of blows "to see" if they hit the target: it is about every single blow to be a "final" and decisive strike.

How do you see the art of Karate evolve in the future?

Nobody knows what the future will bring but as long as we keep the Budo spirit in all the karate dojo around the world, the art will be safe. Unfortunately, if we focus too much on the sport, medals and trophies, the true art of karate will disappear. Be humble, dedicated, disciplined and serious about your training. Budo as a foundation for teaching karate-do is the key to preserve the art for the future generations. Never forget that the students are the reflection of their teacher.

What advice would you give to an instructor who is struggling with his or her won development?

All teachers find some kind of difficulty during their teaching years because they must still keep training and developing themselves. Teaching and self-training are two very different things. Many of the difficulties found can be overcome simply by keep training and sticking to the Budo principles. A good relationship between the teacher and his/her Sensei is very important. Keep training, focus on your personal development, maintain relationship with your teacher and above all, stick to the principles of Budo and the "warrior spirit".

What karate can offer to the individual in these troubled times we are living in?

Karate training offers a diversity of things for all people in our modern society. Kids learn motor skills, they have fun, they develop discipline and manner inside the dojo. They learn to respect the teachers and seniors students, to overcome difficulties and of course it is an "anti-stress" medicine. It is a perfect vehicle for education and good health.

Shotokan, Shito Ryu, Goju, Ryu etc...How do you think the different styles affect the art of Karate?

I personally recommend stick to one style and not jump from one style to another. Find the one that you like and enjoy training and stick to it. There are differences between Shito and Shoto, between Wado and Goju but at the end, karate is karate. However, I believe that is good to have a basic understanding of other styles too, because it teaches us more about the one that we practice and shows us how same things can be done differently.

What are your views on kata bunkai?

Bunkai is a very important aspect of kata study. In the past, when there were no kata competition and 'bunkai' was the center of study. I believe that when a practitioner does not know the bunkai, they perform the kata differently. Understanding bunkai, gives a different flavor to the way a karateka performs the form.

What do you consider to be the major changes in the art since you began training?

Obviously karate has changed throughout the years but the main thing would be the big emphasis that is put nowadays in competition training and sport development instead of focusing in Budo karate.

What is your philosophical basis?

The concept of "Mae"... keep moving forward, keep advancing. This principle was taught daily by Manzo Iwata Sensei. Keep moving forward....

Finally, what advice would you like to give to all Karate practitioners?

Karate is a way of life. The principle of "shoshin shogai" ("with the same heart we start something, we must finish it") should be part of our life and our karate training..

SHIGERU SAWABE

A LEGACY OF EXCELLENCE

Sawabe Shigeru is one of the most senior Shito-ryu practitioners alive today. A direct student of both Kenwa Mabuni and Ryusho Sakagami, Sawabe Shihan has kept the essence of the valuable teachings he received from these legendary masters of Budo pure. "Karate is not a sport. It should be used for self-defense as a last resort only. Karate-do is a way of life ... a means to achieve security and fearlessness." As well as his career as leader of Japan's largest corporate security company, he has long been a leader in Japanese Karate-Do and has held several top positions with several karate-do's governing bodies. He has also authored several highly regarded texts on karate and is the leader of the Japan Karate-Do Shubu-kai. Sawabe Shihan remains active and eager to share the gifts he received from his masters and epitomizes the true definition of the "warrior spirit." In his teaching, he stresses that as one gets older continuous training becomes increasingly important. And, although he is considered among the most knowledgeable of living karate masters, Shigeru Sawabe stresses that he has not arrived. Instead, he is still a student with much to learn, and he intends to continue his quest for knowledge as long as he lives.

When did you first meet Sakagami Ryusho?

I met Sakagami Sensei during wartime. I was in junior high school at the time. At that time in school we were required to do either judo or kendo. I chose kendo, and Sakagami Sensei was the kendo teacher. One day I saw Sakagami Sensei punching a tree. I asked him what he was doing, and he told me that he was practicing karate. Not long afterward I enlisted two of my friends, and we asked Sakagami Sensei to teach us. After the war in 1945, General MacArthur banned the practice of martial arts and Sakagami Sensei decided to stop teaching. After several months, my friends and I found where Sakagami Sensei lived. We went there and asked him to keep teaching us karate. We had to insist a little, but he finally agreed.

How were you introduced to Mabuni Kenwa?

Sakagami Sensei took me to Mabuni Sensei's dojo; that's how I met him. I continued studying karate-do with both Sakagami Sensei and Mabuni Sensei. After high school, I entered Osaka Kogyo University, where Mabuni Sensei was the instructor. I trained with the university club during the day and at night went to Mabuni Sensei's dojo to train more. During my third year at the University, Mabuni Sensei passed away. After that, I continued my training with Sakagami Sensei at his dojo. At that time, his dojo was located at his home.

How was the training under these two great karate masters?

The training under Sakagami Sensei and Mabuni Sensei was very different compared to what we see today in any martial arts school. During the war, when I began, we had no gi and no dojo. We just trained outside. We trained barefoot even when it was quite cold with snow on the ground. The main thing then was the constant training. I would train for three hours at the university and then take the train to Mabuni Sensei's dojo for more training. The morale and mentality after the war dictated how all the practitioners felt and how dedicated they were to the training. It is difficult to explain, but there were mixed feeling inside each and every one of us. From the technical point of view, we weren't concerned about sport and our kata training was a method of training and researching for the most efficient self-defense techniques.

How was the approach to kata training?

Well, to begin with, we didn't really care at all about the look of our kata. This is something that you see today. At that time, kata was not for show. By this, I mean that we never tried to make it look good. It was like a textbook in which you could take technical information. The essence and meaning behind the form were the most important things. The outside or mold was simply perfected to match the proper delivery of the physical technique.

Can you give us an example?

Sure. When we did shuto-uke, we did not hold our fingers perfectly straight. The idea behind shuto-uke is to use the outside edge of your hand to block or hit; therefore, if you straighten all of your fingers, you take force away from that specific area of the hand. We kept the fingers bent to focus more of the tension in that zone. The movement doesn't look as pretty as the "perfect" straight hand, but it is the correct way of doing it …when you are doing it for real use.

The technical approach to the movements was more natural and the human body was taken more into consideration. The main idea in fighting was not to score a point based on speed and power. Instead, it was to attack the vital points in the opponent's body. This is the reason why we develop each part of our body as a weapon. We used fingers to the eyes ands throat, side of the hand to the neck, instep to the groin, kicks to the legs and every other technique that allowed us to seriously hurt the opponent. That's how we learned karate. It was a method of self-defense and not a sport.

Are you against sport in karate?

No, I am not as long as the true spirit of the Budo stays during practice and training. Sport can be seen as a small part of the whole art called karate. That small part never is more important than the art.

How do you remember Mabuni Kenwa?

He was a very special individual. His goal was to try to gather as much knowledge as possible, and that's the reason why he studied so many styles and accumulated so many kata. I understand that modern practitioners do not need to study 60 or 70 kata, but Mabuni Sensei was in a very important position in the history of Budo. He was the link between several styles in Okinawa and the acceptance of karate in Japan. He was in a very important position, and he had to communicate and impart the knowledge in a proper way with the right information. He became a repository of traditional knowledge and kata and many other outstanding karate masters went to him for study and advice. For instance, Master Funakoshi studied with him and sent several of his main students [including M. Nakayama Sensei] to learn from Mabuni Kenwa. He was highly respected among all karate teachers and masters of his time.

And Sakagami Ryusho?

He was a very special individual. His knowledge of Budo was outstanding. Not only he was a master in karate but also in other arts like aikido, kendo kobudo and iaido. He trained with some of the best teachers ever and his understanding of how the different arts fit together in the perfect format for a Budo warrior was amazing. He was capable of relating different techniques and explaining why they could work or why they couldn't. I haven't seen anyone like him, and his memory and legacy will stay with me forever.

Did he teach kobudo, too?

Yes, and he was extremely knowledgeable about the history and application of each traditional weapon from Okinawa. He could relate history to technique in every weapon. He truly was an encyclopedia of knowledge.

Why did he become the leader of the itosu-kai?

According to what I know, Mabuni Sensei had to leave the leadership of the style [shito-ryu] to his son. This is the Japanese tradition in Budo. Sakagami Sensei was older and senior to Mabuni's sons so Mabuni Sensei gave him the leadership of the Itosu-ha legacy that he had received from Grandmaster Itosu Anko. It was a way of allowing him to take the leadership he deserved, but Mabuni Kenwa couldn't give it to him for traditional reasons. Sakagami Sensei became the leader of the itosu-kai style of karate, but it is interesting to note that he was including the entire syllabus from naha-te and tomari-te in his teachings … not only those techniques and kata from the Itosu lineage. The teachings of Kanryo

Higaonna were present in the curriculum and syllabus of Sakagami Sensei. In fact, his teachings were pretty much the same as Mabuni Kenwa's. There were no substantial differences. And by all means, you can consider what Sakagami Ryusho Sensei was teaching as pure shito-ryu.

Do you think that it is important for a shito-ryu or itosu-kai student to know all the complete kata syllabus of the style?

Not really. Each kata represents and teaches certain fighting principles. We have to look into kata using the following approach: Kata was not [originally] a set of fighting techniques. The fighting techniques were separated and they stood by themselves. Then, the old masters put them together in an organized format and created the kata. When you study the application of the movements, you must think this way and try to discover the meaning behind the technique. Sometimes you even have to reverse the kata to understand the bunkai!

Don't try to make sense of the complete kata at once because it was never meant to be that way. Pay attention to the little details in the structure of the form. There is more than meets the eye. Each kata requires time and effort to fully understand its meaning. Therefore, I think that the student in shito-ryu must learn those kata that provide him with the essence of the different flavors found in the shito-ryu style (naha, shuri and tomari) and develop an appreciation for them. Then, focus on those kata that he feels a more natural inclination to and go deep into each one of them. Study the bunkai and oyo bunkai, research the history of kata and find the true meaning behind the form. To be a master of shito-ryu doesn't necessarily mean you need to know 60 different kata. Nobody can master this number of forms equally. Not even Mabuni Sensei had the same amount of knowledge about each single kata he knew. Instructors and professional teachers need to have an extensive knowledge of the complete kata syllabus in order to pass them onto the new generation.

Is it necessary to know different versions of the same kata to completely understand the form in all its interpretations?

Let's take passai kata. According to the opinions and interpretations of the different masters, there are many different versions of this kata. We have matsumura no passai, ishimine no passai, passai dai, passai sho, et cetera. All of these are simply versions of the same. To really get the proper benefit from the form, you don't need to know all of them. Some versions are closer to others, and others are very different to the point that they can be considered a different kata all together. This doesn't really mean anything because the practitioner should take maybe two or three different versions and try to understand their origin and differences. Also, it is important to start with an easier version before learning a more complex or advanced interpretation of the same form. Teachers need to learn more to be capable of passing these different interpretations to future generations.

Are different kata used to develop specific qualities in the student's training?

Definitely. That's one of the advantages of the shito-ryu style. The teacher should use specific kata to develop the student in different technical and physical areas. For instance, you don't use passai dai to develop the student's strength and body conditioning. Other forms like sanchin and tensho should be used to that effect. Each kata has its specification, and it has to be used for that specific purpose. This is one of the reasons why it seems that Mabuni Sensei used the naha-te forms in the beginning of the student's training. Maybe he used that to develop the body so he could later introduce more subtle technical actions based on speed [shuri-te]. I think that basically it all depends on the student you are teaching. The training was done in almost one-on-one situations so the teacher used to give each student specifically what he needed. This doesn't happen today, and the instruction is more mass oriented. This reduces the possibility of the instructor giving the student those things that he really needs for himself.

How does shito-ryu combine (under one format) the presentation of different styles (approaches) and fighting ideas from shuri, tomari and naha?

It is a difficult question to answer because it would take hours to explain all the details, but I'll try my best to keep it short. It is clear how the format of shotokan karate works, and it is also clear how the style of goju-ryu performs the kata. Shito-ryu doesn't use any of these extremes [if we can use this term]. It makes every form more natural ... more in an Okinawan way of performing the techniques. It is not as physical and strong as shotokan, but it is neither as hard as goju. This approach is something that people understand with time. When their bodies change and they get older, the hard approach can't be used any more because it is not natural for the body. Then you have to use a more natural way of doing the kata. Let me cite an example from shotokan. In this style, the kata has been changed and designed for young and strong people. So, when they get older, they can hardly do the kata as they used to. If you look at senior instructors of hard shotokan in the past, you'll see that now they do the forms very differently. They look more natural and closer to the way shito-ryu does the forms. They even use shito-ryu kata in their curriculum now because they have realized that the approach is more natural for the body and you can use it for a long period of time. Karate was never meant to be practiced only by young people. So, in my opinion, the idea of formatting karate for strong and physically talented students was not a very good move.

Do you separate your teaching in basic and advanced techniques in kata?

Not really, because that is a mistake. I don't look at karate techniques and separate the movements into advanced and basic. There are no basic or advanced movements. Techniques are the same. Techniques are something that develop and improve with time and training. A fundamental technique becomes "advanced," as you like to describe, when it becomes a natural movement and a reflexive reaction. An intermediate movement can counter every basic technique, and an advanced movement can easily counter every intermediate movement. What people don't understand is that any advanced movement is very easily nullified by a basic technique. Please note that when I use the terms "advanced," "intermediate" and "basic" that I'm only referring to the technical difficulty of the physical action. Simply, don't forget that the more complex the technical action is, the less likely it will be successful.

What is the difference between a sport coach and a karate teacher?

Many, but unfortunately and due to the fact modern karate is moving more and more into a sportive approach, teachers are becoming like football coaches. They use the sport approach to make students better and this is wrong. On the other hand, many karate champions become instructors immediately. Dan ranks are given to competitors because they have won a tournament. Then, you have a 5th dan instructor only because he has won an international championship. How do you think this instructor will coach his students? A competitor is focused on being better and stronger himself. Usually, they don't teach the student how to be great because they still have to think about themselves. And it is actually quite normal to think about your own importance when you are young and competing. A true sensei is a different thing all together. I have always enjoyed making my students better than me. Fortunately, young students have great teachers around the world they can go to for information, training and assistance.

In modern competition, different scores are given to different techniques. Do you agree with that idea?

I like the idea of shobu-ippon because it represents what Budo is all about. One punch, and you are dead. You can't get up and keep fighting. Even if you don't put your opponent down with one single technique that is what you should strive for. Even if you don't knock him down completely, he will be in very bad shape. In this condition, there is no guarantee of victory. When you know there is only one opportunity of doing it right — because otherwise you'll be doing it wrong — you pay more attention to everything. You know that a small mistake can be fatal. You know you can score three or four more points afterward … like in soccer. It is only one clean shot. No second chances. Like the old samurai duels. You miss, and you are killed. This is Budo, and I like this idea. Of course, it may be boring for spectators. For a Budoka who understands what is happening, however, it is very interesting. This approach influences the mental state of the fighter because of the relevance of a single action. The fighter needs to render himself empty as a mirror's polished surface reflects whatever stands before it. His mind should be empty of selfishness in an effort to react appropriately toward anything his opponent may give him. He finds himself fighting in a controlled environment, but he maintains an attitude of facing death. This is the only way we can bring true Budo spirit into modern competition without losing the traditional fighting spirit of the arts.

Is it more difficult to perform proper kicking techniques or punching techniques?

Every technique has its difficulty, no matter what it may be. Personally, however, I see the necessary coordination, balance and use of all the proper lines of power in the body to be more difficult in the punching techniques. I know many people think that kicking techniques are very difficult. However, if we understand all the body mechanics involved in a simple gyaku-tsuki, we'll realize that it is extremely hard to master the correct body positioning, hip rotation, back alignment, shoulder push, torque action, et cetera. Understanding the different types of kime when punching is extremely difficult. For instance, I see many practitioners only using their arms and hips when they punch. They don't know how to use their shoulders correctly in the movement. If they did, that would fully bring the back muscles into the punch. They, because of the lack of knowledge and understanding, use too many chest muscles to compensate for the technique. They also keep the muscular tension too long after the final part of the technique. Because of this, their breath stops, which is completely incorrect.

Also, the idea of snapping your body like a whip is something that has been developed in the last decades of research. It is important to fully understand how the body works and try to get the most out of it in every physical movement.

What is the traditional model for teachers and students in Japanese karate and how do the Western students accept it?

The technical model is presented to the students, and they try to copy it as accurately as possible. They have faith and confidence in the sensei, which eliminates the need for lengthy verbal discussion about the technique. The student doesn't question anything. He accepts his role and the training environment. For a Western student, all this is really strange because it is a cultural thing. They accept more personal responsibility in their own progress in the art, which compels them to continually question the structure and content of each lesson. The questions need to be answered immediately, and students are not satisfied with the Japanese answer of "because the sensei says so." Considering all these differences, it is not difficult to understand why there are sometimes misinterpretations and misunderstandings. I believe that these important cultural aspects are the key to many problems in the art of karate today. For instance, many Japanese instructors living abroad need to find a reason for every technique they teach. They also feel they have to justify everything taught in class, as this is a desperate attempt to reassure the students that they are not wasting their time. Therefore, the value of the technique is expressed in relation to the potential such techniques have for scoring points and winning tournaments.

What are the most important qualities of a good instructor?

The main point is that the instructor must know himself. He must understand his strong and weak points – both physically and mentally. From there he can look to the students and try to work with the capabilities and limitations they may have. This is very basic philosophy. Only when you understand yourself can you understand other people. Without this, it is impossible to teach other people properly. Also, a good instructor keeps training himself all the time. He doesn't stop his personal training or his learning process, and he places emphasis on the basics movements and techniques.

A good instructor should be hard and dedicated to what he does. At the same time, he has to be understanding to the student's needs and be there to help him when he needs it. This applies not only inside the dojo but outside as well. A good sensei in the traditional Budo concept is much more than a simple teacher of a fighting art.

What should an instructor be looking for in a grading session?

From the technical point of view, it depends on what dan level the student is testing for. Based on this, the requirements are different. But there are basics concepts and principles the students must physically display according to the rank they are testing for; such as body control, hip action, kime, zanchin, stances and overall coordination, et cetera. These are some of the elements that every karate practitioner should have, depending, of course, on their skill level. Regardless if they pass or fail, students should present themselves with etiquette and decorum. If the attitude is wrong, I personally don't care much for the physical ability.

What is karate to you and how would you describe its benefits?

Karate represents many different things. To me, it is a beautiful art that can be used as a physical activity to keep in shape and also a method of perfecting character. It is an art form, but not only because someone designed a set of physical moves that make it look artistic. It is art because karate teaches us to use the body in a perfect way. The movements are designed to be used in the best possible way. Every single muscle and body part work together to generate the body's maximum potential in power and speed. Through the attempt to perfect these techniques, you can use your body like a tool for self-improvement. Once you have the necessary skill, that is when the true spirit of Budo must take over. Any technique, regardless of how perfect it may be from a physical point of view, is irrelevant without the correct spirit. I'm not talking about anger or rage. I am talking about good spirit, which is something creative and positive. With it, we can surpass our physical and mental limitations and improve ourselves.

Why do you think students stop training after three or four years?

There is a threshold in which most of the students quit training, and this is between 1st kyu and shodan. After this period of time [three or four years], the student is not motivated any more because the initial illusion has gone away. Now the students realize that to progress there is only one way to go … constant repetition of what they have learned and this becomes a boring chore. Another reason is that their technical foundation hasn't been set properly, and they start to see their own limitations and get disappointed. If they don't have a precise understanding of the art and basics from the very beginning, it is impossible for them to keep motivated to progress. They simply have no desire to stick to it. In the Japanese culture, the student is not supposed to enjoy the training. Training is a challenge and something difficult the student has to face every day. It is not a hobby or a pleasure as it is in the Western world.

Finally, what advice would you give to all karate-do practitioners, regardless of style?

My advice is to keep practicing all the time. Even if you feel tired, bored and with no motivation whatsoever ... keep doing it. You'll understand one day. Because the more you practice, the more you understand when the right time comes. Never neglect the basics and take the kata training seriously. Never forsake one kata for another and treat them all the same because they bring different benefits to you. Dedicate yourself to your instructor. When you become a teacher, teach anyone who is willing to learn. Karate teaches you how to gain and keep control of any situation in life. When you face a difficult task, push yourself into it until you can do it. Don't give up under pressure. Keep a good attitude and strong discipline.

GEORGE TAN

KARATE PILLARS

From day one, Sensei George Tan has been driven by the spirit of Budo in his Karate journey, a journey that started more than 40 years ago.

Shihan Tan is currently the president of "Asia Pacific Shito Ryu Karate Federation" as well as president of the "Traditional Shito Kai Karate-do Association." Awarded a 7th Dan in 1994 by the Japan Karate-do Federation, Sensei Tan went through the "Shihan" exam in 2006 in Japan and was officially recognized by WSKF (World Shito Kai Federation) with the "Shihan" status after passing the earlier Jokyo (2003) and Jun-Shihan (2004) exams.

Although no one can ever question Shihan George Tan's dedication to traditional teachings, his unwavering practical sense of Budo values set him apart from other karate instructors around the world. " I love the focus and the discipline that Karate provides," he says. "Karate allows me to be completely in the moment for myself, with myself."

How long have you been practicing martial arts?

I started training Shito Ryu Karate in the mid-1970s, almost 40 years ago. I was and am still with Shito Ryu. My first teacher was the late Shihan Naser and in Japan, I also trained under other Shito Ryu masters including Ken Sakio and Kenei Mabuni Sensei. So, all along, Shito Ryu is the only style I have ever practiced.

From a physical point of view, I would consider myself talented for Karate. Karate was never physically difficult for me but of course this doesn't mean it has been "easy." Karate requires a lot of work and training but my body always has responded properly to the hard training.

In the early days, we were all extremely serious in our training. I trained seven days a week and since we had movie icons such as Bruce Lee, we all tried to be like him. I think many Martial Arts masters of my generation were attracted to the training by Bruce Lee. This is not bad if we come to understand that movies are not real Martial Arts. My early training sessions were "never ask questions, just do as you are told." We conditioned our bodies for kumite, had many injuries, and never complained about pain. We enjoyed the pain and when limbs were black and blue due to injuries, we were proud of it. Breaking

bricks, boards, tiles, and blocks of ice were part of our way to show how strong we were. I did not come from a wealthy home so I cherished the training as I had to work hard to get the money to pay the training fees.

How has your personal expression karate developed over the years?

The "Do" or " Way" of karate is a lifelong process when it comes to learning. Karate is now so natural for me that sometimes I wonder whether I was a warrior in a past life. "Bunkai" or analysis from kata also comes so naturally to me that sometimes it surprises me. I have been asked so many kinds of questions that I almost instantly answer when it comes to kata application. I guess it could also be because of my experience in attending a lot of seminars and interacting with the Shito Ryu masters I had the opportunity of training under.

What are the most important points in your teaching methods today?

The most important point is to be serious in training. It is something very simple but very difficult. Discipline is the most important thing. Students come and go because they lose interest. It is common to have only one person out of one hundred achieve the black belt status. Most students drop out ... they find many excuses, tuition, homework, pain, no time, no money, school exams, parents object ... the list goes on and on. These people only need to find an excuse to stop training because they simply don't want to keep training.

What do you think has been lost from Okinawa to Japan in terms of Karate evolution?

I have trained in Okinawa and most people there keep their traditional values. Believe me that the Okinawans treat Karate very seriously and they make the modern Japanese Karate look like kids' stuff. It is because too much sports-karate in Japan currently spoils the value of true karate and Martial Art.

The normal objective of sports today is "win" and be rewarded. Although one also to condition the body for sports, that is not Martial Arts. It is better to train in running because your opponent will never be able to catch you. In real karate, it is important to remember that the adversary is not defeated by the technique, but well before, right at the precise moment he has lost the initiative in the fight. It is exactly because the adversary is already defeated that it is possible to apply the technique on him to concretize and carry out his defeat.

What are the most important qualities for a student to become proficient in karate?

I teach both the traditional and the sport aspect of it, but they all have to go through the normal traditional training procedures. Basics, or kihon, is the most important. If one's basics are weak, the foundation will be weak. It is like the foundation of a building; if it is weak, the building will collapse. There is no other way around it.

When teaching the art of karate, what is the most important aspect the student should be aware of?

Kihon and kata as kumite will come naturally. One should overcome the fear of pain. The principle of "shin-gi-tai" (heart, technique, and body) should be emphasized as "one" – otherwise it is incomplete. The art of karate-do allows us to be ourselves, humbly but firmly. Our internal weaknesses do not instantly disappear, but it takes time to change our perception of what karate is and begin to actually "see" what karate can provide to us. We still must persevere as progress in Karate-do is not measured by immediate result but over the long term.

What do you think is more important, the technique itself or the principle that the technique represents?

Practice of the physical techniques permits us to arrive at an understanding of the principle, but the proper understanding of the principle will help us to improve the physical technique. Therefore, both are extremely important. At the end, it is important to understand that karate is not simply a matter of technique. The physical techniques in and out of themselves are not what karate-do is all about. Techniques have no meaning whatsoever if we take them out of the context in which they have to be used. It is like the actual words and their meaning … two different things.

What do you mean by that?

When you try to communicate a "feeling" or a "lesson" to somebody - in any field, the meaning of the words used matter less than the impact of their evocative power. But in order to fill words with strong and pure energy, you have to be more than a teacher; you have to be a "master." The words become a simple instrument to communicate a concept; that is why the entire act of a true karate master is based on the right choice of words, actions or symbols that truly represent and communicate the thought that he wants the student to grasp. In true Budo teaching, the student needs a very special kind of predisposition or receptivity to understand the hidden meaning of words and ideas, and find out what its real meaning is. This is the true way of teaching traditional Budo.

So, is there a chance that the student misinterprets the teacher's words?

Of course. That is the problem when we use words to communicate. Between the thinking of the master and that of the disciple, there is always an ambiguity of words that can be misinterpreted by the student and prevent him from actually fully understand what the master is trying to convey. That is why in all Budo arts, "feeling" is more important than "talking." The problem is that the student can train for 40 years and still not understand things. Then the teacher has to use words to clarify things.

Within kata, where are the actual fighting/self defense principles? How we can learn to "connect" kata with actual fighting?

Performing kata repeatedly to perfect the kata can give you the reflex as you are in an imaginary combat with your opponent. The directions you face from all over gives you a sense of facing several opponents from different angles. Imagine in sports kumite that you are only facing one opponent and he is always in front of you. Kata is very different but we need to know how to look at it and how to learn from it.

How do you think a practitioner can increase his/her understanding of the spiritual aspects of the art?

You become almost a spiritual leader and practitioner if you can answer all your students questions at ease. You need time and there is no short cut to it. To be a champion in sports Karate, you may need only five years, but the spiritual aspects of Martial Arts need many decades of training and study to understand. Please note I did say "study" and not only "training." Many people "train" Karate for 40 years but they do not "study" Karate.

Is there anything lacking in the way Karate is taught today compared to how it was when you started training?

Unfortunately, Karate has been diluted to make it easier to understand. Students easily get their black belts so that they can retain the interest to carry on. In my early days, just being a brown belt commands a lot of respect from all … more than what you see in black belts today. It took more than four years to obtain a black belt, but today students train less and expect to get their black belt in less than three years. The color of the belt is more important than the training. Students today look for the shortest and fastest way to obtain this status. And this is not right. Many teacher see how students show lack of interest because they are bored or maybe because they find that their limits has been reached. With these idea hanging over their training, the temptation of others are likely to occur example staying at home, watching a movie, computer games, hanging out with friends, etc.

Do you feel that you still have further to go in your studies?

Definitely. I am a 7th Dan Shito Ryu and have obtained my Shihan status from Shito Kai in Japan but I still have many higher stages to go through. I obtained my 7th Dan in 1994 and I am one of the youngest to obtain this grade at the age of 39.

What advice would you give to students on the question of supplementary training?

Using light weights is very good for speed training. However, students are advised to do more in repetition rather than overstretch with force to avoid muscle tear. Running is good for stamina training. Yes, all these additional physical trainings are good for body conditioning … but in no way can they substitute for the actual Karate training.

Have there been times when you felt fear in your training?

There were a few times when I have got hurt really bad during sparring and this affects your confidence, but you have to push through. Spirit is very important in Karate and all Budo arts. As martial artists, we are not controlled by the flesh but by the spirit. Only the spirit defends the body and frees the mind of the karate-ka.

Do you think that Olympics will be positive for the art of karate-do?

I have heard of Karate in the Olympics for more than two decades and it is still not a reality yet.

What are your views on kata bunkai?

Bunkai is the most important after one learns to perform the Kata. Without bunkai, it is just a dance. It is like you are singing but without the music. Understanding and performing the bunkai is very important for Karate training – especially in Shito Ryu because this style has more than 65 katas, which is the most amongst the four major styles of Karate in Japan.

What are your thoughts about doing thousands of repetitions of one single technique in training as in the old days? Is it a good training method?

Of course it is good, but it needs time. Today, most instructors teach the easy ways in order for their students to excel in training. Students like getting their belts upgraded fast. Never forget that the level of a karate-ka is not judged by the number of techniques one knows but by the manner in which one uses them. What is important is not the technique itself but the right attitude to apply it.

If you had only a one-hour class with a student, what would be the most important thing that you'd teach him/her?

It depends on the rank or the seniority of the student. If he/she is a beginner, correct kihon such as proper stances, how the defense blocks are done, etc. If he/she is a more senior student, I would concentrate on reviewing the katas and to perfect the performance. In Karate, it is important for the practitioner to understand that when we get to control the intent of the attacker, he/she loses all possibility of resistance. It is only then that we can apply any technique we wish. The technique we actually decided to use is of little importance because hopefully we have trained enough to be able to adapt to all circumstances. Basically, we should lead the adversary to a situation where the application of our technique becomes possible.

What can Karate offer to the individual in these troubled times we are living in?

Mentally, you have to be strong in Karate, and when in troubled times, a good workout will release the stress that is accumulated in your body. After a strenuous workout, you should feel more relaxed. This is just from a physical point of view. As a philosophy, the art of Karate-do can help the practitioner look at life from a well-balanced inner center.

After so many years of training, what is so appealing to you in the Shito Ryu style of karate and why?

Shito Ryu is a fusion of Naha-te and Shuri-te, an excellent combination of power and speed. Shito Ryu has both and that makes it unique. In simple laymen's terms, power does not necessary means speed and likewise speed does not necessarily mean power.

How do you like to train yourself? Has this changed over the years?

My training at this age is to maintain my form and not let it slide too quickly. I enjoy kata as one can go on and on. Kumite movements are limited and I have been more careful at my age, as injuries take a longer time to heal.

Westerners generally are physically bigger than Okinawan/Japanese (Asian) practitioners; how do you think this has affected their karate?

The Europeans are very good in sports kumite. They move very fast. It is all in the training and basically for competition. Your body structure will depend on the events in which you can excel. For example, for kata division, tall persons don't look as good as short practitioners. However, for self-defense, it is generally known that big and tall ones' moves are much slower than the smaller-built ones. In terms of defense, the smaller, shorter moves can be deadly as they are taught to attack only the vital parts of the body.

Is your style of teaching the same as the traditional Karate-do method or do you have your own ideas?

Basically, we have the same principles of training as found in many Japanese dojo. Different instructors have their different ways of teaching but the essence is more or less the same. The only difference is whether you are teaching from your heart or your mind is concentrated on going to the dojo to collect training fees only and do it just like a business.

What advice would you give to an instructor who is struggling with his or her won development?

I would advise instructors to learn from different masters. That is the only way to improve. Of course, we have to be loyal to our own masters first. But other masters can identify your mistakes easily and you will learn more. If you are Shotokan, go learn from Goju Ryu masters, too, and vice versa. If we are from Shito Ryu, learn from Shotokan and Goju masters ... each master and style has individual good points.

Finally, what advice would you like to give to all Karate practitioners and martial artists in general?

If you are trained in sports Karate only, do not expect to defend yourself on the streets. Be realistic and true to yourself. If anything happens to you on the streets, you should not blame Karate because you only study sport/competition Karate and not real Budo Karate. Budo karate is totally different. We are trained to protect and really defend ourselves, whereas in sports Karate, the ultimate goal is "winning a trophy." I am not against sports Karate as I have also represented my country in tournaments. It is fun and it is all about winning and losing. Lastly, I would advice teaching students first in traditional Karate and later they can decide whether to excel in the sports areas, as not everyone can be a world champion.

KATSUTAKA TANAKA

THE TRUE WAY OF BUDO

SENSEI TANAKA IS ONE OF THE MOST WELL-KNOWN MARTIAL ARTS LEADERS IN AMERICA AND A PIONEER OF JAPANESE KARATE IN THE WEST. BUT MORE THAN THAT HE IS A REMARKABLE MARTIAL ARTIST AND A TRUE ICON IN THE WORLD OF KARATE-DO.

KATSUTAKA TANAKA'S SKILLS IN THE TRADITIONAL WEAPONRY ART OF KOBUDO HAVE IMPRESSED THOUSANDS OF PEOPLE THROUGHOUT THE YEARS. SENSEI TANAKA WAS BORN AND RAISED IN JAPAN AND LEARNED HIS ART THE HARD WAY - A WAY THAT CAN ONLY BE FOUND IN THE ORIENT. ALTHOUGH DEEPLY INVOLVED IN THE TECHNICAL COMMITTEE OF THE WORLD KARATE FEDERATION, TANAKA'S VIEWS ARE A RETURN TO THE TRADITIONAL VALUES OF THE MARTIAL ARTS. "THE SPORT ASPECT OF KARATE IS VERY IMPORTANT NOWADAYS, BUT WE CAN STILL MAINTAIN THE TRADITIONAL ROOTS AND MORAL VALUES OF BUDO. BOTH WORLDS CAN LIVE TOGETHER - THEY ARE NOT THE OPPOSITE OF EACH OTHER. IT'S UP TO THE TEACHERS TO PRESERVE THE ETHICAL PRINCIPLES OF KARATE-DO FOR FUTURE GENERATIONS, AND AT THE SAME TIME KEEP IT AN INTERESTING SPORTING ACTIVITY." RESIDING IN ALASKA SINCE HIS FIRST VISIT TO AMERICA, SENSEI TANAKA HAS TAUGHT MARTIAL ARTS TO THOUSAND OF STUDENTS FROM ALL OVER THE WORLD. HE STILL TEACHES HIS DAILY CLASSES AND STICKS TO THE TWO MOST IMPORTANT PRINCIPLES OF KARATE - HARD WORK AND INNER SPIRIT. HE IS TRULY A MASTER OF THE OLD WAYS.

When did you start training martial arts?

My first experience was at the age of 14. My brother came home one day and found me kicking at some decorative beads hanging from the ceiling. "Hey!" my brother yelped. "Do you want to learn karate?" I shrugged my shoulders and said: "I don't know." "Come on, then," he said. "Let's find out." He took me to a karate school in the city where my brother's friend was an instructor. When we arrived,

we found that there was by a guest from one of the university karate teams in central Japan - and he was really tough! One by one, he fought all of the school's black belts. Not one of them could go the distance against him in a two-minute match. He was too awesome. Knees, elbows, head butts - everything. He was crazy.

What was your impression?

I was terrified. That was not something I wanted to study. I went home and tried to put the incident out of my mind. But the memory haunted me. I was forced to consider my reaction more profoundly. "I know I'm scared," I thought to myself. "And I don't want to go back. But if I don't, I might do the same thing with everything in life. I don't want to go, therefore I must."

Did you immediately enroll in the dojo?

Yes, soon after I began my karate lessons. And, of course, the karate supplemented the judo and kendo classes which were a required part of junior high school physical education in Japan. Yet being a student following a college prep curriculum, I did not have much time to devote to serious study of the art. Then in 1965 I joined the new karate team at Nagoya-Gakuin University, where I was studying for a Bachelor's degree in Economics. The karate team practiced three-to-four hours a day, six days a week. I submerged myself in the training. The art I practiced at the university was seidokai, a sort of cross between shotokan karate and Japanese kempo, but with a lot of boxing-like footwork. However, I soon grew dissatisfied with the karate team, and especially with the team seniors. A karate team at a Japanese university is much like a football team at an American university. Personal pride and school spirit are invested in the team's performance. But Nagoya-Gakuin's team was still inexperienced and not very successful.

What do you mean by that?

When the team showed up at major tournaments, the other university teams would laugh at us. The team seniors were often chastised and mistreated. I really took the insults personally. I wanted my seniors to stand-up to the abuse, physically. They did not. They lacked the mental component of the art - the self-confidence and determination. I felt that I had to do something. I wanted to silence the laughter and restore respect for the name "Nagoya-Gakuin." So one member of the team and I approached our seniors with a proposition: "Please. Treat us rougher! Make us do the things we must to become winners." The seniors listened but they did not act. They seemed almost afraid of our fervor.

What happened then? Didn't they react to your words?

Not really - and in free-sparring practice, on occasion, I would defeat one of the seniors. Several months passed and I progressed to the point where I consistently defeated my seniors. As a freshman I was inexperienced compared to the polished technique of the seniors - but spirit-wise I was superior. Unfortunately, as my skills became more improved, my seniors grew more removed. Once again, I called the seniors aside and said, "Look. Even though my friend and I can beat you in free-fighting, we still respect you. You are our seniors. So go ahead and give us orders. Tell us what we must do to become winners." It was there when I really began to wonder if my seniors even knew how to train champions.

How did that affect the way the team performed in competition?

Soon afterwards, the seniors entered Nagoya-Gakuin in the team competition at the Central Japan Karate Championships. Team competition in Japan is conducted much like the team competitions in America. One squad of fighters faces another one-on-one, utilizing the point system of scoring. The team that scored the most points at the conclusion of the last match was declared the winner. However, the nature of the fighting in Japan was radically different from that in the West. The competition was more blood and guts. There was no safety equipment. Broken bones, knockouts, and an assortment of other injuries were commonplace. The Japanese style of fighting was based on stability. They charged straight ahead, never backed up, and never quit. Back-fists were rarely scored as points, and the hit-and-run tactics of the mobile fighters were never seen.

Do you have some special memories of your competition days?

Yes, I remember that in the first round of the team competition, my school had to confront our closest rival, the team from Nagoya Commercial College. The rival school's team was anchored by one of the most feared fighters in all of Japan, a man called "Monster." He stood five-foot-ten inches tall, was built like Joe Frazier, and liked to knock people out. Nagoya Commercial College sent out Monster - and we sent out our own giant, a friend of mine who stood six foot three. Monster laughed when he saw him. Yet once underway, it was the giant who launched the opening attack. Whap! A front kick found Monster's belly. Monster grabbed the leg and cradled it against his side, like a football. Then he looked the Giant square in the eyes, screamed, and charged forward and deposited the giant on the floor in the next ring. Monster turned around and slowly walked back to the starting position. The match was over. Monster's teammates howled with laughter.

What happened then?

Our team fought back in the later matches, and after the last fight the two teams were tied. The captains of each team met in the ring with the referee to decide who would fight to break the tie. When the captains began to return to the sidelines, Monster assumed his position in center ring. I turned to our giant and said, "Who's going to fight that beast for us?" Over the loudspeaker came a sudden announcement: "Representing the Nagoya-Gakuin karate team is Katsutaka Tanaka!" I was surprised and I protested, but the Giant just slapped me on the back. "Well," he said, "you wanted to do anything to be a winner." I shook my head and gulped deeply. "This is going to be your last match ever kid," yelled one of Monster's teammates.   I gulped again and thought to myself: "This is the man to beat. If I can stop him, I can stop anybody. I am not going to back up." I defeated Monster that day and went on to finish second in the tournament.

SHITO RYU MASTERS

Was it then that you were elected captain of the university team?

Yes, and from then on everything changed. I made the practice sessions tougher - much tougher. I trained the team not to back up and not to quit. If they got hit once, they were to hit back twice. Punishment training was emphasized. No one was to get knocked-out in a tournament. The team needed leadership and discipline, and I was determined to set an example. Most everyone thought I was a little crazy because of the kamikaze attitude that I had about fighting - but they did respect my intensity and my results - and that was exactly what I was after. I figured I had three more years to spend at the university, and was going to get as much out of it as I possibly could. The first thing I did was develop a one-year plan, sort of a crash course to get us on par with the rest of the universities. I started a schedule of very hard training and kept pushing them until they fell. Even then, we poured water on them and kicked them until they got up again. They realized they had to push themselves beyond being tired or hurt because I wouldn't accept anything less. We hit them, kicked them, and we made them get used to getting hurt so they wouldn't care anymore. It really worked. We became the roughest university team in central Japan within that first year - not the most technically sound but the roughest. You can't imagine what an intimidating influence that can have on an opponent. They just didn't know what to expect from us because we got a reputation for being a bunch of crazy fighters. This, in turn, pumped-up the whole team and gave them the confidence that they could win anything. I wanted my team to be the best in Japan, and in 1968 I took his team to the Central Japan Karate Championships and came away with the first place trophy. My dream had come true.

When did you came to the United States?

After graduation, I went to the Alaska Methodist University, which had an exchange program with Nagoya-Gakuin University. I started teaching karate during the day as part of the university's physical education programe, and at nighttime I taught a women's self-defense class. When I arrived at AMU, I started teaching the way I was taught in Japan. I had 40 students when we started and two months later I didn't have any. No one came back because I hit them and I kicked them - and if their stance was no good, I tripped them. I was finally told by the head of the P.E. department that I couldn't do that. And I told him, "Don't tell me what to do. This is the way it should be done." He explained that he was getting a little bit scared, and thought we were going to get sued! So I decided not to hit students anymore. I'm getting very Americanized (laughs). But I still believe in the traditional ways - martial arts should be very strict.

So you had to modify the traditional Japanese teaching methods to Western culture?

When I first came to Alaska I was still gung-ho and quite convinced that my training methods would be effective and well-received. But I quickly realized that I was no longer in Japan and that I couldn't treat American people like Japanese people. I tried to take it easy and I really thought I had successfully tailored a program that would be acceptable to everyone. I was wrong. I had one student who refused to listen to my comments on the narrowness of his stance. I came up from behind him and swept him to the floor with relative ease. He stood-up glaring at me and asked why I tripped him. I told him his stance was too narrow and to try again. Again his stance was too narrow and again I swept him to the floor - this time very hard and very fast. Admittedly, I made him look like a fool. The next day he came to class acting really tough, saying that he wanted me to know that he had a gun and that I'd better watch out. I knew that if I showed fear I'd have a difficult time controlling him. When he finally showed me the gun I grabbed it and emptied the bullets. It was then that I realized that I didn't want to have to contend with this type of behavior for the rest of my life, and that many people take the discipline in the classroom as a personal affront. I've since found a number of ways to accomplish the same end by alternative means. It's still rough and it's still intense but I don't find it necessary to pummel a student to get his attention. I've been told my classes are not unlike Marine Corps Boot Camp. That's not so bad.

After settling in the United States, did you go back to Japan to update your training?

Yes, I did. In 1972 I returned to Japan briefly. I found that seidokai stylists were then turning to kickboxing, a move that I could not support. I began to search Japan for a new style to serve as my foundation art. I looked at shotokan, kyokushinkai and goju-ryu, but finally settled on shito-ryu. I don't believe that one system is good enough - none of them. No single one is fully adequate. Each system has good points. So what I teach combines everything. My fighting technique comes from my days with the university karate team.

How can a karate practitioner develop a fighting instinct to survive a real threat situation?

It's a rather simple concept, but it's very difficult to teach. What it boils down to is a person's ability to refuse to be beaten. Injury and pain must be accepted as minor obstacles. The ultimate concern is to prevail and to convince yourself that nothing else matters. To the layman, this might sound a bit extreme, but fighting must be viewed in its own separate context. I agree with those who say that fighting should only be a last resort to any altercation. But there are going to be times when there is no other alternative. When that time comes, there can only be one thing in your mind - get in, do as much damage as possible, and get out. Resign yourself to the fact that you're going to get hurt. Accept it. But be confident in the fact that your opponent is going to get hurt a lot more than you.

What about the idea of pushing yourself beyond your physical limits?

Again, the concept is simple but the execution is difficult. The human body has the ability to go beyond conventional limits of strength. When you feel like you can't go on anymore, that's when you really learn, that is when you really make progress. When you're really tired and you are able to push yourself past the point of exhaustion, you suddenly forget about being tired. You are past that point and you no longer have to think about what you are doing. You have passed all points and your mind is free of your body so you're ready to do anything.

Do you follow the strict shito-ryu method?

I earned my black belt in the shito-ryu, and yes, I follow that style as far as foundation and kata training goes. But 90 percent of what I teach is actually a highly stylized combination of many styles - at least in principles and concepts of technical functionality. I think that a majority of instructors will tell you how to do a technique without telling you why it is going to be useful. I shun soft, flowing techniques and concentrate on hard kicks and punches - particularly punches. The main thing that I want my students to learn is to punch well, because in terms of self-defense, how many people on the street jump up and kick you in the head? They just grab and punch. For that type of situation, you've got to have good, dependable hands - where you're confident that if you hit your attacker he won't be getting up for a while. If you have good hands you feel more secure and will be calmer. You'll see the situation better and maybe try to talk your way out of a fight altogether. I tell my students to avoid trouble as much as they can. My master in Japan said that the highest skill in karate is not winning 100 fights out of 100, but avoiding 100 out of 100 fights. But in order to avoid these 100 fights you must be very smart - you must have good self-control, be calm, and clearly evaluate how the situation is developing. But if they are pushed to the point of fighting, I encourage them to go all the way. Either you fight all out, or you don't fight at all. There is no halfway in self-defense.

So for self-defense, you advocate having powerful and definitive techniques?

Definitely. This is the main reason why I concentrate on what you can be described as "hard" techniques. I stress hard punches and kicks to vital points on the body. If you're fighting someone who is big and muscular, so what? Kick the groin and pull him down. The groin, throat, nose, eyes and neck are basically the only areas that I want my students to attack. Don't even bother with joint locks and throws. Throwing a guy is not going to put him away, it will just get him more enraged. So before you throw him, knock him out - and fast. I want my students to know exactly what's going to work for them and why. This is a bit of a departure from the traditional Oriental approach, where if you have a question about something you are told to practice until you find the answer. I don't agree with this and that's probably why I had so much trouble in school - I always wanted to know "why." When my instructor told me to do a technique I would ask why it was a good technique. In many cases, I don't think they really knew why. They would just say, "That's the way it's always been done, so do it." I think that my questioning attitude brought me to where I am today. I understand now, though, what my instructors were trying to say - most answers in life come through self-realization. They say that studying martial arts is like walking on a stony road. It's very painful - nothing but pain. But that's how you learn the answers of life. The real truths come from fighting with yourself. No matter how good anything seems on the surface, you must be convinced - you have to convince yourself. That is the answer.

How important do you think the study of kata is in the art of karate-do?

It is very important. The more I study kata, the more I can see how important they are for fighting. To fight better than your opponent, you must make him move as you want - with proper spirit, and well-balanced techniques. Your technique has power when your body moves as a single unit. Kata helps you learn that unity. In Japan, maybe we put too much weight on fighting and not enough on kata. I mean, when you think about it, so many masters have practiced this art. Maybe for one master to develop a kata, it took him a lifetime. He thought about a lot of things. You know, if my opponent does this, what can I do? So the katas are the result of all his training and experience. And the more time you spend exploring a kata, the deeper will be your understanding of the art of karate and its uses. You have to go deeper and deeper into the study of the kata. You just can't stop on the surface and simply try to master the physical and external appearance of the kata.

What is your teaching philosophy for the budo arts?

I truly believe the old ways are the best and still work. Perfection in the martial arts is to make the mind and body work together. That's the final goal. I try to teach my students how to perfect themselves. That's the true way - the way of budo.

ALLEN TANZADEH

A WEALTH OF KNOWLEDGE

ALLEN TANZADEH BEGAN HIS KARATE TRAINING IN 1972. EVER SINCE, HIS LIFETIME PASSION FOR KARATE ENABLED HIM TO DISTINGUISH HIMSELF IN NUMEROUS WAYS. AS A COMPETITOR, HE WAS A MEMBER OF THE IRANIAN NATIONAL TEAM FOR SEVERAL YEARS. AS A COACH, HE HAS BEEN NATIONAL TEAM COACH AND CHAIRMAN OF THE COACHING COMMITTEE IN IRAN. AS A TECHNICIAN, HE WAS A MEMBER OF TECHNICAL COMMITTEE IN ALL IRAN KARATE DO FEDERATION, AND CURRENTLY IS A TECHNICAL ADVISOR WITH ASIA PACIFIC SHITORYU KARATE DO FEDERATION (APSKF) AND SECRETARY GENERAL OF PAN-AMERICAN SHITORYU KARATE FEDERATION (PSKF). HE IS ALSO AN OFFICIAL EXAMINER OF THE WORLD SHITORYU KARATE DO FEDERATION, AS WELL AS THE MEMBER OF STANDING DIRECTORS OF WORLD SHITORYU KARATE FEDERATION. RENSHI TANZADEH RECEIVED THE COVETED DISTINGUISHED SERVICE AWARD FROM THE WORLD SHITORYU KARATE DO FEDERATION AT THE 6TH WORLD SHITORYU KARATE DO FEDERATION (WSKF) WORLD CONGRESS IN CHINA IN 2009.

How long have you been practicing karate and who were your teachers?

I started practicing karate in 1972, at the age of 12 with Sensei Farhad Varasteh: the founder and the father of karate in Iran. At that time and for a while after that, he was the vice President of former WKF. The karate style that he introduced in Iran was based on Okinawan style that strongly emphasized on Kumite, which became foundation of Iranian karate.

Before studying and practicing other karate styles, I continuously practiced karate for 8 years under the instruction of Sensei Varasteh and, in 1977; I received my Black Belt Shodan. During those 8 years, I occasionally trained in Taekwondo. I was curious about this form of martial arts and wanted to try it. I also practiced Judo every now and then. Since martial arts in general were new to me, I was eager to try all of them, but karate remained the martial art that seriously attracted me and which I practiced and trained for in a constantly.

SHITO RYU MASTERS

How many styles have you trained in, and who were your teachers? Do you practice any other art in conjunction with karate?

After about 10 years practicing karate, I started studying other Japanese Karate Styles more in depth; more specifically, the four major Japanese karate styles that are Shitoryu, Shotokan, Gojuryu and Wadoryu. At that time I was the chairman of National Coaching Committee in Iran, Member of Technical committee and also the National team coach. Therefore knowing the 4 major Japanese styles of karate was extremely important and essential to me. However, I was more attracted to and more successful in Shotokan and Shitoryu. I was following the fundamentals of different associations, but specifically those of Shitokai in JKF and expanded my study in that particular association.

In 1986, I eagerly and seriously focused on Shitoryu. But at the same time, I carried on my study of other Japanese and Okinawan styles.

One of the reasons for which I then became more interested in Shitoryu was that this style contained all the aspects of Okinwawan karate such as Shurite, Nahate, Tomarite and also part of Crane fist (Kakkaku ken of Master Go Kenki) as well as Kobudo systems. I therefore decided to choose Shitoryu as my major style of karate training.

Were you a 'natural' at karate – did the movements come easily to you?

I am not sure if I can say that karate was natural to me or I was a natural at karate. But as far as I remember, and as everybody around me used to tell me, I was exceptionally talented in karate. My older brother used to practice karate when I was 11 years old, and I remember the time when he was practicing kata and kihon in our backyard. And by just watching him, I could exactly copy his movements without any mistake. Of course, I did not perform them as well as someone who had learned them under the instructions of a sensei, but everyone around me was really surprised to see me performing the movements by just watching them. My brother discovered this talent in me and enrolled me in karate school. By the first time I put on my Gi to attended my karate class, I could already perform the first Heian kata, and everyone in the class was amazed that I could perform this kata without any instructions of a sensei.

I think the reason that I can understand the concept of movements and techniques and digesting and performing them properly is my talent in karate; as has been proven to me and others around me.

Did you train and study in Japan?

Yes, I lived in Japan for 3 years where I trained in Shitoryu, from1990 to 1993. My training took place at dojos in the Tokyo and Saitama areas. In 1990, I received 4th Dan from Master Manzo Iwata. After that, I had training sessions every single evening, even on Saturdays and Sundays. During those years in Japan I trained with some great masters including Genzo Iwata Sensei, Sakanashi Sensei, and Yamazaki Sensei who was the first Japanese Sensei who officially introduced me to Shitoryu Association of JKF (Shitokai) in Japan. I also attended many seminars including the All Japan Shitokai Gassuku, where many great Shitokai masters such as the late Tsujikawa Sensei, the late Sakio Sensei, the late Hisatomi Sensei; as well as Murata Sensei the present WSKF and JKF Shitokai president, and Soke Kenei Mabuni instructed. Before traveling to Japan, I retired from competing. However, while in Japan, I decided to compete again. In 1992, I attended the 32nd All Japan Shitokai Championships and I placed 3rd in Open Kumite. Right after that I attended the 2nd All Saitamaken Championships and won Silver in the Open Kumite division. It was the same year that I attended in All Japan Shitokai Masters Clinic and I as a first non Japanese who could be able to passed the exam for the official Instructor License.

During my stay in Japan, I also practiced iaido and could manage to spend some time on learning this form of martial art. As it was new to me at that time and I found myself very much interested in it and I received the Shodan title in iaido before leaving Japan.

In my opinion, iaido is one of the most beautiful martial arts. In iaido, katas are basically performed with sword, and I was really amazed by the zanshin, focus, concentration and the beauty of movements that were applied in katas. In March 1993, I attended the 1st World Shitoryu Championships held in Tokyo. There, I won 3rd place in the Individual Kata division, which was a great honor and achievement for me. After 3 years living in Japan, I left the country in April 1993 and traveled back to Japan in 2000, 2006, 2008, 2010 and 2013, to attend the Championships, Seminars, Congresses and the exams.

Please, explain for us the main points of Shito Kai and its differences with other styles like Shotokan, Wado Ryu or Goju Ryu?

Any style in karate, emphasis on a specific point, one on power, the other one on speed, another style on defense or counterattack and so on. One of the major and most important points that Shitoryu emphasizes on, is speed. In Shitoryu, we increase speed by shortening the distance and especially through shortening the path of blocking. You may have noticed that in Shitoryu, the techniques and stances are short. For example in shuto uke or gedan barai, the path of execution is shorter compared to the way they are done in Shotokan, Gojuryu or other styles. The reason why Shitoryu emphasizes on this matter is to reach the target faster. As we know, $V=D/T$ (speed equals the distance over the time). The founder of Shitoryu, Master Kenwa Mabuni, was completely aware of this physics formula and wanted to apply it to techniques. Distance is one of the major elements determining speed. So, the shorter the distance, the faster the speed. This fact is extremely important in Shitoryu.

Although it is an endless task, but Shitoryu practitioners strive to master a number of principles. To assist in this mastering, everything in Shitoryu is systematized and organized. This structured approach includes the four elements of martial arts and the main goals of training of Shitoryu (physical education, martial arts or Budo, and education of spirit and mind). Practitioners must also strive to apply the three main elements of Shitoryu (Sappou, Kappou and techniques of mentality), five principles of blocking

SHITO RYU MASTERS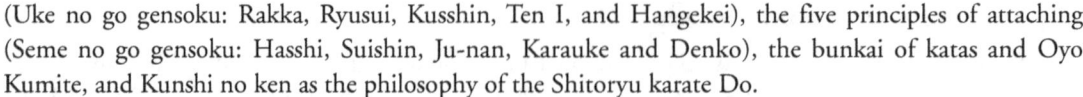

(Uke no go gensoku: Rakka, Ryusui, Kusshin, Ten I, and Hangekei), the five principles of attaching (Seme no go gensoku: Hasshi, Suishin, Ju-nan, Karauke and Denko), the bunkai of katas and Oyo Kumite, and Kunshi no ken as the philosophy of the Shitoryu karate Do.

What can you tell us about the fonder Kenwa Mabuni and the evolution of the style in two different places like Osaka and Tokyo where the late Sensei Manzo Iwata lived? Do these two groups were different in training and development of the style?

Kenwa Mabuni, the founder of Shitoryu was a genius, and everybody is agreeable with this fact. The founder of Shotokan, Master Funakoshi and the founders of other styles always gave him this credit. Mabuni was not only famous as a genius, but also well known as a technical knowledgeable person in Okinawa and Mainland (Japan). Because of this, Master Mabuni had a special position in those days and was greatly respected. Often, he was being asked for technical advices. Some called him the encyclopedia of karate. If they needed to develop a special program, they certainly consulted with Master Mabuni.

Osaka and Tokyo were not and remain not so different. Since Master Manzo Iwata and Master Kenei Mabuni were both two of the senior students of Kenwa Mabuni, the two regions, Osaka and Tokyo developed in parallel and, in 1993; the World Shitoryu Federation was formally established by them. Master Iwata became its 1st president and Master Kenei rolled as the Soke (Governor) of the World Shitoryu Family.

How do you see the different "branches" of the Shito Ryu style...Shito Kai, Hayashi-Ha, Kuniba-ha, Tahi-Ha, etc... and what makes Shito Kai different in comparison to these?

The masters and founders of most branches of the Shitoryu groups were in contact with Ryuso Kenwa Mabuni or were his students. They also had their personal ideas, which they gained from other styles or schools, and added them to their own school or to the syllabus of their own association, and modified them. The difference between Shitokai and others is that in Shitokai, pure Shitoryu is being practiced, exactly following the advices and instructions of Master Kenwa Mabuni.

Do you have any favorite technique?

I have always been using different techniques in kumite particularly in both guards (hidari kamae and migi kamae), but I can say that there are a few techniques that I have been using more than others. One of them is the sweeping of both legs (moro ashi barai). My other favorite technique is front leg jodan kick either mawashi or uramawashi.

The other technique that I have always used is counter attacking or doing Deashi with Zuki. But I have always been trying to use as many techniques as possible.

What are the most important points in your personal training these days?

Because of my responsibilities as the technical director of my organization, I have to travel a lot for seminars inside and outside of Canada. My goal has always been to transmit proper technical points of Shitoryu Technique, katas and principles. So, most of my personal trainings are the subjects of my seminars, which emphasize on karate in details, bunkai, main principles of training in kata, footwork and how to apply them to Kumite. And... I always try to stay in good shape, because I know that although my explanations are good enough to get the concept, I also would like to apply and perform these points in my seminars and in my classes, so that attendees and students would be able to learn more by watching and copying.

Are you against sport karate?

Absolutely not! Karate is a martial art and has been popular in the last decades, and we owe this to sport karate. The way sport karate is done, has led karate to be recognized in the world. For years now, we can see children as young as 3-4 year old in dojos, practicing karate. There are also summer camps for younger children teaching them karate. The sportive aspect of sport karate has promoted all this. This is a great thing.

We may think that sportive aspect of karate can take us away from the real or traditional karate, but as we can see, there are a lot of people who practice sport karate and traditional karate at the same time. The most important point is that as long as sportsmanship is considered, respected and applied in sport karate, as well as traditional karate, they can coexist at the same time. In other words, as long as the true spirit of Budo is applied in the training sessions and competitions, it's positive and beneficial.

What are the most important qualities for a student to become proficient in the Shito Kai method of karate?

Karate is a lifetime study: it's a lifetime journey. To be able to proceed in this long journey, just like to achieve any goal in life, we need to have love, while being patient and perseverant.

As a teacher of the art of karate – what is the most important element of your teachings?

There are many important elements in karate. I have students at different levels and with different motivations. Some of them are very young and interested in the sport aspect of karate. So I teach them the sportive elements of karate in their training sessions. Some are very much into traditional karate and are way more than those who would like to compete. But in general, I strongly emphasize on the proper form of karate techniques, correct posture, strength and speed to techniques and I also try to give them the concept of karate do and how to exactly apply katas and techniques in reality.

The word "Do" in Karate Do means "way". Do will never come to an end, the art of karate do is the way for a life time. So, the most important element to me is Budo or lifetime karate. However, as I mentioned, I train my younger students to be able to compete. Even when they get older, they become interested in Karate Do: and by all means, I train them Karate Do.

Kihon, Kata and Kumite: what's the proper ratio in training?

It depends on the season of training: whether it's competition season, a special occasions or regular training time.

In general, I recommend that in every regular training session, 30% kihon, 30% kata and 40% kumite and bunkai being practiced. But as I mentioned, it depends on the situations. For example, if more emphasis is supposed to be on kata, because of upcoming exams or championships, or during seasonal training, the ratio must then change to 10% kihon and 90% kata. The 10% kihon here must be practiced in order to improve kata. The same change in ratio can also be applied on Kumite when necessary.

Kihon in karate is divided into several groups and the whole point in practicing kihon is to get prepared for kata or kumite. So kihon trainings must be systematic. The combination of techniques in kihon must be determined very carefully, according to its goal. Kihon training is extremely useful for the improvement in kata and kumite.

How has your personal expression of karate developed over the years and what is it that keeps you motivated after all these years?

My personal expression of karate has developed over the years to "My Life Style". Karate, now, to me is how to communicate with others, how to think, how to deal with problems in life, how to help, how to improve and how to make changes, which are all the philosophy of karate. What keeps me motivated is to share my karate and what I have learned over the years, with people around the world. I would like to transfer my knowledge to others. I like to be useful in any way possible, using my life style which is karate.

Although knowledge is power, I think applying knowledge is real power and sharing the knowledge is a way to apply that knowledge.

How important is competition in the evolution of a karate practitioner?

Sport karat and competition can be done in a limited time of one's life which, is during youth. In general, competition is not necessarily applicable to all karate practitioners and I cannot say that it has a great effect on their evolution. There are a lot of karate practitioners who are not young enough to compete, but still have the motivation to continue practicing. But for those who are able to compete, the competition motivates them to train more. Competition also has a lot of positive points.

What really means "Ikken Hissatsu" and how it applies when used in Shito Kai Karate?

"Ikken Hissatsu" literally means "killing with one strike". The katana or sword is the symbol of Budo in Japan. I believe "Ikken Hissatsu" origins from Budo culture or symbol. But in karate we certainly do not want to kill with one Strike and do not want to think this way!

I think the concept of "Ikken Hissatsu" in karate would be to "knock out", as it has happened at times and as it's possible to knock out the opponent with one strike.

Having that said, I believe there's a mental statement in "Ikken Hissatsu" which is to encourage the students mentally, particularly while training in kata. As we know, kata is to combat different imaginary opponents, in different directions. When we finish with one direction, we should make sure that the opponent in that direction has been knocked out, and then start with another direction and so on.

How do you see the art of Shito Kai evolve in the future?

After the 1st World Shitoryu Championships in 1993, every year, more countries have been joining Shitoryu. Last summer (2013) the 20th anniversary of the world Shitoryu federation was held in Japan. During this event, the number of participations was twice as much compared to 10 years prior to that, as about 1000 athletes participated. This shows that every year, the number of Shitoryu fans and participants increases in different countries and will increase in the future as well. I believe that one of the reasons behind this is the beauty of the technical aspect in Shitoryu.

Do you feel that you still have further to go in your studies?

Definitely, these studies will carry on. I am still studying every single day and improving my knowledge, using different articles, older books and new ideas. I try my best to use any available source to learn more and more about different methods of trainings, even basic techniques. I try to find out the best way to perform techniques, how others practice and perform them, and what their point of view about them would be. I want to understand the motivation of masters and pioneers in creating these techniques. So by studying every day, I will be able to have a more detailed and comprehensive view of these. This has a great effect on my personal practices: particularly when I train my students. I have noticed that by having more knowledge about karate, I can better transfer such knowledge to my students.

During all the years practicing karate, I have gathered more than 1000 books, magazines, articles and videos. I have studied a lot of them and I don't know how many more years I would need to read to finish all of them, considering that I keep on adding new ones! I will do my best to take advantages of all these sources.

What advice would you give to students on the question of supplementary training?

Since physical activities are greatly involved in karate training, using supplementary training can therefore be beneficial in the physical aspect of karate. Supplementary training can be done by elastic bands or weights to improve the strength and speed of the movements (techniques). Cardiovascular practices such as jogging and running are also very helpful.

We can also use sport science (physical education) or kinesiology to improve the physical aspect of karate and our techniques. For example, pushups on the knuckles have been done at the end of the training sessions for many years. But nowadays, a simple pushups has many variations and can be done in 20-25 different forms. These supplementary pushups are kind fun and also makes different muscles stronger, which helps in physical movements in karate. There are also plyometrics exercises that can be added to karate sessions in to give practitioners speed and give agility to their body and techniques.

Have been times when you felt fear in your training?

As far as I remember, I've never felt fear in my training. Perhaps because of my passion and love for this art, such a feeling never occurred to me.

Do you think that Olympics will be positive for the art of karate-do?

It will be absolutely positive in terms of more recognition for the art of karate. But I think traditional karate Do with its specifics and as an art will never go to Olympics. Nowadays, a lot of younger people are interested in sport karate and are involved in it. So a lot of countries are trying to get sport karate into the Olympics and if they succeed, it will still be useful for more recognition. Some people agree with the idea that karate do may disappear eventually because of Olympics but we should not mix sport karate and karate do. These are two different things. There are a lot of people involved in sport karate and, who at the same time practice traditional karate. Also, training in karate Do is still being done in a lot of dojos all around the world. So, I think by sport karate going to the Olympics, karate do will still survive. It will go on and will not get hurt nor will it disappear.

What are your views on kata bunkai? Is bunkai really important?

Bunkai in Shitoryu is one of the most important elements in practicing Shitoryu Karate. In Shitoryu, a kata does not exist without practicing Bunkai and applying Bunkai. In all katas, even in primary ones such as Heian, the application of Kata in the attack and Block techniques must be completely understood and practiced.

Bunkai is one of Shitoryu syllabuses component and is mandatory in the exams and tests.

How important is for a Shito Kai practitioner to know all the Kata of the style?

Although in Shitoryu, there are numerous katas from Shurite, Nahate, Tomarite and Hakkaku Ken systems. However, particularly in the beginner's level, it's not necessary or mandatory to train and practice all those katas. If we notice, there are some katas with 2 or 3 versions such as Naihanchi (Naihanchi Shodan, Nidan and Sandan). Even in Okiniwa, all masters and pioneers of karate emphasized mostly on the first (Naihanchi Shodan) version of the kata, because all the technical aspects of the kata are included in the first one. The 2nd or 3rd versions do not include much more than the first one. Therefore in some styles such as Wadoryu

or other Okinwawan styles, only Naihanchi Shodan is being practiced. There are other katas the same as Naihanchi, where the first version is more important than the others like Itosu Rohai series. However, a master in Shitoryu, in high levels, must eventually know, be able to teach and perform all of the katas in this style.

I need to mention that right now in All Japan Karate Federation (JKF) and All Japan Shitokai, there are 4 designated katas as the mandatory Katas for the style of Shitoryu for those who want to upgrade their Instructor's level or to become a judge or examiner and... These 4 katas are the representatives of 4 major systems in Shitoryu, Bassai Dai represents Shurite, Seienchin represents Nahate, Nipaipo represents Crane Fist or Hakkaku Ken and Matsumora Rohai represents Tomarite.

How do you like to train yourself? Has this changed over the years?

I practice almost every day between 45 minutes to 2 hours. I try my best to practice everything in every session, which is sometimes not possible because I need more time to practice katas, kumite and kihon. I have to say that the methods of trainings change with the age of trainers. The more we age, the less pressure should be applied during the training sessions. Obviously, the way I used to practice in a session when I was 30 years old was different from the way I did it at the age of 40 or now. This is an important point and must be taken under consideration. But I still enjoy every session of my trainings and try to practice bunkai, kihon and kumite and of course katas as much as possible and every time, I start with kihon and basics.

Do you recommend "cross-style" training in karate?

Knowing and doing cross-style training in karate is a good thing and it is an asset, but certainly not at the beginner's level. I recommend that everyone who practices any karate style, fist improve to a very high level in their own style and master that style. Then, they should start to get familiar with other styles and gradually, but seriously practice the main and basics of them. There are and there have been karatekas mastering different styles equally. So cross-style training is possible. If someone realizes in himself that he is able to do it, he should go ahead and do it. For those who are active in Sport karate, whether for training athletes or judging, and athletes themselves, cross-style training can be beneficial. By training cross-style, you should pay attention to details of not just the styles, but also paying attention and putting time on training for different moving and turning mechanism. For example some styles emphasize on heal rotations and some other styles emphasize on rotations on toes. So it is necessary to understand all those mechanism, not just doing different katas from other styles.

What is your opinion of makiwara training?

In my opinion, makiwara training is very important because it not only improves the strength in hands and knuckles, but also has a great effect in understanding, feeling and practicing Kime: which is the essence of karate techniques.

Makiwara training has also other important effects, which are the increase of confidence for the karateka and the improvement of concentration and focus. All these are in fact, included in Kime.

Therefore, makiwara training is extremely important. However, I must mention that, before starting makiwara training, the technique itself must first be fully understood and properly applied by karateka. The precision of the technique is of a very high importance and it's not just about punching and kicking on the makiwara pad.

As I mentioned, makiwara training improves the strength of hands and knuckles and kime, therefore it is necessary for those who are interested in Tameshiwari to have a lot of makiwara training. Since the main goal of makiwara training is to improve kime, I recommend that in the beginning, karatekas start this training under the supervision of their instructors and, after a while, when they master the techniques, they can continue on their own.

Do you consider kata an important part of karate training?

Definitely yes! There are a lot of technical points including applications, blocking techniques that can be learned by practicing kata. Every single kata in karate includes a specific usage in terms of technical aspect and certain technical abilities. Therefore, practicing kata is extremely important in karate.

If we look at the history of karate, we can see that in the past, they used to teach the kumite strategies, by teaching kata. So, kata is a useful tool in learning self-defense and kumite.

We can practice and learn a lot of basic movements in kata. As a matter of fact, kata consists of kihon and complex techniques including punches and blocks and counterattacks. It's important to know that we should not perform a kata just for the sake of performing it. What we should do is to understand and analyze all the movements in each kata and have enough knowledge of their application. By understanding what we are exactly doing and why, we can actually perform the kata and every single movement in a kata, in a more advanced, perfect and beautiful way. Therefore, I strongly recommend that while performing kata; it is important to understand the movements and their applications.

What are the main aspects of your teaching?

As we are aware, karate develops in different aspects. One of them is Budo or combat and self defense. The other aspect is health. Karate training can make us healthier and stronger. Other aspect would be sport. Another one is the mental aspect and is aimed at perfecting character.

I have always tried to teach all these aspects to my students. Nowadays, the students enter karate dojos willing to practice karate with different reasons and motivations in their minds. I have always tried to

give the proper response to their motives. Some of them come only for the sport aspect of karate and would like to attend the tournaments. So, in my trainings, I emphasize on the ways of combat and sport karate more than other aspects.

Some come to my dojo to learn martial arts. I certainly consider that while training them.

But in General, although each individual starts karate for different reasons, I have always tried to teach them the moral and mental aspects of karate. Kenwa Mabuni has a famous saying: "kunshi no ken" which means "Fist of a Nobleman" that means use your fist and power in the right way. So we can simply interpret that to: "power brings responsibility". By talking about kunshi no ken, I try to teach the development of character and spirit which is the essence of karate and this is extremely important to all of us with any motivation. I want my students to understand the real meaning of Kunshi no ken and apply them in their life.

Shotokan, Shitoryu, Gojuryu etc. How do you think the different branches and styles affect the complete art of Karate?

We are all happy and satisfied with the style of karate that we practice in. But we are all also aware that no style is perfect. Therefore it could be beneficial that masters and instructors study other styles too in order to be able to use one another's point of view. In the past decades, different styles have influenced each other and sometimes, some masters have even combined different styles. Some Shotokan masters have added Gojuryu and Shitoryu katas to their trainings and syllabuses. In general, I think that studying other styles can have a very positive effect on the art of karate.

Do you think Kobudo training is beneficial for a karate practitioner in general?

Kobudo and karate do were developed in Okinawa almost at the same time and parallel to each other. I am confident that to learn Kobudo, one must learn and know karate techniques first. In fact, we use karate blocks and strikes to be able to use those weapons. So, having karate training is very beneficial for those who practice Kobudo. However, Kobudo training is also, in a way, beneficial for karatekas, because you can apply karate techniques to use the weapons.

What is your opinion about the "Shobu Ippon" division in Karate competition?

Sport karate and its rules are going through a lot of changes and we all know that Shobu Ippon is still a part of Sport karate. Shobu Ippon in general is tougher than most resent regulated rules within WKF (World Karate Federation). Therefore, I don't mind it to be just a division.

In Sport Karate, techniques are limited and you can wrap it up with a Chudan geri or Jodan geri or Chudan zuki and Jodan uchi. Sport karate is expanding in the world and students start competitions at a very young age, like 12 year old in an international competition. So I think the high quality techniques of shobu ippon for these young athletes are not appropriate. Different rules and regulations can be tried, but eventually they have to come up with a logical conclusion. Perhaps in the future, we can achieve and observe something better and more advanced than shobu ippon.

What can karate offer to individuals in these troubled times we are living in?

We are all aware that people with depression and mental problems, in long term, will end up having physical problems as well. Their bodies will get damaged because of the damage in their souls. It's also true that if we have positive and healthy minds, the positivity and health will transfer and affect our bodies. Since there's a discipline in karate training, such as in blocks, in

different forms of kata, stances, etc. the repetition of this physical discipline can have a direct reaction on mental health. So, in long term, a karateka will be able to deal better and easier with the troubled times we are living in.

During our karate training, for years we do blocks, counter attacks, we use different strategies in kumite and so on. All these have a very positive and constructive affect on one's mental state because one learns how to block or avoid problems, and how to use different strategies when dealing with problems and so on.

After so many years of training, what is so appealing for you in Shito Kai and why?

Different styles of karate overall pursue the same goal. But as I have already mentioned, Shitoryu includes Shuri, Naha, Tomari and Hakkaku Ken "Crane fist" systems: and that's why I look at it as a complete style. This advantage in Shitoryu gives me the motivation to study more and more, and it was through Shitoryu that I could more deeply understand and comprehend the concept behind the techniques and therefore found them more enjoyable.

The nature of the practices and trainings in Shitoryu gives me a better and particular appreciation of karate and practicing it. I have been able to get familiar with other karate styles through Shitoryu because of its nature: that has made me significantly detail oriented. So, with the studies that I have had through many years and am still pursuing, I could understand karate much better. The way Shitoryu looks at the technical aspects of this art is very realistic. In Shitoryu, katas and bunkai in particular are being noticed realistically; therefore all the movements are being done naturally.

Is Shitokai in constant evolution?

Shitokai and Shitoryu karate are not excluded from other karate styles and schools. Karate has gone through lots of changes during many years. This evolution will continue in the future too, and all these changes will bring better and more positive results. The same is with Shitokai. As master Mabuni, the founder of Shitoryu has said, karate do has never been perfect and will never be. This means that evolution in karate do makes it more and more perfect as the time goes on. For example, the way kata trainings were done in 40's or 50's was in many ways different from the way they are being done today. I am sure that there will be more changes and evolution in karate in the next years and decades, which will all be in a very positive way. I hope that I live long enough to see some of these changes that will occur in the future, in Shitoryu or any other styles.

Finally, what advice would you like to give to all Karate practitioners?

The most important advice is that karate must be accompanied with respect, discipline and good manners. Without respect, discipline and proper manners, karate would be nothing but throwing some kicks and punches: it would be nothing but fighting. In fact, understanding and training in any style in karate must become the life style of the individuals. So, applying respect, discipline and proper manners in karate is critical and extremely necessary as they are in our lives, in our communications and relationships with people, and also in different situations.

My other advice is that in your training sessions, be honest with yourself and others and take your training seriously. Try to pay attention to details in every single point that you learn. Try to feel and comprehend them. It's extremely important to do your best in every training session and take them seriously as well as enjoying them. This way, after every training session you will feel satisfied and joyful. If not so, then you have to consider that something should have gone wrong in that session. Think about it and figure out what the problem was. At the end of every training session, you should strongly feel that you have gained a benefit out of it, if not, find out why.

I would like to add here that an athlete, an instructor and a referee, all together make a triangle and are closely related to one another. My advice to athletes is to try and practice different ways of training in their sessions, use different samples that have already been used by masters and champions. Always respect your instructors and referees. Always trust them.

My advice to instructors is to keep updating their knowledge. Just like physicians, constantly study and improve your knowledge about new sport technologies, information and physical trainings in order to be able to adapt yourself to the evolutions happening in sports.

My advice to referees and judges, especially in Kata, because of their huge responsibility, is to choose the right athletes for the podium and to improve their knowledge about different styles and katas as much as possible, to be able to judge easier and more accurately to pick the right athlete.

KEIJI TOMIYAMA

THE CHALLENGES OF BUDO

HE IS ONE OF THE ICONS OF TANI-HA SHITO-RYU KARATE. A DIRECT STUDENT OF FOUNDER CHOJIRO TANI, TOMIYAMA WAS CHOSEN BY TANI TO SPREAD THE ART IN EUROPE ACCORDING TO THE ETHICAL AND MORAL PRINCIPLES OF THE OLD JAPANESE TRADITIONS. ONCE KNOWN ONLY FOR HIS FEROCIOUS FIGHTING SKILLS, SENSEI TOMIYAMA HAS MATURED NOT ONLY AS A KARATE-KA, BUT ALSO AS INDIVIDUAL. WITH THIS MATURITY HAS COME A PHILOSOPHY THAT PUTS A PROPER PERSPECTIVE ON WHEN TO FIGHT AND WHEN NOT TO FIGHT. HOWEVER, HE STILL BELIEVES THAT THERE ARE TIMES WHEN A MAN MUST NOT RETREAT. "TO FIGHT WITH ANOTHER IS WRONG," SAYS TOMIYAMA, "BUT TO LOSE A FIGHT WITH ANOTHER OVER PRINCIPLES YOU DEEM HONOURABLE IS WORSE. TO FIGHT WELL IS AS PROPER AS BEING ABLE TO STUDY CORRECTLY OR WALK PROPERLY. BY LEARNING TO FIGHT, YOU ARE ACTUALLY EDUCATING YOURSELF TO AVOID BATTLE." DESCRIBED AS A TEACHER WHO GIVES AS MUCH AS HE DEMANDS, TOMIYAMA CONTINUES HIS DEDICATED TASK OF SPREADING THE MESSAGE OF HIS TEACHER. HIS SCHOOLS AROUND THE WORLD CONTINUE TO FLOURISH BECAUSE THEY HAVE BEEN ESTABLISHED ON A NUCLEUS OF LOYAL INSTRUCTORS AND STUDENTS WHO LIVE BY THE SAME BUDO PRINCIPLES THAT FOSTERED THE SPIRITS OF THE ANCIENT WARRIORS OF JAPAN.

How long have you been practicing martial arts?

I started karate at the age of 17, so I have been practicing for 35 years. However, I did a little kendo at the age of 13 and judo at 16 as they were compulsory at school. I hold 7th dan in shito-ryu and 6th dan in goju-ryu, but I do not actively teach goju-ryu as everything I have learned in it is included in my shito-ryu teaching. Shito-ryu is a broad style which includes both shuri-te and naha-te. Moreover, my teachers learned their goju-ryu from master Kenwa Mabuni, the founder of shito-ryu, who also taught goju-ryu just to my teachers. I still practice with my teachers in goju-ryu every time I go back to Japan. Also, I have been practicing shinto muso-ryu jodo for the last ten years or so.

Who were your first teachers?

I started with my cousin who was studying shito-ryu, but my serious training started when I entered Doshisha University in Kyoto and joined its karate club at the age of 18. The teacher there was Sensei Fukuda. Master Chojiro Tani, one of the senior students of Kenwa Mabuni and founder of tani-ha shito ryu, was the technical director and came to the dojo and taught regularly.

What do you remember most of your early days in karate?

I was doing boxing at high school. At the same time my cousin, who is two years older, was studying karate. So one day we decided to fight to see which was better. I was beaten conclusively. He just kept kicking me and I had no answer for that. At that point, I gave up boxing and started learning karate!

At the university club, we trained for three hours every day - one hour of fitness training, one hour of basics and katas, and one hour of kumite. Sit-ups were a important part of fitness training and we did a minimum of 500 every day. We jokingly called ourselves members of the Doshisha University Sit-Up Club. When you do so many sit-ups, inevitably the skin around your backside forms a callus. At public baths, which were quite common in those days, we could recognize members of the karate club by just looking at their backsides! At training camps, where we practiced three times a day for one week, we used to do 1,000 sit-ups in the morning, another 1,000 in the afternoon and another 1,000 in the evening. Our record was 2,500 sit-ups at one time. We also had training camps at Sensei Tani's dojo in Kobe.

Smoking was the norm in those days and almost every adult male smoked. It was a sign of adulthood and almost every male student started smoking upon entering the university. Sensei Tani, myself, and everybody else in the dojo were smokers. There was a big ashtray, maybe two feet in diameter, at the end of the dojo and, at the break in the middle of training, everybody, including Sensei Tani, sat around the ashtray and smoked while discussing techniques. On finishing a cigarette, we resumed training. Both Sensi Tani and I stopped smoking quite soon after those university years, and the dojo became a non-smoking zone several years later.

How has your personal karate has changed over the years?

I was fairly successful in competition, winning second place in the All-Kansai Individual Championships - so I was one of the top university fighters. Master Tani tried to modernize karate and developed a unique theory consisting of many new ideas such as "double-hip twist," "zero-tension-zero," "kick shock," "recoil," "changing weight," "dropping body," and more. Following his instruction, I developed very good speed which helped me to be successful in competition. When I came to Europe by Master Tani's request in 1972, after graduating from the University, I realized that European people were thicker and heavier than the Japanese. So I tried to develop more power. Luckily, Sensei Yasuhio Suzuki, Chief Instructor for Europe, had very powerful techniques and he taught me how to use body weight more effectively.

When I visited Japan in 1980, I met Master Yamashita and Master Uehara of goju-ryu at the university dojo. To enable you to understand the situation more clearly, I will briefly tell you the history of the Doshisha University Karate Club. In the 1930s, some students from Doshisha University and Ritsumeikan University, both situated in Kyoto, got together and sought instruction from Master Chojun Miyagi, founder of goju-ryu. These two universities are the birthplace of goju-ryu in mainland Japan. The famous master Gogen "The Cat" Yamaguchi and most other senior instructors of Japanese goju-kai are graduates of the Ritsumeikan University Karate Club. On the other hand, Doshisha University Karate Club sought instruction from Master Kenwa Mabuni, who had settled in nearby Osaka, following the advice of Master Miyagi who could not stay in mainland Japan all the time.

To show respect to his fellow master, Kenwa Mabuni only taught naha-te at Doshisha University, thus the club remained a goju-ryu school. Master Tani, a graduate of Doshisha University, eventually became a shito-ryu stylist and, with permission from Master Mabuni, started tani-ha shito ryu. So the university club is basically goju-ryu, but I followed Master Tani and became a shito-ryu stylist. Both masters showed and explained some goju katas as taught by Kenwa Mabuni, and I was quite impressed by the theories and wisdom contained in these forms. Master Tani must have also learned these, but his instruction was more geared towards his modern theories so their explanation was quite eye-opening to me.

In 1982 my father fell ill and I had to go back to Japan to look after him and his business. I stayed there for three years and, during these three years, trained with both masters every week. I was also very lucky to be able to train with Master Fujimoto, the most senior instructor on the goju side of the tradition, who had refused to teach previously. I absorbed a lot during this period. I also managed to train with Master Tani quite regularly, learning many more shito-ryu katas.

Upon returning to Europe, I had to train and think hard to combine Master Tani's modern theory with goju's traditional wisdom. The answer came to me fairly quickly because it had already started to form within my body during my three years in Japan. The key lay in Master Tani's teaching. When he had taught his theory, he had always said that once mastered, these movements would become smaller and smaller and eventually invisible. Once these invisible, or internal, movements were mastered, there was no conflict between his modern teachings and the traditional teachings. In 1990, I wrote my book "Fundamentals of Karate-do," explaining these traditional teachings in a more modern approach.

For the last ten years or so, I have started realizing that one has to reach a high spiritual level in order to reach a high technical level. So that is what I am trying to achieve at the moment. Although I have almost all the information material needed, I have to further refine my techniques and reach a higher level. The border between spiritual and physical states gets blurred at the higher levels. So I still have a long way to go.

How did Westerners respond to traditional Japanese training?

Very well, actually. When I went to Europe for the first time, I was in Paris and I could not speak a single word of French. I was also young and inexperienced. So I just kept training normally and everybody had to follow and copy me. I remember the language barrier but I do not remember any differences in training between the Westerners and the Japanese. It is rather impossible to categorize Western karate and Japanese karate. There are many kinds of karate and karate-ka in the West as well as in Japan. Some Western people are far more advanced than some Japanese. What I can say is that there are a small number of old generation karate-ka in Japan who reached quite a high level, just because they practiced for a longer period and were closer to the source.

How has your teaching philosophy evolved?

Until 1982 I was teaching what I had learned from Master Tani and Sensei Suzuki. I was just a messenger. However, when I came back from Japan around 1985, I started to teach my own ideas, which does not necessarily mean my creations but rather my understanding of what karate should be. I had to explain and convince my old students of the validity of the teaching, as my approach was different from my pre-1982 period. The majority understood or trusted me, but some failed to understand and left, which did not bother me too much as I was convinced that my new approach was far superior to the old one. In 1990 I decided to spread the word outside Western Europe and started to travel the world. Within a few years, I had established branches in Eastern Europe, Southern Africa, the Middle East, and the Indian sub-continent.

With all these changes, do you think there is still pure shito-ryu and goju-ryu?

It is very difficult to define what pure pure shito-ryu, goju-ry, or even shotokan is. The first established shotokan club was the Keio University Karate Club. Their techniques are different from the JKA, for example, but nobody can question their pedigree. I believe in my version of shito-ryu, but another shito-ryu instructor will probably disagree with me. Also, my goju-ryu is quite different from other goju branches. Having said that, there are distinctive differences between the shotokan group and the shito group, and between the shito goju groups. When you see people from reputable shotokan organizations, although there are some differences, you can recognize them as shotokan people from their movements. The same can be said for shito, goju, wado, uechi, shorin, et cetera. On the other hand, I admit that there are some people whose style we cannot recognize by just observing their movements. Generally speaking, the technical standard of these unrecognizable people is poorer.

I do think that different schools are important because one cannot just learn one style of karate. There is no such thing as a standard karate. Different styles exist because of different historical ideas and principles. At the higher levels, all styles become quite close and similar. It is like climbing a mountain. There are many paths to climb a mountain. Although all paths lead to the same summit, one has to choose a path to climb. On the other hand, there are people who are only interested in competition fighting. They train only how to move around and how to score points. For them, different styles are not important.

What is your opinion of full-contact karate and kickboxing?

People who are engaged in full-contact karate and kickboxing are very committed and very strong. I respect them very much. Although these activities are combat sports, they are not budo. So they lack the philosophical aspects that balance their existence as human beings.

What are the main characteristics of your shito-ryu method compared to other branches?

Master Kenwa Mabuni taught shuri-te first in order to acquire basic fighting skills. Then he taught naha-te to develop power. So all other shito-ryu groups are shuri-te based and put naha-te on top of the shuri-te base. On the other hand, Master Tani and myself

learned naha-te or goju first, then shuri-te was added on top of the naha-te base. This is the main difference. As I explained earlier, I now practice the invisible version of Master Tani's theory and, as a consequence, our movements may be slightly smaller and more subtle than other shito-ryu groups. Moreover, as our techniques do not require great muscular strength or big dynamic movement to produce power, it is well suited to older practitioners who have started to reach limitations in their external power.

Do you feel there are any differences between Western karate-ka as compared to Japanese karate-ka?

None whatsoever. Japanese people used to be smaller than Westerners, but the younger generation Japanese are now quite tall due to the change in lifestyle and nutrition. Also, Japan is no longer a poor country with strong social discipline whose people readily accept harsh discipline.

How do you see Japanese karate in the West compared to the rest of the world?

For me, karate is a whole package - physical, technical, spiritual and cultural. Therefore, etiquette and discipline are quite important. There are many Japanese instructors resident in the West who teach this wholesome karate. Many Western instructors who learned from them also teach this kind of karate. But there are many instructors who did not learn properly or did not like this kind of approach. They usually teach karate as just a physical and technical exercise. On the other hand, there are some people who have gone in the opposite direction and teach mystified karate which, in my opinion, can be harmful to

one's mental health. Karate has been in the West for quite a long time now, so it is quite diversified.

Do you think it helps to train with weapons?

It generally does, although it is not essential to train in weapons to progress in karate. One has to have good stances and postures as well as the correct distribution of strength in order to handle weapons properly. So training with weapons will help to develop the aspects which are equally essential for karate. On the other hand, people who are already quite good in karate can learn weapons fairly quickly as they already possess these qualities.

What's your opinion about makiwara training?

Makiwara training is good for developing focus and power and strengthening the body, but it should be done correctly. Moreover, a makiwara board should be flexible.

Do you think an instructor's personal training should be different than what he teaches his students?

Definitely. When you teach people, what they need for their development should be your main concern. This can be quite different from your own needs. These are two completely different things which need to be approached separately and individually.

Kata and kumite - what's the proper training ratio?

In general, I would say 50-50.

What determines a karate-ka's level?

The quality of your karate is determined by the quality of your basics, so you have to practice basics regularly and try to improve them whatever level you are at. This does not mean you can neglect kata and kumite practice. You should practice kata and kumite to improve your karate, but do not neglect the basics. Tradition is the most important element. Tradition includes self-defense techniques, self-development exercises, and personal ethics.

Is going to Japan to train necessary?

Not really. It depends who you are learning from in your country and who you are going to learn from in Japan. Of course it is nice to visit Japan and see the culture, but whether it is highly necessary or not depends on each person's circumstance. I have great respect for many of the Japanese instructors

teaching outside Japan. They are much better than the average instructor in Japan and, moreover, can speak the local language.

What are the major changes in the art since you began training?

During the last three or four decades, karate has spread around the world and become one of the major combat sports. So this worldwide development of karate as a sport can be seen as the major change, although traditional karate is still mostly unchanged.

Who would you like to have trained with that you have not?

I consider myself extremely lucky to have met and trained with so many legendary teachers. I do not feel a need to have trained with any other teachers, although I try to learn something new from everyone I meet. As a shito-ryu stylist, you might expect me to say Master Kenwa Mabuni. But since all my teachers are direct students of Master Mabuni and I learned a lot about him I do not feel a need. Perhaps the only person I would like to have trained with is Master Choki Motobu.

What would you say to someone who is interested in learning karate-do?

Well, I would say, "Karate is good for you, so start straight away." Some people are very natural when it comes to any kind of physical activity but It was never this way with me. Even if you are 'gifted', I always believed the factors to determine the quality of your karate were the quality of instruction you receive and the amount of work you put in. At the University Club, we gave several hundred repetitions in each technique with senior grades constantly correcting junior grades. If we did not correct ourselves following their instruction, senior grades did not hesitate to slap our face or kick our stomach. So, to avoid getting hurt, we learnt fairly quickly.

What keeps you motivated after all these years?

My teachers have constantly given me inspiration and motivation. I have formed ideas about karate should be and I try to implement it in myself. It is the main motivation for my own development. On the other hand, I would like to help others to develop themselves. That is why I keep traveling and teaching.

What is your opinion about mixing karate styles. Can it be beneficial?

There are styles which are compatible and others which are not. I do not think practicing two incompatible styles is beneficial. For example, I myself train in shito-ryu, goju-ryu and uechi-ryu. Moreover, some ryuei-ryu katas were included in the shito-ryu list in recent years. I have no problem with this because the underlying principles of these styles does not conflict. On the other hand, I think I would have a problem with mixing shotokan and shorin-ryu. Some branches of goju-ryu are also too different from mine, and thus incompatible. As I explained earlier, shito-ryu is a very broad style and I teach all these styles or katas under one roof of shito-ryu. To avoid confusion or conflict, I teach all of these with the same principles.

How important do you think bunkai is in the understanding of kata?

Originally, to learn karate meant to learn katas and their bunkai. It still applies to traditional karate. Although practicing a kata and improving its techniques is most important, the performance becomes incomplete and hollow without understanding and practicing its bunkai and that is exactly what is happening in competition katas. To combat this, the World Karate Federation has put kata bunkai in the finals of the team kata event. So we shall see what happens.

What is the philosophical basis for your karate training?

In common with most Japanese martial artists, I have learned, and am still learning, the budo philosophy of the samurais, which is based on Zen Buddhism, Confucianism and Shintoism. But I believe the majority of its virtues are universal and can also be found in other religions and philosophies of the world. Although they also apply to life in general, I believe the most important virtues specifically to martial artists are mushin or "no mind: and muga or "no ego." One has to empty ones mind to be able to understand the opponent's intention and get rid of ego to harmonize with the opponent in order to control him. In other words, the principles are "understanding" and "harmony." It is easy to say but not that easy to achieve.

Do you have a memorable experience that inspired your training?

Yes, when I saw Master Fujimoto for the second time. When I saw him for the first time, I was still a white belt and could not understand what he was doing. But when I saw him for the second time, many years later, I was actively seeking knowledge and I can still remember the shivering which went through my spine with excitement and elation. I get a similar inspiration every time I train with him.

What does the practice of karate-do mean to you?

Another grand question! In short, it is the continuous betterment or improvement of one's technique, understanding and personality. But the baseline is to enjoy the training and to achieve your goal - whatever it may be. It can be to get fit, to pass the next grading, to master a technique, to learn a new kata, et cetera. Once your current goal is achieved, set a new goal and keep enjoying the training. Hopefully, this contributes to improving the quality of your life, for which the social side is also quite important.

How can a practitioner can increase their understanding of the spiritual side of karate?

Primarily by reading relevant materials containing correct information, and meditating and practicing kata with the right attitude and state of mind. One has to try to achieve the state of mind I explained earlier - mushin and muga. But if you behave aggressively with a big ego in daily life, the higher levels of spiritual development are impossible to achieve.

How much training should a senior karate-ka be doing to improve?

Everything, every single day, has to be impregnated with the spirit of karate-do. One has to incorporate daily life with karate practice - how to walk, how to breathe, how speak, et cetera. Karate is not only a way of simply punching and kicking, it is a way of life and as such affects all the facets of your existence. At least this is the way it should be.

Is anything lacking in the way martial artists are taught today, compared with your day?

What do you mean by "your day?: I am still learning, you know. Well, again it depends on the instructor. As I said earlier, maybe etiquette and discipline are missing in some dojos. But the world and its people are changing constantly and there are varied cultures and customs in the world, so certain changes are inevitable.

What are the most important qualities of a successful karate-ka?

Perseverance and modesty. Open-mindedness to absorb the teaching, and friendliness to get on well with fellow students also helps. Enthusiasm is also important, but many over-enthusiastic students burn

out quickly and leave. Steady students who keep coming regularly and persevere are the winners.

Do you recommend supplementary training?

Stretching and running are very good and very important for the overall physical condition of the karate-ka. But one has to be careful about weight training. Although it is very good to strengthen the whole body, I have seen too many people who started to use brutal force rather than technique as they grew stronger due to weight training. This is detrimental to karate practice. It is very important to remember that it is "supplementary" training and put the primary emphasis on karate training and not on the other aspects.

Why do many students fall after two or three years of training?

There are so many things to do these days and many people tend to do a little of everything rather than stick to one thing and reach a high level. Also, there are some barriers to break through in order to progress in karate. The first barrier is to become a brown belt and the next is to become black belt. Two to three years is the time when students face these barriers. Probably these barriers are too much for some students. There are also people who successfully overcome the barriers but have no energy left to carry on. The next barrier is between 3rd and 4th dan. People can progress up to 3rd dan with plenty of spirit and enthusiasm, but refinement is needed to pass to 4th dan and many people find this quite difficult. Those who made the 4th dan grade generally continue to train for the rest of their life and keep progressing.

There is very little written about you in magazines. Do you avoid publicity?

My two main teachers, Master Tani and Master Fujimoto, both did not like publicity so perhaps that influenced me. Master Tani could have gotten an important position within the Japan Karate Federation but he declined it. Master Fujimoto was positively against publicity and believed that those who wanted to learn from him had to seek him out. Although I would like people to know what I am doing to a certain extent, as I might be able to help some of them, self-glorification is against my beliefs.

Have been times when you felt fear in your training?

At the university club, our seniors did not use control at all during free sparring. Talking to them after graduation, I found out that they had sincerely believed that it had been beneficial to us. Many of us got broken noses and teeth because of the free-sparring sessions everyday. We all felt some kind of fear as the free sparring session approached. Having once started fighting, you are too busy dealing with the job at hand and have no time to feel fear.

What is the key to gaining a deep understanding of karate principles?

Time is an important element in ones progression. If you do not understand something straight away, you have to keep practicing it. Then one day, if you remain diligent, you will suddenly understand like a ripe fruit dropping off a branch. If you do not keep practicing, you will never understand. It is important to give yourself time, be patient, and just keep practicing.

ERIC TOMLINSON

THE WAY FOR PERFECTION

SENSEI ERIC TOMLINSON STARTED TRAINING IN THE MARTIAL ARTS IN 1971 IN ENGLAND. HE HAS TRAINED IN SHUKOKAI KARATE HIS ENTIRE MARTIAL ARTS CAREER. IN 1996, HE MOVED TO THE UNITED STATES AND OPENED A SHUKOKAI DOJO IN MISSOURI AND ALWAYS REMEMBERED HIS TEACHER AS A TRUE EXAMPLE TO FOLLOW: "KIMURA SENSEI WAS ONE OF THE MOST EXCEPTIONALLY POWERFUL MEN I HAVE EVER KNOWN. IN TERMS OF TECHNIQUES, I REGARD KIMURA SENSEI AS THE MOST OUTSTANDING PERSON IN THE PAST 20–30 YEARS OF KARATE. HE WAS THE TYPE OF PERSON WHO STOOD OUT BECAUSE OF HIS CHARISMA. I BENEFITED FROM KNOWING HIM AND FROM THE OPPORTUNITY TO TRAIN WITH HIM. BECAUSE OF THE TEACHER/STUDENT RELATIONSHIP WE HAD, WE BECAME VERY CLOSE." IN 2002, HE JOINED THE "SHITO RYU SHUKOKAI UNION" AND EVENTUALLY WAS GRANTED THE FREEDOM BY SENSEI YAMADA TO ORGANIZE A UNION IN THE UNITED STATES OF AMERICA.

How long have you been practicing karate and how many styles of Martial Arts have you trained in?

I have been training for more than 39 years – primarily Shukokai with Chojiro Tani, Shigeru Kimura, Haruyoshi Yamada and Tsutomu Kamohara. I've also trained with Kanazawa Sensei and Higaonna Sensei in Shotokan and Goju Ryu styles. It was a lot of hard work. I wasn't really good at kicking, but I was quite good with my hands and (foot) sweeps. I did train in Kobudo but I didn't get into it much because I wanted more of what Kimura was teaching. I trained nunchaku for a short time under Hanai Sensei in England. Tani Sensei sent him over from Japan. The truth is that I never practiced other arts on top of Karate-do. When I think I've perfected my karate, then maybe I'll move on to something else. But honestly, I think they'll be putting flowers on my grave before that happens.

What is your most memorable moment in your karate career?

I remember, in 1978, the English National Shukokai Team was invited to Finland to face the Finnish National All-styles Team. Well, all I can say was that it was a blood bath. The team managers were Stan Knighton and Eddie Daniels. They told us just go for the points, so we did. Then the Finns started to come really hard at us. That's when the blood bath started. Anyway, we eventually won. The British ambassador was in the audience – it was the biggest tournament we'd ever seen. We were then invited to the British embassy for supper.

When did you move to the United States?

In 1996. I opened a Shukokai dojo in Missouri, hoping it would be a small step to promote Shukokai in United States. In 2002, I joined Shito-ryu Shukokai Union under Yamada Sensei. The same year in October 2002, I met Yamada Sensei for the first time at the European Championships in Manchester, England. Although Yamada Sensei is one of the highest ranking instructors in JKF (Hanshi, 8th Dan), he is a very humble and open-minded person. He granted me the freedom to organize the association within the United States as one of the Union's branches. In March, 2003, I attended Yamada Sensei's seminar and Gishinkan Championships in Amagasaki, Japan. Yamada Sensei and other instructors welcomed us and showed us the warmest hospitality, which made me feel that to be a member of Shito-ryu Shukokai World Union was a great honor. Yamada Sensei's students (even small children) were well disciplined and showed great respect for their sensei and senpai, which made me realize that this is the essence of learning traditional karate-do. This is what we often fail to teach in our dojos, and I believe this is something we need to improve upon. Discipline and respect should be evident in our instructors so that this important element is taught to our students.

What is opinion of fighting events such as the UFC and Mixed Martial Arts events?

I think it's good for other Martial Arts to come along. It is interesting and makes you look at the way you train and how you can improve yourself.

What are the most important qualities for a student to become proficient in karate?

Well, I think some students are naturals, but some maybe not as talented. Everyone has different abilities, but the most important qualities are tenacity and perseverance. Sometimes, the most talented (students) get bored and quit early because it comes too easy for them. They never get to experience the really deep parts of karate. Then there are others who keep pushing through. They take their time and eventually experience all the important things karate has to offer.

When teaching the art of karate, what is the most important element; self-defense or sport?

I teach from a traditional or self-defense way. I then add in a competitive element to keep sharp. Personally, I look at karate as an art, but it's also good to bring in the tournament side to make it more completive. It's like training in soccer but never actually playing the game. How many times does an average guy defend himself in a year or lifetime? Competition is just another part of your training – the exciting part. There's no pressure to compete, but it's an important part to get and keep students. After competition starts to be less important, the student is ready to learn the deeper parts of karate. Karate has changed a lot, but I feel more passionate about karate now than when I started and the essentials are the same: body mechanics, breathing, and relaxation. I didn't really understand their importance many years back, so now I emphasize it as much as I can to my students.

Kihon, Kata and Kumite: What's the proper ratio in training?

I don't think there's any formula because it all comes back to the basics or Kihon. When you improve your basics, you improve everything else. All these aspects are interrelated.

Who would you like to have trained with that you have not?

Bruce Lee was very inspirational and open-minded. It's obvious that he was very passionate about his Martial Arts.

What are the real technical differences between the Shukokai method and other karate styles?

I think that training in traditional Shukokai methods forces you to analyze and adjust your techniques. Sensei Kimura and Sensei Tani taught this way. They would teach us to pay attention to the feedback, especially during impact training, and always adjust to make it better. Kimura said that in karate, we should "study" more than "train" – basically constant personal inspection rather than just repeating techniques over and over. If you delivered your punch or kick with true impact, it will "shock" your (training) partner's body. He'll look like he's just been rear-ended in a car accident – even when holding a six- or eight-inch thick impact pad. His hair will fly or his glasses will fly off because his head will jerk – like whiplash. If you hold the (impact) pad long enough, you might even develop a headache because of the constant whiplash. You need to actually hit something, not just the air. A makiwara or big bag can't tell you if the shock was on the surface or six inches inside the body. That's why holding the impact pad is so important to both practitioners. By the way, the pads themselves are a key part of training because they aren't the soft or squishy foam that you find in most pads. They're also not filled with rags like heavy bags. Kimura searched for many years before he found the correct foam that imitates the human body.

SHITO RYU MASTERS

Tell us about the Shukokai style...

As I mention many times, the characteristics of Shukokai are relaxation and breathing which increase speed and traction to create impact. It's not enough to be fast if you don't shock your opponent's body. To the head, it's a knockout. To the liver, it's tremendous pain. To the heart, it can mean death. Also, perfecting your body mechanics. You have to have the right structure or the energy "leaks" out of joints that are not aligned correctly. This allows your body to move quickly, efficiently, and powerfully. Most times, all you get is one punch, so it has to be as close to perfect as possible. If you're not relaxed, you're muscles are fighting each other and your brain is in overload. That's when you freeze. Knowing you can deliver true impact cuts down on that momentary mental "freeze" and physically allows you to deliver that life-saving blow smoothly and powerfully. As relaxation, breathing, traction, and body mechanics improve, so does speed and timing. It all comes together for the best stopping power. In the old days, many experienced karate men and boxers would talk about Kimura's punch. They would say that it was like getting hit with a cannon ball. That's why so many karate clubs in England switched from their original styles to Shukokai many years ago.

Do you feel that you still have further to go in your studies?

Yes. Looking back on my early days in karate in the mid-70s, I worked very hard to perfect my style to compete in tournaments. I was just a hungry fighter. All my pains, bruises, and sweat were rewarding as they gave me a great drive for perfection in life. Although my mind is still willing and continues to push me, my body finds it physically difficult to attain success. It is difficult for a man in his mid-50s, with aching arms and hips from years of training, to continue at peak performance, no matter how much his mind pushes. As time passes, I must admit that my punches and kicks are not as fast as they used to be; however I can still pass these moves on to all of my students because this is one of my responsibilities. I earned the recognition that I received through hard work, and now my goal is to help the next generation have the opportunity to reap the same rewards that I had. I also wish to keep the high standards and the spotless reputation held by karate-do professionals for the sake of the future of traditional karate-do in the United States. I tell students that it's like looking for piece of a jigsaw puzzle that you can't find. When you stop looking, it's time to stop training. I'm very traditional, but when I came to the U.S., I found out the hard way that students want to be entertained, for lack of a better word. If I still taught the way I did in England, I wouldn't have any students, so I try to balance the two.

What advice would you give to students on the question of supplementary training?

I would do whatever kind of training you feel is right to improve yourself. Everybody has different thoughts on this subject, but I believe that it's a personal decision.

What advice would you give to an instructor who is struggling with his or her own development?

Don't ever stop pushing yourself. This is one of the defining factors of karate-do: the way or path you have chosen for your life. If you want a new path, OK, but as long as you choose the martial path, keep pushing to improve, not just physically, but mentally and spiritually as well.

Have there been times when you felt fear in your training?

Not really fear but maybe frustration and there's always the adrenalin rush.

Do you think that Olympics will be positive for the art of karate-do?

As I said before, you also have to have a competitive side and the Olympics is the world's biggest stage for competition. However, I've heard that in order to become an Olympic sport, karate will have to drop kata competition. If that happens, I can't support it. Kata is very important to keep karate a martial art and not just a sport.

What are your views on kata bunkai?

Bunkai and kata are very essential parts of your Karate training. When I look back to my early days, I just wanted to compete in tournaments and spar, but now it's the other way around. But now, I'm getting more into the bunkai of kata, especially since affiliating with Yamada Sensei. He's been researching the original kata and their bunkai for several years.

What are your ideas to improve judging and refereeing in Karate competitions and what are the main problems you see in sport karate refereeing these days?

I personally think you'll always get good decisions and bad ones. It's very difficult because everything happens so fast. If (as a referee) you've been competitor, sometimes you can see a point before it actually happens. It's gotten better since I was competing, mainly because of good referee training. It wasn't always this way. There was a lot of favoritism (years ago). I remember a match many years ago with a well-known karate man in the England. He was one of the best fighters in his day. I won't say his name because he's still very well-known and highly respected. Anyway, I wasn't well known and I wasn't getting the points so I went harder. I kicked him in the ribs and I was sure I broke some ribs. I didn't get a point either. Many years later, we came across each other. I was surprised that he remembered me and he said, "You know, Eric, you broke my ribs that day."

What are your thoughts about doing thousands of repetitions of one single technique in training as in the old days?

Well, when I was taking a course with Kimura Sensei in England, I was also preparing to take my Shodan exam. All week we concentrated on gyaku-tsuki (for impact development). Anyway, there were 40 of us taking our Shodan exam and we all failed. Then six months later, only four of us came back to take it again. Many years later, I asked Kimura Sensei about this and he said, "If you buy a bag of apples, what do you do with the bad ones? Throw them out." Personally, I think he was trying to find out which of the students were committed enough, especially for Shodan. He would do this sometimes.

Itosu Kai, Shukokai, Shito Kai, Hayashi-ha Shito Ryu, etc. ... How do you think the different branches within the Family may affect the style?

I don't think the various groups really affect the style of Shito-ryu because each chief instructor has his own interpretation of how to perfect their individual system of techniques.

How do you see the art of Shukokai evolving in the future?

At the moment, my organization ["Shito-ryu Shukokai Union"] is growing very fast internationally. Not so much in the USA. Argentina, Chile, Bolivia, South Africa, Botswana, Zimbabwae, and just recently, the Phillipines have joined. There are a lot of sensei who are coming aboard to share their ideas of karate. Under Yamada Sensei's guidance, I'm studying the bunkai and trying to see where Kimura's method of impact would fit. He used a modified Sanchin-dachi as his base so impact is a part of kata.

What can you tell us about Sensei Yamada?

Yamada sensei is a traditional type of karate-ka and has a different approach to karate-do from Kimura sensei. They were both Tani Sensei's students, although they applied the fundamental basics of Shukokai karate with their own interpretations. Throughout his life, one sought a specific perfection of technique that is focused on speed and power through the perfect application of body mechanics. The other saw karate as a lifetime process that leads a person to become a mature human being. Performing karate for one's whole life without tearing muscles, excessively pressuring body parts, and causing physical problems later in life is the goal. To study Shukokai is to study body mechanics in order to generate maximum power and speed. This is also the point where my karate-do started and the core of my karate training. I do not want to lose this basic principle whatsoever.

What is your opinion about the use or non-use of protective gear in Karate competition?

In the early days we had no protection. It was forbidden. A lot of people got injured so I'm all for it. We need to protect our students from injury.

We know loyalty is an important aspect in your teachings. How does this principle affect the character of the practitioner?

I believe loyalty and respect are the foundation of karate, but it has to come from the sensei as well as the student. Students should trust their sensei to develop them into the best karate-ka they can. They're getting the results of their sensei's lifetime of blood and bruises. Not letting your ego get in the way of your training is the foundation of karate. This goes both ways. Sometimes there are differences as a student becomes more advanced and goes his own way. Tani said that we all make our own karate so if a sensei is fair and understanding, he shouldn't be offended or angry when his student goes his own way. It's not disloyalty so the sensei shouldn't let his ego get in the way. Leading by example goes a long way.

What does karate offer the individual in these troubled times we are living in?

Well, I had some very bad times in my business and personal life – losing my business and my previous wife of 17 years. It was my karate that gave me the strength and determination to keep going and never give in. It's the same as in tournament competition. If you lose a fight, you don't give up. You move on taking it as a lesson in life. We all have bad times and even tragedies so we need determination and perseverance to win – on the mat and in life.

After so many years of training, what is it for you that is so appealing about Shukokai and why?

My secret is I wanted perfection. I may never get it, but I will never stop trying. That is what karate has made me today – very strong and determined - whether in karate, family, business, or life in general. It's the same with impact training. You constantly study and analyze your technique based on the feedback you get from your training partner (when you punch or kick the impact pad). His body will react differently depending on the amount of impact you deliver. Is it more of a push or did you deliver real shock? Then you analyze and adjust. You eventually learn to deliver impact more consistently as all the parts come together instinctively.

How do you like to train yourself? Has this changed over the years?

Yes, it has changed quite a lot. When I was young, I wanted to spar all the time. Now I want to improve my technique and hand it down to my students. That is my priority. Also, my body has changed so I can't jump around like I used to, but my spirit is still the same. I remember Kanazawa Sensei say many years ago, "When you're 45 years old, you body is very fit. When reach 50, your muscles start to deteriorate. When you're 60 years old, you tend to lose your strength, but it is your spirit that drives you on." Now I'm 63 and my body has changed, but my spirit – Kokoro – keeps me going.

Finally, what advise would you like to give to all Karate practitioners?

Don't stop. Never stop seeking perfection. As a last word, I'm always grateful to all the sensei who have taught me, especially Kimura Sensei, who is no longer with us. My goal is for Shito-ryu Shukokai Union USA to take the Shukokai techniques I earned from Kimura Sensei such as kick shock, recoil, dropping the body weight, and so on, and merge them with Yamada Sensei's knowledge and experiences in developing a mature human being by following the traditional karate-do philosophy.

284

TAMAS WEBER

BUDO ON THE BATTLEFIELD

A DECORATED VETERAN OF THE FRENCH FOREIGN LEGION, TAMAS WEBER HAS USED KARATE-DO TO PREVAIL IN LIFE-OR-DEATH COMBAT SITUATIONS, AND ALSO TO DEAL WITH EVERYDAY LIFE.

FEW PEOPLE IN THE HISTORY OF KARATE ARE MORE RESPECTED THAN TAMAS WEBER. POSSESSING A COMPLETE KNOWLEDGE OF KARATE LORE AND EXPERIENCE, SHIHAN WEBER HAS PUT HIS LIFE ON THE LINE ON MANY OCCASIONS, IN MANY WARS, WHILE SERVING WITH THE FRENCH FOREIGN LEGION. HIS BATTLEFIELD EXPERIENCE IS PUNCTUATED BY THE MANY BULLET SCARS ON HIS BODY. IT IS IN HARD MEN LIKE HIM THAT THE TRUE CONCEPT OF LIFE AND DEATH IN THE MARTIAL ARTS TAKES FORM. HIS KARATE-DO TRAINING HAS BEEN HEAVILY INFLUENCED BY HIS APPROACH TO THE BATTLEFIELD; AND ALTHOUGH HE APPRECIATES THE SPORTIVE ASPECTS OF THE MARTIAL ARTS, KARATE FOR HIM IS SIMPLY BUDO. AS A MASTER OF THE ART, THE EXTERIOR STRENGTH AND INTERNAL POWER HE DISPLAYS ARE UNDENIABLY APPARENT. HOWEVER, HIS WARRIOR SKILLS ARE COMPLEMENTED BY HIS DEEP LOVE OF FAMILY AND A GENUINE CONCERN FOR THE STUDENTS UNDER HIS TUTELAGE. AS ONE OF THE HIGHEST RANKING MASTERS IN THE WESTERN WORLD, TAMAS WEBER IS RESPONSIBLE FOR COACHING MANY OF THE OUTSTANDING CHAMPIONS OF EUROPE. CURRENTLY LIVING IN SWITZERLAND, BUT POSSESSING SPIRITUAL QUALITIES THAT CROSS ALL SOCIAL AND POLITICAL BOUNDARIES, TAMAS WEBER IS A TRUE ICON OF WHAT REAL BUDO SHOULD BE.

How long have you been practicing karate-do?

I started my training in martial arts in November of 1951, more than a half-century ago. My first teacher was Masafumi Kawata, who was nidan at that time – the highest rank in those days was godan. Straightaway, I had a good feeling for the art, but it was never easy for me. After some time of hard and dedicated training, my personal understanding and knowledge of the art increased very much. The kata, bunkai and kumite aspects became part of a complete new dimension, compared to my previous understanding. I improved my technical skills and developed more speed and power, and a mature way to move. This was much better for focusing power and controlling distance. Today my karate is like a tidal wave, with high-explosive power mixed harmoniously with the calm of the ocean sea. I strive to develop deeper and more focused types of movements based on internal strength and not muscle power.

Was your early karate training difficult?

I remember when we where training ippon kumite (free sparing) very late at night – we would nearly fall asleep. To wake-up we kept a bucket of cold water in the middle of the small dojo. Every fifteen

minutes or so we each dipped our head inside the bucket to avoid falling asleep. Despite dripping water all over the floor, we kept on training. Often the dojo was in half darkness. The purpose was to give us an instinct and feel against unknown attackers. We were totally devoted to the art – the attitude and approach to training was very different than what you see today.

With all the technical changes during the last 30 years, do you think there are still pure styles of karate?

I don't think that a pure style has ever existed in real terms during the history of karate. Like painting or writing, nothing can be described as a "pure" art – everything is a combination of several influences. You often have a strong and charismatic personality who serves as a basic initiator and reference of a particular style; but if you compare the previous forms performed by the old masters you will find a huge difference between their way of interpreted the techniques and the way the modern karate is perform today. For instance, there are now very deep stances and unnecessary movements with no meaning at all – these movements have been added simply to make a more visually attractive performance. In the old times the main purpose of the art was a self-defense, and was based on each individuals capability to adapt karate to his body structure, understanding, and knowledge. Karate was a highly efficient fighting tool that used the entire body as a weapon. Because of its killing efficiency and the great danger of misuse, it become necessary to restrict abuse. For this reason, a set of strict rules of honor, respect and humility was established. Karate today has lost part of is fighting fluidity; the stances are more like movie choreography – very deep and stiff with a limited correlation to practical fighting.

I sincerely think that natural development and adaptation is the natural essence of all life on earth – why should karate be any different? Every sensei has their own interpretation. This interpretation is transmitted to the students who, hopefully, will soon take their teacher's approach and raise the art to a higher level. It is a fact that the execution of techniques and movements have special flavors peculiar to each style. However, it is not the physical difference of technique that makes the distinction in style, but rather the mind of the student. The thinking and strategy dictate the technique to be used; which in turn requires a special way to initiate the application of power suited to the tactics. It is this means of applying strategy in combat that creates different styles.

What is your opinion of full-contact karate, kickboxing, and MMA?

Basically, kickboxing and full contact karate are very demanding sports. You need a high level of physical conditioning, but they are still sports with rules, gloves, referees, and judges. In the true art of combat there is only one rule – to defeat your adversary as fast and efficiently as possible. The MMA events are very hard, violent, and physically demanding. For the audience, it is like the Coliseum was for Rome. There was a reason why the Romans had the gladiators fighting and there is a reason why these kind of events fit into our society today. The smell of blood makes the audience feel the savagery of combat without actually bleeding or suffering pain from wounds themselves. They use these events to release the aggression they have inside and can express their violent feelings about their home and working lives. Like the gladiator, the purposes of the fighters in this brutal game is to survive the match and make money. I wonder if all this is really worthwhile, though. Are we getting something of real spiritual value out of it or just watching Roman gladiators without the lions?

Do you think Western karate has caught up with Japanese karate?

In the sportive aspect, definitively yes. The European teams are much better in kumite than their Japanese counterparts. However, as far as understanding the principles and essence behind the art, probably not – besides a few rare and exceptionally knowledgeable and experienced Westerners. Unfortunately, when a Westerner wins a world championship they immediately think they are better than the Japanese in the art of karate-do – not in the sport but in the art. This is not the case. Many Western kumite champions don't really know how to execute a perfect zenkutsu-dachi, for example. In the kata aspect, just because a Westerner wins a world title it doesn't mean they are better than a Japanese or Okinawan performing kata. Kata has nothing to do with the acrobatic performances that we see today. Changing the technique to make it more appealing to the judges and increasing the breathing volume to pretend to have more kime is a joke to the real art of karate-do. In martial arts you can learn a simple movement quickly – but knowing the correct usage of the body in relation to the movement takes few years.

So you don't think of karate as simply a sport?

Karate is not, and will never be, simply a sport. If we allow that to happen then we'll be responsible for a major crime. Of course, the scale and range of techniques will always include the techniques needed to score in tournament kata or kumite. But karate is a martial art and a martial art includes many lethal techniques such as the finger-jabs to the eyes and attacks to the throat that are very valuable self-defense weapons. This makes it too dangerous to become only a sport. The bottom line is that karate-do is a violent art. Because of the times of peace we are living in, however, a part of that art can be used as an enjoyable sport activity. The important point here, though, is not to lose the direction and real meaning of the training.

What connection do you see between the art of karate-do, budo in general, and the life-and-death battlefield environment?

Like on the battlefield, a warrior should be well-prepared for the coming battle by good training basic. When the first explosions detonate and the first bullets whistle in the air, there is a short moment of surprise and stress before you can assess the situation, control your fear, and go to immediate action. This control is only possible because of your military and technical skill, your inner strength, and the confidence in your own knowledge. Reflexive action is based on systematized training learned through a wide range of drills and exercises. The martial artist, before a fight begins, should feel like a warrior in the battlefield and have a short moment of stress mixed with fear. Then when you control your fear and stress, you turn it into a source of a positive energy and use it as a power source to neutralize and destroy the challenger or the target. All your internal power and all your physical energy should be released in an attack or counterattack. This ability to move efficiently and quickly, and adapt to a combat situation, will depend very much from your preparation, basic training, knowledge, and self-confidence in your capabilities. This is what is incorrectly called "reflexes."

There is no difference, in principle, between the martial artist and the soldier on the battlefield. The only difference is the goal for the actions and the tools used in combat. The warrior, like the soldier or the true martial artist, feels the same stress and fear before he starts the battle. But when the combat action begins, the technical skill, the readiness to go to action, the first move, and the readiness for an ultimate sacrifice of life, is the difference between victory and defeat.

Did your experiences as a soldier help you to understand the concept of "one killing blow" in karate?

I sincerely think that the "one killing blow " concept is one of the myths of martial arts. On the battlefield, nobody know exactly how an enemy was killed. In an assault, everybody fires in all directions and hundreds of bullets have to be fired for one kill. Why does the martial artist or karateka think they can kill with one blow when bodyguards and police officers always fire two bullets to the chest? Of course, it might happen that one blow can kill – but it is not guaranteed – and what will happen if it doesn't? You will get killed in return. Makiwara training and a fast and strong technique do not guarantee will efficiently deliver a lethal blow to your target. The way you train is the way you fight; and if the way you train is traditional, chances are the way you fight will be effective.

Do you think that dealing with a life-and-death situation changes the whole concept of karate as a sport?

Yes. The basic concept of karate is to use all the mental and the physical abilities of the human body as a tool for self-defense. To achieve that goal, an arsenal of techniques was created and combined, and the human body transformed and reshaped by an intensive and systematical training method into a lethal weapon. The purpose was to severely defeat any challenger with a graded response from a harmless disarm up to a lethal blow. Karate was too dangerous to be taught to everyone because it could easily be misused. This is why it was necessary to frame the training with a code of values, honor, humility and respect. This code is similarly to the military and bushido code. Karate was a way of life – a life of training and devoted commitment with great respect for the sensei.

The purpose of sport, in contrast, is to score. To score you need a very limited arsenal of non-lethal techniques authorized by the rules. You can only score if the judge agrees to give you the points; the criteria is often very subjective and is a game involving you, your opponent, the judge, and the referees. Today you are on top, and tomorrow you are history. You will never know if your techniques will work for real – it is not a way of life, but just a game for children. The rules change not to make the fighter more efficient in combat, but rather to make the competitions more attractive to the spectators.

The whole picture of karate has evolved in two totally different directions. One direction is a sport, and the other is trying to keep the old concept of martial art. These two different and distant concepts can't be evaluated with the same criteria. Sport misuses the karate traditions when the competitors insist that they are practicing a martial art. The titles and the medals should be enough. Why should sport fighters keep a ranking system related to more formal achievement, technical skill, and combat fighting experiences? For me, personally, after my experiences on the battlefield it is very difficult to take the powerless scoring techniques seriously. I feel that I am not a part of that game. I like a more realistic and useful approach to combat. But I am a dinosaur.

You are one of the highest-ranking karate practitioners in the Western world; do you feel that you still have more to learn?

Rank has nothing to do with the idea of learning. The higher your rank, the more time you have to dedicate to the art to reach higher levels of understanding. I think that in any subject, you should analyze the past to avoid the previous mistakes. Stagnation does not develop human skill in any field or science. There is no limitation in the understanding or technical development you can achieve in karate. The teacher should always try to improve their skill level by gaining new experiences, more knowledge, and a deeper understanding of what he is doing. When you just transmit your knowledge to the students you may be losing part of your sharpness and the necessary physical condition you need to master the art. Therefore, it's paramount that the instructor dedicate a certain amount of time to his personal training and not mistake his teaching time as his training time.

SHITO RYU MASTERS

A good karate-do instructor teaches a student the way to teach himself; how to take all the elements of the art and weave them into his own experience and self-realization. The teacher, of course, cannot kick or punch for the student – only show, tell, and do everything necessary to make the student aware of what punching and kicking is. We live in a world where everything seems to be done for us; but the art of karate-do is not that way. It doesn't follow those rules. In fact, it's just the opposite. It's extremely important that the instructor has a firm grasp of all the fundamental elements of his style. His understanding should be deep enough to interrelate all the philosophical and technical principles of the art, and show the student how to incorporate those into his training and life. This will take him to a higher level as a teacher himself. A good instructor is not greedy, and his goal should be to make his students better than himself. That's the real challenge. He should love the success of his students, not be threatened by it.

I have always devoted time for my personal development and my private training. I like to push beyond my physical limitations and go further in my research of the relationship between muscle power, technical skill, and devastating concentration. In a way, it is a great fight between the inner part of myself and the natural aging process. It's a challenge between my body and my spirit. Time will tell who is the winner!

What are the major changes in the art since you began training?

The art didn't change as much as the people did. The mentality is different these days when compared to what we used to have 20, 30, or 40 years ago. Before, the world of karate was very mysterious. It was a strange form of superpower that provided skill to face any challenge and confront anyone earth. The people who were attracted to the training were stronger physically and mentally. Everyone was ready to undergo many years of hard practice and have a great respect for the sensei. Today, the practitioners are only interested in the physical appearances, superficial knowledge, and a fast black belt degree guaranteed and signed by a famous teacher who is only known in his small city. More often than not, that "master" promoted himself to higher degree. The rank and not the knowledge become a major tool for the economical competition between the different dojo.

Who would you like to have trained with?

I regret the fact that I never trained under the supervision of Motobu Choki. I grieve the fact that Fujiwara disappeared in the early '70s. I truly believe that a lot of knowledge has been lost, not in a technical sense but in a more philosophical one. Losing these old masters is not about losing an unknown kata or secret application, but about losing the right training spirit, the correct attitude, and the proper state of mind to train karate-do.

Do you think it is necessary to engage in free-fighting to achieve good self-defense skills?

Free sparring in the dojo gives you the opportunity to improve, in a practical way, your technical knowledge. Of course, you have to really understand what you are doing. You can't lie to yourself. All psychological conditions are not the same in sparring as in a real situation, where panic and stress are at a very different level. But it is true that free-fighting is the closest to a real fighting situation you can come to in the dojo. Just like hard military exercises are not like real war, but are useful because they bring a certain kind of experience, feeling, and a knowledge that prepares you mentally and physically to adapt yourself to a real war situation. The truth is that you never know how you are going to react until that moment arrives. In karate-do, kumite is very important for the development of efficient, economic footwork, precise alignment, and fast, fluid action. It also trains the acceleration of body parts to deliver maximum power and gives you a highly refined sense of timing and rhythm for the development of proficient combat skills that might be used in a self-defense situation.

What is your opinion on mixing karate styles?

Every style and every instructor has its own character, profile, personality, and way to teach. To be a sensei means having the ability to transfer your knowledge to students in an appropriate way. The emphasis of every particular style is mostly due to a charismatic leader and his capability to emerge among the others and pave the way for his approach and concept. So it was the case for Funakoshi Gichin, Mabuni Kenwa, and others. All of them – with their own way of understanding – have contributed to a common karate history that brought benefits to the entire karate community. No style stands alone today like in 1922. What we know about the history of each style is a series of tales with few eyewitnesses and foggy memories. What is the truth? Every student starts his own history with his first sensei. For him, the style of his teacher is of no meaning at all. What is more important is the student's physical compatibility with the characteristics of the chosen method. For the practitioners, the style is an abstract reference with very little value beside the fact that you will feel safe when you belong to a group that uses a reference code and a emblem or symbol to tell you apart from others. This belonging is something usual all mankind, and its role in the martial arts world is simply a reflection of our society.

What is your philosophical basis?

My philosophical basis is very simple, and I understand it may not fit into everyone's mind. Through the hardship of training, through the continuous challenge against your personal physical and psychological limits, through pain and discipline, every individual develops self-control and an internal harmony that leads to a higher quality of life. The discipline in the dojo, and the way you learn to respect the rules and your partner or opponent, will be reflected in the way you handle your private life outside the dojo. It will give mankind a noble attitude in society. I believe that karate gives everyone a code of honor that can and should be used in their approach to life.

Did you have a memorable experience that inspired your training?

One of the karate experience I remember most is when I came back from the war. All my friends in Paris were talking about a new master that had just arrived. They described him as fast, strong, impregnable, and very impressive. I was waiting to see some Japanese giant – a kind of superman from the Rising Sun empire. When I came to the dojo, I didn't find that at all. I only saw a very short man with a massive body structure that made him to look shorter than he actually was. I was totally disoriented because of my preconceptions about things. That man is recognized today as one of the greatest karate masters in the world, and a true icon of what tradition, science, and evolution means within the art of the "empty hand." His name is Taiji Kase. Enough said.

What is the meaning of karate-do for you?

The meaning of karate-do and budo is a way of practice with no real end or beginning – it is a perpetual stream of conceptions and principles. Everyone should try to read and educate themselves about the art of budo. Historical facts, geographical influences, style particularities, different philosophies, and correct attitudes are all very important things to learn if one wants a complete education in karate as a way of life.

What are the most important qualities of a good karate-ka?

I think that the most important aspects for a karate-ka is humility, respect, and devotion to the art. The strength should be inside yourself and not a attribute you display in front of others to show off. You only reveal your strength when needed. Endless training is good, but rational training is much better and will help to reach higher goals in the art and in the sport as well. Karate is a lifetime commitment. It is not something to be done for a few years and then quit, like they do in the universities in Japan or in the Western world after getting the rank of black belt. I understand that there is an enormous gap between that philosophy of budo and our modern way of life. But everything should be enjoyable and not evaluated in terms of money. Unfortunately, karate is a very demanding activity with much involvement and dedication if you really want to reach the higher levels of the art – and it returns no money at all. Very soon, training becomes one of the last priorities and people leave. The fear factor is important in training and the student should be able to deal with it in a positive manner. Feel it but control it in such a way that you'll be able to do great things.

What is the future of karate-do?

The future is very a big uncertainty, but I firmly believe that true karate will survive our generation – but the question is for how long? It's sad, but in many ways I represent an old guard of instructors who

accept the new direction the art is taking as a sport, but yet are struggling to keep the old traditions and principles of budo on the battlefield alive. Karate-do is something that we own ourselves. It doesn't belong to any association or federation. It's ours. It becomes part of our own texture, learned in the bones, a kind of fixture of heart and body in cooperation with the mind. Karate is a vehicle which, used in the proper way, will set us free as individuals because we do it ourselves and for ourselves – allowing us to know ourselves and understand other people as well. We must start continue on as students and teachers because, in the end, the candle is not there to illuminate itself.

ONE-ON-ONE with Jose M. Fraguas

Drinking from an Empty Cup

BY ANTONIO SOMERA

As evening falls, a warm orange-and-black glow, painted by sunlight and shadows, spreads over Sunset Boulevard in Malibu. Jose M. Fraguas is seated in the corner of a coffee shop, relaxing after a long day of writing. Clad in faded jeans and white tee-shirt, the creative writer and martial artist is remarkably still. Quiet though he is, his hands are never still. He drums the fingers on the table, and gestures with a mixture of cultural hands signs, from Italian to Japanese. He seems to delight in paradox. Everything he does is accomplished with a sense of economy, without deliberation or hesitation. It's a quality of contentment that goes beyond confidence and exceeds mere self-possession. "You are responsible for your own happiness," Fraguas says quietly. "You have to make yourself happy - but sometimes you have to go through real unhappiness to get there."

The Spain-born, Los Angeles-raised native is not keen on giving interviews. More often than not, he refuses. Fraguas fell in love with the martial arts when he was only nine years old and pursued his Karate ambitions by joining a school in his neighborhood - but things definitely weren't easy. "In the beginning, some training sessions were so intense that I couldn't fall to sleep and my body couldn't stand still in bed. I could get no rest at night," Fraguas recalls – philosophically, with a soft laugh. "I sure did learn how to drink tea from an empty cup."

His face still retains a glimpse of his young days in the streets of Madrid. His fingers compulsively running through his hair as if holding forth on the evils of the past as he says "I knew since I was a kid that the way was long and there were many difficulties ahead, but I believed, as Mencius said, that 'The way is lofty and beautiful. It leads to Heaven. It is far in the distance. But should we not try to bring it nearer by advancing a little, day by day?'"

While Fraguas – with more than 1,500 articles written and over 30 books published and translated into five different languages - still pursues martial arts and writing with as much youthful passion as ever, he now has a much more mature viewpoint of himself. "Everything in my life is based on a straight, logical approach. I'm committed to expressing myself as a human being. Some martial artist and writers doubt what they are doing and wonder if their success or recognition is just an illusion. But I know what I do is simply a natural expression of who I am, so I'm not afraid of looking into the mirror with strict eyes, empty my cup, and grow. I don't try to find in that mirror who I was once. I embrace who I am today and feel grateful for a great and challenging journey called life."

What's enviable about Fraguas isn't his life journey, but the way he has learned to come at it, uncomplicated by the self-lacerations that plague most creative individuals. He is ready to laugh [at himself too], able to relish the moment, even as he works for betters ones. "I have plenty of fight in me," he says, "I'm simply not wasting any of it fighting myself. I think I probably have a lots of drive. But I don't have any ambition. I never really had any. I don't have a hugely high opinion of ambition. I think of ambition as the need to prove something to others, and the need to be recognized. A need for regards outside of the works. Drive motivates you to do whatever it is you are doing as well as you can. That's an important distinction and always has been for me".

He has a reputation as a generous person and an unhealthy even sickening, work ethic [that makes him to get up everyday at 3am], a trait he shares with the most successful people I have met. All what he has accomplished in his life didn't come from luck or a cosmic fix. Every time I have spoken to him he's been in some state of intense emotional and existential transformation, I am not sure people really understand that level of daily commitment and what it takes to maintain it over a span of years. His "sickening" writing routine matches perfectly with his martial arts training, almost no days-off. "Once you are in shape you can get away with a few treats," he says. "But every day off, requires three days of work."

A perfectionist, Fraguas is aware that anyone who strives for absolute precision tends to have a very narrow focus. He also knows that when a person reaches their peak, it's not acceptable to go back and just be acceptable. "The difference for me as a writer is that I'm used to living in a constant state of anxiety that is driven by my desire to make very personal writing works and the need to make it commercial enough to please the public. You have to have the book there in your mind before you write it because if you don't, you are not a writer, you are a guesser. The same thing happens with martial arts. It's like walking on a tightrope – you need to have a good balance knowing where you are going and what you want. You need to conquer the heavens without burning in hell - you have to challenge them both. You have to give your best, regardless of what you're doing in life. I'm always strive to be better at whatever I do. It is not what do you, what is important, but how you do what you do, that really defines who you are."

"We have to differentiate between a challenge and a goal. Goals are single-minded pursuits and therefore limiting. Challenges can expand," he says. Fraguas makes it sound simple, and on one level it is. But is not so simple on a-day-to-day, real life level when we are all faced with personal choices and challenges. If you want to bring it back to simple – permanently – he advises first 'to bring yourself to a point of reckoning', just like he did. "Don't have this feeling that more is better. If you are doing a lot, people respect you more. It is like you are winning the game of life. That's wrong. Instead, learn a lot about yourself. Push yourself, challenge yourself, you should go to difficult places emotionally and you not always will be willing to do that. Our tendency in life is to narrow everything. Worldwide view, friendships, choices, feelings we have, our reactions to things become smaller and narrower. We lose our range."

Without seeming to do so, Fraguas through his articles, books and publications in Europe and USA has played a critical role throughout his career influencing people's mindsets in Martial Arts around the world. "I just like to write works that are positive in the sense that they deal with the dignity and essence of the true Martial Arts spirit," he says. "A writer [or martial artist] must never be satisfied with what he

does. The writing piece or the martial arts technique never is as good as it can be. Always dream and shoot higher than you know you can do. Don't bother just to be better than your contemporaries or predecessors. Try to be better than yourself. I believe a genuine artist [of any kind] is a creature driven by demons. The only thing that can alter the good writer is death."

Back at his residence, Fraguas pulls up a collection of pictures of himself with some of the most respected Martial Arts masters of our time, music icons and movie celebrities. Japan, Hong Kong, Thailand, and several European countries, in traditional Japanese dojo, Thai training camps, historical "kwoons", the legendary "Mejiro Gym' and "Chakuriki" in Holland, etc. are the locations of these coveted collection of photos and training journey.

His more than 40 years of martial arts involves direct training under legendary masters, a resume that makes practitioners [who would give up their firstborn for 10 percent of this man's experiences] looking at him with healthy envy.

SHITO RYU MASTERS

1. With Angel Lopez and Felipe Hita. Spanish National Team at 5th W.U.K.O. World Karate Championship. Madrid, Spain. (1980). 2, With Shigeru Sawabe Sensei (2005). 3. Practicing "Sepai" kata (1980). 4. With Fumio Demura Sensei (2007). 5. Practicing "Mawashi Geri" (1980). 6. With Y. Tsujikawa Sensei (1980). 7. With Ishimi Sensei and Sakumoto Sensei (1985). 8. Makiwara training: "sweat, blood [lots] and no tears." (1985).

1. With Y. Inoue Sensei (2010). 2. With Coach Antonio Oliva (2012). 3. With Kenzo Mabuni Sensei (2001). 4. With Teruo Hayashi Sensei (1980). 5. First generation of certified "Official Spanish National Karate Instructors" (1981). 6. With H. Nakahashi (1980). 7. With Kenei Mabuni Sensei (1980). 8. With Masahiro Okada Sensei (1978).

In the writing field, although he appreciates the many influences he received from a wide spectrum of individuals, he specially treasures his friendship and "cathartic experience" [as he likes to describe it], with Noble Prize Camilo José Cela, whom he met in Madrid, Spain during his youth.

"Camilo José Cela was a legitimate black belt in Judo and I wanted to do an interview with him because of my personal journey in writing and martial arts. He accepted and eventually I ended up having a friendship with him that I greatly treasured. He opened my mind to what a 'true' writer really is. He told me that a 'writer needs three things, experience, observation, and imagination — any two of which, at times any one of which — can supply the lack of the others. If he is interested in technique he should take up surgery or bricklaying. There is no mechanical way to get the writing done, no shortcut'. I was extremely lucky that I met him and that he shared his insight and wisdom with me. He passed away in 2002, but his many words of advise still echoing on my mind."

He still keeps some of the trophies and medals won during his competition days but they don't seem to be as much as relevant for him – the photos are a different sort of award, "I really don't show them to people. Some years ago, I have reached a point in life where I don't feel like letting others to know what I did in the past. One day I found out that it is no longer necessary for me to have a history to explain when I meet people. If you have no personal history to tell, no explanations are needed; nobody is disillusioned with your acts because nobody knows what you did or did not in the past. There is no label. No expectations to be met. And above all no one pins you down with their thoughts. This makes me completely free from the encumbering thoughts of other people. It is not bad to create, little by little, a fog around you and your life, so nobody knows completely who you are or what you do. I follow these four rules that were given to me by a very wise person: never ever talk about your weaknesses, personal finances, plans for your future and who you know."

He is a interesting bridge between tradition and progress, intellect and emotion, body and spirit. To all outward appearances Fraguas is a contradiction in terms. Yet with one foot planted firmly in yin and the other in yang, he is not divided by the light and the dark but rather is the line between the two.

"I believe that in order to become a man of accomplishment, one had to encompass what the Japanese call 'Bunbu Itchi' (the sword and the pen). Such parallel disciplines filled the life of the Japanese nobility, whilst this ago-old doctrine was expounded by Plato in his 'Timaeus', in which it was argued that the balancing of activities relating to mind and body were important in the pursuit of excellence. Only when these two parts are exercised equally could one rightly be called a fully developed personality. It is a regrettable feature of the martial arts in the West that much emphasis is placed on physical attributes, and so little on the mental development of practitioners," he says.

"On the other hand, philosophers do not, as a rule, have an easy relationship with their bodies. Descartes recognized that he had a body but insisted that it was not the same thing as himself. Plato sneered at the body's demands and shaped his philosophy from the desire to overcome them. Berkeley's body was a bundle of his own ideas, while Hume had great difficulties in establishing that his body existed at all - which is why he got so fat. Socrates is remembered by his body, but largely on account of its ugliness.

Nietzsche took exercise, fruitless attempting with his dumbbells to overcome the "blond beast" of his dreams. And Sartre took no more exercise than was required to get from his downtown apartment to the bar across the road. For some people both

things don't match. As a martial artist, I like to train physically since that training reminds me that the body and the thinking of the self are one and the same."

A fervent admirer of Yukio Mishima - he owns all Mishima's works in their first edition - Fraguas founded in the prolific Japanese writer, a mirror image of his personal journey; the dichotomy of writing and Martial Arts impregnated with the samurai spirit of Bushido. "I was fascinated by this fact and eventually I became friends with people who knew him personally. For me, Mishima was about as famous as he was infamous. The enormous legacy left behind pretty much outshines his public suicide. When he was 30 years old, conscious of the inevitability of aging, and desiring bodily "perfection," he started a strict bodybuilding training that lasted for the rest of his life. His longing for a return to a spiritual Japan which respected the Bushido (way of the warrior) code inspired his training in Karate and Kendo. True Martial Arts, for him, allow one to experience the border between life and death. Regardless what anyone can think of him, no one can deny the symbolic significance of his life [and death] for Japan's post-war cultural identity, an identity that was rapidly changing in a country where Mishima seemed to embody the ultimate "lost samurai." Like the samurai of old, he succeeded in achieving the perfect death," he says.

"His philosophy was hard to understand for the Western world, even for a modern Japan. Mishima was seeking a faith, a religion, a God he could not find. Man cannot live by beauty alone: the esthetic and the romantic idea, when divorced from the whole context of existence, contains the seeds of extinction. They are death bearers, and his formula was one "in which Beauty, Ecstasy and Death were equivalent and together stood for his personal holy grail." The equation is suicidal. He was a man of a frightening talent."

It is clear that every one of us will some kind of leave a legacy behind when we die. The challenge is the same for all of us. So for Fraguas, the important question is what kind of legacy will I leave? Although he recognizes that does not spend much time thinking about his, he seems to have a clear idea about it. "I believe our main legacy as writers is to educate or even just re-echo those things that we believe are worthwhile - a subjective matter. Even if the idea is obvious or simple, we believe it deserves to be kept alive, and we do that using different ways current with the times; we broadcast our worldview with our family, friends, co-workers, and so on, " he says. "Ideally we live by our beliefs so as to lend them credence; the "unfollowing adherent" is just a meaningless mouthpiece - a preacher not following his own sermon. A legacy of values proven out by the bearer's own life would be a very good legacy for anyone. Life is motion, and the real goal of a writer should be to arrest that motion [which is life] and preserve knowledge by artificial means, and hold it fixed so that a hundred years later, when a stranger opens a book and reads it, it moves again since it is life. Since man is mortal, the only immortality possible for a writer is to leave something behind him that is immortal since it will always move. This is the writer's way of scribbling "I was here" on the wall of the final and irrevocable oblivion through which we all must someday pass."

A perpetual student of world cultures, a passionate reader of Eastern philosophers like D.T. Suzuki and Jiddu Khrishnamurti, and classic European thinkers such as Albert Camus, Soren Kierkegaard and Jean Paul Sartre, Fraguas prefers spending his free time reading and keeping in contact with the "real world," instead of pursuing the glamour of glittering ceremonies and social parties. "The other day," Fraguas says softly, "I was just walking barefoot around the block and the wind was blowing…" He stops momentarily, his gaze focusing inward, then continues. "…it was one of those perfects moments…like a perfect technique, like a perfect kata. Like Sisyphus, I think I have reached a point where I find contentment and meaning in pushing the rock uphill. What always mattered to me was to find a purpose, to see what it really was that I should be doing in this world; to find a truth which is truth for me, to find the idea for which I am willing to live and eventually…die."

Sometimes is hard to differentiate between Fraguas the man and Fraguas the martial artist. "The true greatness of martial arts lies in the depth and immensity of their underlying philosophies. They are the guiding aspect of our psychological unification and, most importantly, are the moral foundation of us as human beings. Martial arts, in the end, transcend the idea of winning and losing, and become a way of thinking and living. They become less about relating to the opponent's movement and more about

adapting and coping with the changing aspects of daily life. This is the real battle - to become the best you can be as a human being. Martial arts can aid the spiritual refining and polishing process and help to guide you toward the achievement of your goals, whatever they may be," he says. "Like Mishima said: 'A samurai is a total human being, whereas a man who is completely absorbed in his technical skill has degenerated into a 'function', one cog in a machine'. We need to strike that balance or we'll be defeated in life. It is either fighting or polishing your spirit. Following the first will take you to use your power to defeat others. In the second path, you struggle against yourself but the reward is much better. When you read in some places that martial arts are for peace, it means about 'polishing the spirit'. When the old Japanese swordmakers compared the value of their swords everything was boiled down to how the metal was tempered. Well, that's the real challenge of martial arts for me, instead of the blade there is only ourselves and our quality is tempered only by our spirit."

Certainly, if contentment can be attained through the gradual diminishing of worldly ambition, he seems well on his way to achieving peace of mind. This "polished spirit" is what Fraguas has been searching for, in one way or another, his entire life. It's where his stillness comes from today, and it reflects the peaceful state that readers and acquaintances can perceive while enjoying his works or simply by having a conversation with this unconventional "tea master."

Note: This article written by GM Antonio Somera was completed 4 months before his passing on October 21, 2013. It has never been published until now.

DOJO KUN

五誓訓

一、和して乱れざることを誓う

一、懈怠の心なきことを誓う

一、気迫に欠けざることを誓う

一、艱難に挫けざることを誓う

一、言行に恥じざることを誓う

www.ingramcontent.com/pod-product-compliance
Lightning Source LLC
Chambersburg PA
CBHW081344080526
44588CB00016B/2373